D0188944

Dr Roberta Sykes was born in the 1940s in Townsville, North Queensland, and is one of Australia's best known activists for Black rights. In the 1980s she received both her Master and Doctorate of Education at Harvard University. She has been a consultant to a wide range of government departments, including the Royal Commission into Aboriginal Deaths in Custody and the NSW Department of Corrective Services, and was Chairperson of the Promotion Appeals Tribunal at the Australian Broadcasting Corporation. A guest lecturer at universities and tertiary institutions throughout Australia, and in demand as an international speaker, she is also the author of seven books, including *Eclipse* (1996) and *Murawina: Australian Women of High Achievement* (1994), as well as having written, contributed to or co-authored numerous publications, journal articles and conference papers. In 1994 she was awarded Australia's highest humanitarian award, the Australian Human Rights Medal. She lives in Redfern, Sydney.

Snake
Cradle

Roberta Sykes

ALLEN & UNWIN

Copyright © Roberta Sykes 1997

All rights reserved. No part of this book may be reproduced or transmitted in any form or by any means, electronic or mechanical, including photocopying, recording or by any information storage and retrieval system, without prior permission in writing from the publisher.

First published in 1997 by
Allen & Unwin
9 Atchison Street,
St Leonards NSW 1590 Australia
Phone: (61 2) 8425 0100
Fax: (61 2) 9906 2218
E-mail: frontdesk@allen-unwin.com.au
Web: http://www.allen-unwin.com.au

National Library of Australia
Cataloguing-in-Publication entry:

Sykes, Roberta B.
  Snake dreaming.

  ISBN 1 86448 513 2 (v. 1).

  1. Sykes, Roberta B. 2. Aboriginies. Australian—Biography.
  3. Aboriginies. Australian—Women—Biography. 4. Authors.
  Australian—Biography. 5. Aboriginies. Australian—Civil
  rights. 6. Aboriginies, Australian—Land tenure. I. Title.
  II. Title: Snake cradle.

920.00929915

Set in 12/15 pt Novarese by Bookhouse Digital, Sydney
Printed by Australian Print Group, Maryborough

10 9 8 7

1

My younger sister Dellie and I lay sleeping in the bed we shared when Mum's scream interrupted my dream. Hurrying footsteps of one of the two older girls my mother cared for assured me the scream was real. Dellie barely stirred.

I slipped from the bed and, in the warm night air, made my way in the dark to the doorway of the verandah where Mum had her bed in a corner closed off from the world by three-ply. I was wearing bloomers and singlet, our usual nightwear.

'He was here. He was here.' Mum's voice was urgent. She tugged the bedclothes back and forth, peered under the bed, and, ridiculously, slapped at the mosquito net.

'Who, Rae? Who was here?,' asked Dessie, who'd come to her aid.

'A man. I don't know. A tall man. I didn't see his face. He walked up to the bed and stared at me through the mosquito net.'

'A dream—a nightmare. Here, I'll give you a hand.'

Together they straightened the sheets and mosquito netting.

'You, back into bed,' Mum hissed towards the door-way where I stood, filled with fear and curiosity. I slunk off; back to the safety of my side of the bed. The night returned to normal as I listened to Dessie's soft foot-falls pad down the hallway to the room where she slept.

But peace was short-lived as we were woken by another scream. Even though I'd quickly gone back to sleep, this time I was ready. I was the first one up. The verandah was alive with moonlight and shadows, and Mum's eyes were wide with horror behind the mosquito netting. She struck out at me.

'Get back. Get back.' I watched her rising, gasping, sobbing. Again, she tugged the sheets and pillow from the bed, and with them bundled in her arms, used them to push me back. Suddenly there were other people, the older girls, and I stood near the wall to watch what happened next. It was all so strange to me; I was only about four years old.

Mum said the 'man' had returned, walked up to her bed and was wearing some sort of hood so she couldn't see who he was. When she screamed, he'd run 'behind the bed'. But there was no 'behind the bed'. The bed stood in a narrow corner, its length along the wall, the top pushed up against three-ply lining, the bottom against one of the internal walls. There was nothing on the verandah but a few pieces of old cane furniture, a low table and chair, otherwise there was nowhere for anyone to conceal themselves, but Mum would not be pacified.

They dragged the bed out from the corner and walked around it. I was shunted away from getting under everybody's feet. I sat down in the shadows on the floor beside the cane table, making myself small and unnoticeable so I wouldn't be sent back to bed.

Mum continued to insist that the man was real, that he'd come up to her bed, that he was still hanging around, somewhere. One of the older girls was sent to look around the yard. Nothing, no one. My mother kept on, fretting and anxious, and Dessie asked who she thought the man might be. They'd slotted the narrow bed back into its space, replaced the sheets and tidied the net. Mum sat on the bed, bent over, her head in her hands. 'Old Nick,' I heard her whisper. 'Old Nick—I think he's come for me.'

'Who?' I said, brightening at the sound of a name of someone I didn't know, wanting to learn more about our late-night visitor. Mum threw a look of aggravation towards where I sat in the shadow of the table, and one of the girls came and picked me up by the back of the singlet, shuffling me off to bed.

They all went to the kitchen for cups of tea to settle themselves down. I lay in bed, wondering briefly, but was soon swallowed back into the deep warm sleep of childhood. When I woke in the morning it was because my mother's stirring disturbed me. She had eased us littlies over and lain down beside us rather than return to her own bed.

Later that morning I was at my usual pastime under our house, making mudpies from the fine sand gathered by ants, when a shrill whistle let me know someone had arrived. A boy, his leg casually over the bar of his pushbike, waited on the path outside our house, and Mum's dog raced me to the front gate. I took the telegram and bounded up the stairs to where Mum was standing at the door, come to find out what was going on.

Ashen-faced, she took the telegram without her usual rouse about me minding my own business. I hurtled along beside her in the hall, urging her to open it and tell me what it said. I loved telegrams, letters, visitors, anything new, anything that tied our lives into whatever went on in the big outside world. But, as usual, I was given a scrap of food and sent back to my games, while the news of the telegram was shared with an older audience. I hated being small and too young to be in the confidence of older people.

When we littlies were called in for lunch, we got an announcement. Mum was somewhere else in the house, we could hear her rifling through clothes and bags and papers, and one of the older girls put our food on the table.

'Your Gran's dead. Your Mum's going up to Cairns for the funeral. She's packing now, so don't disturb her. *Don't make noise.*'

I picked over the food with my spoon and thought about this. Dellie, two years younger, who normally took her lead from me, watched me carefully to see what our response to this news ought to be. I'd never met Mum's mother, indeed I don't know if it had ever crossed my mind in any serious way that she *had* a mother, although in the abstract way of childhood I suppose I knew it must be so.

A far more intriguing question surfaced in my mind from the disturbances of the previous night.

'Who's Old Nick?'

Early childhood memories are like pieces of a giant jigsaw puzzle. Whole days, weeks and months slide by, full of mangoes and mudpies, of being banished into the yard to play, while life ticks over fairly uneventfully,

and these days are the background pieces—the yawn-
ing sky, the forest of leaves of similar colour—of the
picture. Other events stand in stark contrast, forming
the hard and complex part of life's puzzle. It is not the
background to which we refer when we point to our
completed picture, tedious and nit-picking though it
may have been to assemble the setting.

I remember the fact of the mudpies, and that we
would commandeer any small round or shaped hol-
lowed item to be pressed into service in our mudpie
kitchens, and the highly prized fine dirt that enabled
our pies to set nicely and firmly in our sunshine 'ovens'.
I remember the fact of the mangoes, the hundreds, perhaps thousands, devoured throughout our childhood.
These are, without doubt, the 'background' days.

Also, and again without doubt, there were incidents
of great and immediate urgency—a piece of drama at
that moment—which end up being nothing more than
'background' in the long run. A sharp knife sliced accidentally and carelessly across one's own fingers, a
piece of broken glass or tack embedded in one's foot,
the immediate flash of pain followed—often—by basking briefly in the attention of adults, and then the little
flag that singled one out as having been the object of
such attention and affection: the bandage or band-aid
or sling. But these, too, are mainly just part of the background of life. For us, they did not occur with any great
frequency. Years later, despite my panic at the time at
the sight of the deep red splash of my own blood, I'm
unable to attribute any particular incident to most of
the small scars which pepper my soles, feet, legs and
hands.

Events which constitute the main picture are also
often tiny, and some seem not to have been so

dramatic when they occurred. It's in retrospect, as they come together to form important pieces of the whole, that their weight and significance become more meaningful, that they can be seen to have contributed to, or detracted from, the essence, the central core, of life and our understanding of our world.

So it was with Old Nick visiting Mum, and her mother dying at the hour of this visitation. Is this my earliest memory? No, not quite. But it is one of the memories that come to mind when I try to reconstruct my mother.

Mum, who lives on still at over 90 years old, has curled back into herself, her mind completely gone. I am drawn to wonder to what extent was she ever really here.

The physical form—the skin and bones which we, my sisters and I, discuss as 'Mum'—is just the husk of the woman who once lived right here amongst us, the minder and nurturer whom we suspected of having eyes in the back of her head, and who was the central and most powerful influence in our early lives. But did we know her? The answer is no.

The tables have turned. Mum's now the one minded and nurtured. She doesn't know her own name, much less any of ours. Trapped in the rigid confines of overwhelming memory loss, unable to recognise which bodily feelings are associated with which bodily functions, she peers out from beneath heavily wrinkled eyes at a world that must consist, for her, of truly fragmented pieces, a fearful kaleidoscope.

But even before this complete retreat, how much of herself did she reveal? Why did she not want to be found?

In many of my earliest memories, Mum was either

the central player or a physically close bystander. This is the case even in events where hers were not the pivotal actions nor her words the source of any enlightenment. I remember Mum as always 'being there', although she shared little of herself.

Memories stand, and time has given some of them a dreamlike quality, especially the memories of events which I enjoyed and from which I drew strength. Indeed, when these memories occur to me, they often begin at a point which is neither the beginning nor the end of the event, but centre on that part where the intensity of the experience burnt itself into my psyche.

I have many such memories. In one, I'm being lifted through the air and put on top of the petrol tank of a shiny motorbike. Someone, a man, is holding me between his forearms while his hands work on the handlebars. A sudden loud noise, the engine kicks into life and we start to tremble and vibrate. I am quickly fearful.

I look down onto chrome and pipes, and see that stones and clumps of grass are moving beneath me. A few seconds later we're rolling and I gasp as the air hits my face and, for a moment, takes my breath away. Soon I'm having my first, and very memorable, experience of travelling faster than air. I can feel the wind in my hair, my throat, tearing at my skin and flapping my clothes. I laugh out loud with delight and the wind whips the sound and my own warm breath back onto my face.

The ride is probably very short because almost as soon as it starts we pull up, back alongside my mother. She is reaching her arms towards me and I'm hanging onto the forearms around me, trying to prevent her lifting me. I want to do it again, feel it all again, but that's the end. Mum wrenches me from the bike, I hurl myself onto the ground, then I can hear their voices laughing. Their laughter is brief, after which they ignore me and resume their conversation.

At the time of this event I was less than two years old, perhaps even eighteen months. The clear, sharp memory it left with me was to play an important role in my search for my mother more than a decade later.

The shadows of some of Mum's friends and relatives, the few I was allowed to meet, were oft times also revealed to me in this way; they appear in my memories, but their relationship to me was never made explicit.

We are walking along a track in the bush. My legs are short and have to walk fast to keep up with Mum, even though she's walking slowly. Dellie is dawdling a bit behind us. Uncle George is carrying my youngest sister, Leonie, a very tiny baby wrapped up in a shawl. Mum and Aunty Maggie are talking, just big people's talk.

I glance at my hand to admire a little gold ring Mum had recently given me—and I realise I've lost it. My fingers are bare. Then I'm frightened. The ring had belonged to Mum and she'd had it cut down to fit me. We're poor and owning a gold ring is a very big deal. Mum had told me a jeweller cut the ring down in exchange for the little fragment he'd cut out of it— that's how precious gold was. I begin to cry because I'm too afraid to tell her it's gone.

Mum's carrying a cane basket with a big check pattern tea towel over the top and tucked in around the sides. My crying is completely silent, I can feel myself sobbing inside. Tears run down my face as I struggle with this dilemma. I've fallen behind, almost as far back as Dellie, and Mum turns casually to check on our progress. Her sharp intake of breath at the sight of my face causes Uncle George to look, too.

The baby and food basket are juggled around between the adults, leaving Uncle George free to scoop me from the ground. When he asks me what's the matter I tap one hand on top of the other and blubber quietly, 'My ring.' Uncle George lifts my hand to his mouth and kisses my wet fingers, looking in my eyes all the while. I watch him but his outline is distorted through tears. A small smile crosses his black face, and when he relays the bad news to Mum, I feel very safe.

A psychiatrist would probably come up with a profound explanation for why this incident remains frozen in my mind. It's not that I don't recall what went on before or after this event, because, to an extent, I do. It's only that the entire episode seems to have collapsed itself neatly and tidily around this one moment. From the size of my sisters I know I was four years old at the time. Mum, almost forty when she had me, produced both my sisters in the next four years.

Uncle George and Aunty Maggie lived in a humpy or shack beside a river outside Townsville, probably in the area now known as Upper Ross River. But this is in the Townsville of fifty years ago, when the town had only one main street and now quite central suburbs, such as Aitkenvale, didn't even exist.

We visited them from time to time, although I have no exact memory of how we did that. We didn't own a car. In fact, no one we knew then had a car either. But a reliable and frequent bus system operated in Townsville and around the district throughout my young life which makes the present bus service look like a joke. We were most likely walking back to catch a bus into town.

I've no idea how, or even if, Uncle George and Aunty Maggie ever knew when we were coming. None of us had a phone; very few people did then.

In her basket on our visits, Mum carried shop-bought goods, such as flour, tea and sugar, which were contributions to Uncle amd Aunty's stores rather than fare to be served up at the time. Uncle George caught fish for us, sometimes crabs, and Aunty Maggie cooked, and her garden and surrounding bush yielded a rich cornucopia of vegetables and fruits. These were the things we were fed on our visits.

Uncle George, Aunty Maggie, and the absolutely wonderful times we had out at their place, splashing in the clear, fresh, and often very cold, water and playing in the unspoilt bush, would probably have faded into obscurity amongst many other pleasant childhood memories if I hadn't lost my ring.

Uncle George, carrying me on one shoulder and Dellie on the other as we hurried towards the bus stop, said he thought the ring had most likely fallen into the river. The jeweller had left a little 'growing room', which enabled it to slip off easily and unnoticed. Although upset by its loss, Mum said she didn't blame me, which made me greatly relieved. But there was no time to go back to look for my treasure, and with the current running so rapidly we were sure the ring had been swept away.

That night, when Mum put us to bed, I shed a few tears for the loss of the ring, but she said sternly, 'Forget the ring. It's gone. George is probably on the turps already.' My ears tickled at another new word.

'What's turps?'

'Go to sleep!'

Next morning, a faint tap on our front door woke me.

I heard low murmurs, Mum talking with a deep-voiced man. After a short, whispered conversation, I heard her urge him to come in and 'at least have a cup of tea'. I slipped out of bed, dropped my dress over my pants and singlet and bounded out. The front door was closed, Mum stood with her back leaning against it, frowning in the half light. By the time she moved out of the way and I could get through the door, the visitor had gone. I tripped down to the front gate and peered down the track which led to our house, but could see only the rapidly disappearing figure of a man as he passed over the crest of the hill in the distance.

The details of Uncle George's early morning visit were revealed to me only in small pieces over time. Was this because I had lost the ring, a gift to me from Mum? Was I to be punished by being kept ignorant of its return?

During the next week I learned of the ring's recovery, and Mum said I could have it back when my finger had grown a bit fatter. In the meantime, it was to stay in the wardrobe in an old handbag in which she kept her trinkets.

I was amazed by Uncle George's cleverness at locating the ring as I was so sure it had been lost forever. He had told Mum the ring had fallen straight down and lay glinting in the sunlight through the clear water. He'd retrieved it at first light and walked in the cool morning air for over two hours to bring it to our door, and then he hadn't even come in for a cup of tea.

But who was 'Uncle George'? And 'Aunty Maggie'? This was the last time I saw either of them, and references to them, of which there were very few over the years, made them figures of even greater intrigue. George was a very black man with loose but kindly features and, beside him, Maggie was pale, probably a white woman, with limp brown hair. Her most startling feature, to my young eyes, was that she had all her front teeth missing. Mum said they lived in the bush because they wanted to be free and because they liked 'a drink'.

Years later, Mum evaded my questions about Uncle George and Aunty Maggie. It was her way to become angry when pursued on subjects she didn't want to answer. I gathered she was related to George in some way, and that they were the parents of a young girl roughly the same age as me, my cousin Betty, a pale girl with lank hair who lived with adoptive parents not far from us.

Betty's adoptive mother was an obese woman with a huge suppurating tropical ulcer on her leg. She was married to a quiet, nondescript man who'd made Betty the most wonderful rocking horse in the world—which she seemed only rarely permitted to ride. Generally speaking, theirs was not a happy household, as the woman could barely hobble about and Betty had to do many chores and errands, including bathing and dress-ing the ulcer; a nauseous task which I assisted with on several occasions. Mum said it would be good for me to stay in touch with Betty because she would be handy later. I wondered what she meant at the time, and about her reversal of this advice a few years further on.

Young children accept being kept in ignorance on all sorts of issues and I was no exception. By the time we are old enough to assert our curiosity, we've already, to a great extent, internalised our knowledge about the natures of the people around us—our parents, relatives and neighbours—and we're usually canny enough to know who we can ask questions of and whether they are likely to be answered.

As children, instead of receiving answers, we were often dismissed or given a reassurance in lieu of a reply.

I learned that Mum was from a large family, perhaps as many as sixteen or eighteen children, most of whom lived, during my childhood, in Queensland though not in Townsville. I only knew her sister Gladys who lived in Brisbane.

Our mother was not normally a demonstrative person, and her devotion to us, her children, became apparent—with a few exceptions—only by the commitment she showed us over time.

It's hard to explain why Mum didn't like us to touch her to show our affection. She did all the necessarily close things to sustain life such as breastfeed us as babies, but she could not have afforded to feed us otherwise. Once, when she was lying on her bed feeding Leonie, I pestered her to taste the milk that the baby was gulping down with gusto. She sent me to the kitchen for a teaspoon, rather than allow me to crawl up beside her and taste it from her breast. I was four, and on reflection this seemed cold and fairly typical of her actions towards me.

She didn't allow us to clutch her leg, though we had to hold onto her skirts when we were crossing roads. We were chided and told to, 'Hold on properly,' if our hands brushed her hip or thigh. She picked us up, as parents do, when we had to be any place higher than the floor, but we were constantly admonished to 'sit up straight' and 'stand up straight', which meant we were not to be touching either her or each other.

I imagine I experienced the emotional coldness of

our lifestyle more intensely than my sisters, in part because, as the eldest I was expected to pull the younger ones into line; tell them to stand and sit straight, to be independent and not lean on or touch one another.

Perhaps periods of sharing a bed with my sisters was some compensation, though I certainly didn't think so at the time since one suffered from incontinence until her teens.

Mum shared little of her feelings with us and only in crises did her love for us become obvious. On one such occasion I was playing under the house and poking around in some boxes stored there, which I'd been forbidden to do, when I found a 'lipstick' in a metal case.

Lipsticks represented the epitome of grown-up possessions to me, so I was determined to put some on, but the lid was very tight.

I got a tack hammer and carefully tapped away at it for a long time until I eventually managed to prise the top off. I was terribly disappointed when it was open because it wasn't the bright red colour of lipstick, but a yellowish grey sort of mud. When I couldn't get the lid back on again, I decided I'd have to take it to Mum, even though this meant I'd probably get in trouble for poking in the boxes.

Mum was sewing at her treadle machine on the verandah when I came up the stairs behind her. When she heard me she turned and asked, 'What have you got there?'

At the time, my head was only slightly higher than the top of the bench of her sewing machine. I didn't answer because I didn't know what I had, and I thought she'd tell me.

I recall her shock as I showed her the two halves and asked what was the stuff down the tubes.

With her eyes wide open with fear, Mum made me put the pieces down carefully and back away. Then she picked me up and carried me, held in place firmly under her arm, through the house, out the back and down the stairs to the laundry where she washed my hands with a cake of laundry soap, her body trembling against mine the whole time.

When she'd finished cleaning all traces from my hands, she put me back on the ground and bent so her face was level with mine.

'*Never*,' she hissed, '*never* play with a bullet again.' I burst into tears, blubbering that I didn't know it was a bullet. The more I sobbed and carried on, the angrier she became—but only when she felt assured that the immediate danger was over. She grabbed my head between her hands, shaking it and hurting my ears. 'You could be dead. You must *never* hit a bullet with a hammer.' She began to shake and weep, repeating her words louder and louder and shaking me even harder. I felt I'd more likely be killed by her concern for me than by the bullet.

She went inside and I was frightened to go onto the verandah where she was working so I hung around just inside the door, intending to peek outside to see what she was doing.

I could hear her making a noise and it took me a long while to realise she was crying. Even when I knew what the sound was, I couldn't believe it. My mother didn't cry.

When I stepped around the door for a better look, I saw her sitting with her arms folded on the top of the sewing machine, her head resting on them, and yes, she sure was crying.

Torn between taking off to avoid her seeing me and giving me a flogging, and feeling I should comfort her because of the trouble I'd caused, I edged towards her. When she noticed me, she grabbed me close and snuffled in my hair. I didn't mind.

2

Mum was fond of telling us she'd been put out to work at age twelve, that her first job had been keeping things clean in a cafe owned by a Greek, and she'd been barely tall enough to see over the top of the tables she had to wipe. It was a live-in job, and she was given a hessian bag to sleep on in the kitchen. She said the man was 'smarmy', always trying to touch her, and she ran away after working at the cafe for a year. By that time she knew her times tables, could add and subtract money, and she'd heard there were lots of other places looking for girls with these skills.

She could never be pinned down as to where the cafe was, or in what town she'd lived until then, or about virtually anything concrete between that time and when she had us. Mum had a few stock phrases which she uttered that told me a little more. From time to time she'd lose her temper and swear at us, and her language, when I was small, was enough to scare us rigid. She had 'fits of temper', but the rest of the time she was completely under control. After these fits, perhaps trying to explain herself, she'd say, 'My father was a bullock-team driver—that's where I learned those words, and I've got plenty more!' We weren't about to argue.

On other occasions she would tell us she'd once flown into a rage and put a claw hammer through one of her sisters' tongue. One time when she mentioned this and wasn't bordering on another temper fit, I asked her why she had done it. 'Because she wouldn't shut up when I told her to shut up, that's why,' was her short reply.

Mum's temper tantrums, though not daily, were legendary, and they weren't necessarily directed at people, either. Once when I was playing in the yard, a rotary egg-beater came sailing out the kitchen window and into the yard, with a few choice words following it. When I was sure the coast was clear I ran to get it, thinking that she'd thrown it away because it wasn't working properly. I found it worked fine and began using it to beat my mudpies. Minutes later, Mum looked out the window and saw me, raced down the back stairs, grabbed the beater out of my hands and threw it even further up the backyard into the chicken run. I wasn't brave enough to go and fetch it nor question her about it.

When she called us in to eat a short time later, she plonked our bowls on the table with just one comment: 'If the bloody thing won't work for me, be buggered if I'll let it work for you!' After that, lunch was quiet.

Our neighbours were used to things sailing out of our windows. If the cutlery drawer stuck, out went the knives and forks. 'You don't want to wear that school uniform I ironed for you?'—and we'd find ourselves scrambling up onto the next door roof to retrieve it. Books, saucepans, glasses, whatever, they were all the

same to Mum when she was displeased. The neighbours would hear her yelling and come out to raise
their eyebrows and occasionally to smile to cheer
us up.

I always knew Mum was regarded fairly widely in our
area as a 'sinner'. She used to tell us so. When I was
very young I thought it was because she didn't join
those people who rolled up, so spotlessly clean and
often in shining cars, to attend mass at the cathedral
on Sundays. Mum was a single parent before 'single
parent' even became a phrase, and not a woman who
had lapsed once by accident but the mother of three
'mortal sins'. She called herself a widow, but when I
occasionally—and futilely—asked her when her husband, our father, had died, I realised that there had
been no 'husband' in my lifetime, and I was the oldest
of her three daughters.

Dellie looks sufficiently like me to be my sister in the
full sense, but Leonie, younger than me by four years,
does not. She has Asian features. I heard all sorts of
rumours, none of which I was ever brave enough to
bring home to my mother. But from my infancy I have
many memories of us standing outside a shop in
Denham Street run by two brothers, Henry and Dennis
Mah Kong, and of being sent into the store with notes.
Leonie was a baby in a pram, and Dellie, at two years
old, would be sitting on the end of it. The store was
dimly lit and a very old and wrinkled woman would
see me and call to one of the brothers in a foreign
language.

I was told, 'Don't give this note to XX, only give it to
YY', but the problem now is that I've forgotten to which
of the brothers I was ordered to give it. I'd stagger out

under the weight of a bag, flour or sugar, and once we even received a packet of Corn Flakes. I remember this vividly because I was excited to have something so flash as we usually had oatmeal which came very plainly wrapped. When we got home and Mum put some into plates for us and poured milk on it, she cried because the cereal melted down to almost nothing, unlike the oatmeal and Weetbix we were used to.

My role there, I think, was as intermediary between my mother and my sister's father. One or other of the brothers used to go around the neighbourhood in an old truck, set up like a shop with a set of scales and laden with fruit and vegetables. Women lined up to buy food or sent their children down when the truck pulled up at the corner. Whenever I was sent out, I was particularly told to ask for 'pumpkin with no wood in it'. Later, the brothers and their truck disappeared from our lives and I don't recall seeing them beyond when I was eight or nine.

The store remained there longer, and at some stage, perhaps when I was in primary school and in charge of shepherding my sisters to and from school and kindergarten, I was told we were never to go into that shop for any reason. Mum had her secrets and we were obliged to act on them, without knowing what they were. When I was a bit older and had to walk past the shop from time to time, I always did so with an acute sense of embarrassment, though I didn't know why I should feel this way. As soon as I was old enough to jaywalk across Denham Street's wide lanes of traffic, I crossed over to avoid going near the premises.

Whatever my mother's sins were reputed to be, 'the drink' was not one of them. Mum had a friend, Nell, whom she described as 'a spinster', who was the cook at Lowth's Hotel. They met in the local ladies' lounge, known as the snakepit, to have a few shandies on Saturday afternoon while we kids were at the matinee. At a quarter to five, Mum was always standing outside the theatre, waiting for the film to finish so she could walk us the three blocks home. I never saw her drunk in her life, and only perhaps a half dozen times did I see her even tipsy.

Mum was also known as a very hard worker, a fact on which she prided herself and from which she drew great strength. She took in laundry as a living, and our backyard was full of long wire clothes lines which stretched from house to fence posts and back, propped up with lengths of wood, worn smooth and shiny, to keep the laundry from dragging on the ground.

For a few pence, Mum washed and ironed men's shirts, trousers, socks, handkerchiefs, singlets, and, very occasionally, clothes for women. She had a wood copper which she stoked up before dawn, and by breakfast the first loads of washing had been rinsed and wrung out by hand and were drying on the lines. I know, because my job was to walk along beside her handing her up items and clean wooden pegs from the basket. If I handed her a damp or darkened peg which made a mark on the clothes, or dropped an item of clothing on the dirt so it had to be rinsed again, I was in deep trouble.

Our days were spent around the laundry. I'd wake from a nap and Mum would tell me to go 'feel if the shirts are dry yet'. If they were, she'd come down to take them in because I was too small to reach the line. Then we'd fill up the empty space with more things—there was always more wet laundry waiting its turn. Singlets took longer to dry, trousers longer still. By early afternoon, we'd be ready to iron and Mum would light the wood stove on which the iron stood to be heated. Mum did the ironing in the backroom on a table, which was also where we ate. She had two irons, and my early job was to ferry them to and from the stove so she wouldn't have to stop her work. Then she taught me how to spit on my fingers and touch the ironplate to test its heat, and my next job was ironing boxer shorts and men's hankies with a warm iron.

Mum kept lists. Mr Smith liked his shirts starched, Mr Dunn did not. Another would want only his collars and cuffs starched. She had her own methods of sorting out which shirts belonged to which customer, marking long-standing customers' clothes with their initials in tiny letters in indelible pencil. For others who might be occasional or irregular, she lightly stitched a small coloured thread in some inconspicuous place. She boiled the starch and I'd often do the starching, learning my letters and numbers very young in order to read her lists.

These tasks made me feel essential to the family and I never resented having to do them. They were my life. There was a joke in our family about how once, at four years old, I was ironing my quota when I dropped the iron on Mum's foot as I was stepping onto a brick platform she'd made to enable me to see on top of the table. Her scream of pain shocked me so much, and I was so frightened she was going to hit me, that I scrambled under the table and hid, and when she got over the sting of the burn, she couldn't find me. I also recall that when she finally did find me, she went to lengths to tell me that it wasn't my fault, that our lives had just been cut out to be hard.

We lived in a large dip, separated from the main road by a high retaining wall with a fence on top of it which prevented people and cars from falling the twenty or so feet onto our level. Directly opposite us was the Sacred Heart Cathedral and presbytery, in Stanley Street, Townsville. Both our house and the one next door had once belonged to the church and had been the priests' accommodation. Of almost identical structure, they were built of timber, small and plain, with a few stairs leading up to a little verandah running across the front. The house next door had a narrow hallway with four small bedrooms opening off it in which priests had lived, a tiny kitchen and another room at the back, while our house had only three bedrooms and a parlour.

At some stage, when a new presbytery was being built, the houses had been carried across the way and mounted on stilts in the style of all North Queensland houses. They had been placed sideways and side by side across a steep slope of the hill, so on one side there were high poles and enough room for a tall man to pass under without stooping, while on the other even my mum's pet dog could barely burrow her way out. The hillside had been tiered and shored up with rocks to accommodate the houses.

There were three houses situated along our little track, the third was built in the same style but, according to Mum, it hadn't been a priests' house. Our house was in the middle. In the house downhill from us lived old Mrs Scott and her lodger, Edie, a travelling saleswoman for lingerie goods.

Once a cyclone peeled the roof off Mrs Scott's house and sheets of corrugated iron flew under our house, which was frightening because Mum had tied us children to posts under the house in case our house was blown away.

In the house above ours lived old Mrs Sullivan and her assorted lodgers.

From our front gate we could see the grand presbytery which had replaced our little cottages, and although the houses were nestled among large overhanging mango trees, the priests could see our front door from their verandah.

We almost always had someone living with us during our early childhood as renting out rooms was a good way for Mum to increase the household income. With three children to feed and clothe, and a veritable fortune which had to be spent on me for medicines, vitamin supplements and anything else Mum heard or read might help me, she had to watch every penny.

The lodgers were all white and most were women, sometimes with a child or children of their own. The upside of having them stay was that Mum could occasionally ask them to keep an eye on us while she took care of her business. For her, I'm sure the downsides were many, but for us, it was mainly that we had to sleep in a crude shelter under the highset part of the house. Even Mum spent periods living in this room when opportunity arose and she was short of cash. We had to play quietly so as not to disturb her lodgers, whom she called 'boarders', whether they were in on the basis of room and meals or not.

At that time, up to ten years or so after the war, many people arrived in Townsville without anywhere to live. Some European refugees with little money would go along the streets in the centre of town, which was near where we lived, knocking on doors and asking to rent a room or pleading for a little food, or some work in exchange for food. A trickle of these people made their way up the Stanley Street hill and a few left the main road and came into our dip.

Old Mrs Sullivan, who we children thought was a hundred years old already when we were born, always had a house full of boarders, and her place was a well-known address for transients. A few times when she had a room vacant, she had Mum put a small advertisement in the *Townsville Daily Bulletin* for her. She only took 'clean single men', or so her ad stated, but the lodger who was with her longest was by no means clean. Bert Love, who received some sort of pension, sat on her front verandah almost from daylight to dusk, wearing dark trousers and a grey singlet stretched over his pot belly. Mrs Sullivan was very proud of Bert because he didn't drink, but he had other obnoxious habits. He'd cough and hawk up phlegm, which he spat over the side of the verandah or out through his bedroom window until the tracks—along with the tea-leaves that he emptied from his teapot—had stained the house. Mrs Sullivan was too blind to see the stains, and by the time I was six, almost too frail to walk around her own house at all.

Bert often volunteered to watch us if Mum had to rush into town for some business. She was paying off the house in instalments at the bank, whenever she got a few shillings from her laundry work, and there were bills from the gas company and, eventually, the electricity company, so she often had errands to do. When Bert was to look after us, she'd tell us to play in our front yard where he could see us, but not to go over to his house. No sooner was she out of sight than Bert would call out that he had lollies for us, and to come and get them. He would rub his hands over us, always touching us on our arms or backs, and he'd offer to teach us to play cards. First he taught us to play snap, but later he'd ask us if we wanted to learn to play 'strip poker'.

Mum used to question us closely about him, and threaten to belt him over the head with her iron frying pan if he 'ever says so much as a word out of place', but we didn't know what was out of place and what wasn't. As he had often given us a penny or a ha'penny each to say we hadn't even gone into their yard, we weren't able to tell Mum about his groping ways without admitting we'd gone beyond our own fence and thereby risk a thrashing.

Mrs Sullivan had three rooms to rent and, besides Bert, the other lodgers turned over several times. They were the quiet, elderly gentlemen she sought. Mum's boarders during those early years included Mrs Mayers, whom we called Maisie, and her husband, Fred, who stayed a long time and had amicable relationships with everyone in our family. Fred was thin as a stick while Maisie was very obese. She was unable to have children and she lavished all her affection upon us. Also, Maisie was the only person who gave me and Dellie a clue about menstruation.

We also took in a series of refugees from Europe, including children, all of whom spoke English poorly or not at all and arrived at our house late in the evening and desperate for shelter, and several single mothers with a child or children. Most stayed a few weeks until they organised themselves, and because they were often broke when they arrived, Mum fed them until they got on their feet. She also gave advice about where to look for work, depending on their skills, and sometimes I had to look after their children while they sought to establish themselves. This was difficult because the children weren't used to obeying me as my sisters were, and those who didn't speak English would often cry until their mother or father returned because they were afraid they had been abandoned. Mum encouraged us to feel sorry for these children and to help them in any way we could.

Within three blocks of our house was St Anne's Church of England school. We walked by it many times as we passed on our way to town. We couldn't see into the main schoolyard as it had a high fence and tall buildings, but tucked into one corner was a hall, and on some afternoons we'd see girls inside playing, exercising and vaulting, and occasionally singing.

The area consisted of hills and dales, and the hall stood on much lower ground than the footpath which ran alongside it. We'd squat down to peek in to see the girls through the tiny gaps between the open flaps. The hall didn't have windows, just flaps, common at the time, made of timber and propped open with sticks to allow in air and light when the building was in use.

One day Mum said the school was having an open day. Prospective kindergarteners were invited to spend half a day there, prior to starting at the beginning of the following year. She dressed me up and marched me down to the school but from the minute she left me there, I knew I wasn't going to be welcome.

As I wasn't an enrolled student, and this was only to be a 'test run', Mum hadn't gone to the expense of buying me a uniform. I was unaware that there was such a thing as a uniform until that day. Vicious little girls circled me, pulling at the pretty frock Mum had insisted I wear in order to impress the school with my worthiness, and taunting me. I was so taken by all the new things I was seeing, in the schoolyard, the playing courts and the classroom buildings, that I didn't take too much notice of their meanness.

Sometime that morning, we were brought into the hall, and I was excited at seeing it from the inside. The regular pupils knew what they were to do, and soon, under the teacher's eye, had built up a structure of steps and stairs made of forms and positioned themselves in rows. The teacher told us new girls to fit ourselves into the formation. The little white girls were quickly pulled up into the lines, and I was left walking up and down the rows, trying to find a space for myself anywhere, while the teacher moved her papers and song books around on her stand out the front.

I went to all the lines along one side, but could find no room. The girls were shuffling around to fill up the gaps and not let me in. The structure was close to the wall but not tight against it, so I decided I'd cross behind it and go along the lines on the other side. As I did so, two girls began kicking me around the head and shoulders. When I looked up I saw that they weren't looking down at me, their heads were facing straight in front so that the teacher wouldn't know what they were doing.

I put my arms up around my head to protect myself, and I noticed that the girls kicking out at me were holding onto other girls in order to keep their balance. I slid past them, but behind the lines it was dark and I felt hot, terribly hot, and my perspiration and tears were making the top of my dress wet. As I continued along a third girl struck her foot out at me and hissed, 'Get away.' The wooden forms they were standing on rocked when she moved so suddenly and viciously.

I could see daylight at the end of the formation and I stumbled on towards it. The girls tensed and I sensed the teacher coming towards the back. One girl said, 'Don't telltale, darkie.'

The teacher's voice came clearly. 'Who said that?'

There was no reply. The teacher reached the end of the row and peered towards me. She reached in and grabbed me by the arm, dragging me clear of the desks and the wall. Everyone had turned and was watching me.

I'd like to think the teacher just didn't know what was going on, that she was busy with her work and failed to notice the increasing skittishness of the group of girls as they realised that by shuffling around they could keep me out and torment me.

After a moment of excruciating embarrassment and agony, which stands out in my memory of this event, the teacher hoisted me up by the arm and toted me outside. She carried me at arm's length away from herself to a tap in the playground where she put my head under the cold running water several times, and between each dumping I was drawn up, spluttering and coughing all over myself.

Sufficiently wet to please her, she pulled the skirt of my pretty frock up to wipe my face dry with it. Another teacher came towards us and asked if anything was the matter. She was told that I was having a turn from the heat, and asked to look in on my teacher's class until she got me 'settled down'.

Eventually, I was left sitting alone on a low bench that was nailed around the bottom of the thick trunk of a tree, with my new little school port beside me, watching the dappled sunlight as it played between the leaves, making interesting patterns of light and shadow, keeping my mind blank and waiting for my mother. After a long wait, Mum appeared around the corner of a building across the schoolyard just as the girls were filing out of the hall. I picked up my port and walked towards her, ignoring the girls, and when I came up level with her I put my hand in hers to pull her out of there as fast as I could. The teacher ran over, calling, 'Mrs Patterson, Mrs Patterson,' and when Mum stopped, she was told, 'Your daughter had a turn from the heat.'

I already knew this was not the sort of thing I could tell my mother about. At other times, people had called me and my sisters names in the street when she was with us and Mum had just said, 'Don't take any notice of them,' and dismissed the incidents. On a much earlier occasion, after a similar occurrence, I had asked Mum, 'What's a "nigger"?' She was powdering her face and paused but didn't answer. So I pressed on. 'Well, what's a "black gin"?'

'Where did you hear that?' she reluctantly replied, her lips pursed tensely. I could sense that she had become angry because I hadn't backed off when she didn't answer my first question, so I ran away.

Later that day she told me, not for the first time and probably by way of explanation, 'When people say rude things to you, just remember you're as good as anyone else.' I recall thinking then that I'd seen some ugly people in town, drunks rolling around in the streets and the like, and it hurt me to hear her say I wasn't any better than these people—which was probably a very negative reaction to what she thought was good advice. 'As good as anyone else' was one of Mum's stock phrases in the peptalks she gave us about racism, and every time I heard it, it grated on me. It always seemed to me that she was putting me on the same level as racists themselves.

Although I didn't bother her with the details of what went on during my 'open day' at St Anne's, I let her know I would not be happy to go to there, even though it was the closest school. Mum tried to terrify me by telling me stories about what sort of things might happen to me if I went to the state school, but I already knew what sort of things happened at St Anne's.

Not long afterwards, we had a visit from a priest from across the street. He was a small man with a kindly, moon-shaped face, called Father Gard. We were having our nap when he knocked on the door and Mum made me put a dress on over my bloomers and singlet as soon as she saw who it was. Then she and I dragged kitchen chairs out onto the front verandah so they could sit there in full view of everyone to have their conversation.

I had to look after the two littlies while they talked, so I don't know what was said. He called back several times over the next few weeks, and each time they sat on kitchen chairs on the verandah. The initial visits were very quiet, but after a while Mum began to like him and we could hear the occasional hoot of laughter from where we were playing under the house.

Each year, Mum's sister, Aunty Glad, travelled through Townsville on her way to Cairns by train to visit their mother and, when she'd died, other family members. On the return trip she shared the latest gossip with Mum. On one such stopover I overheard Mum telling her about Father Gard's visits.

Father Gard had said to Mum that he'd seen her around with her three girls and the oldest one must be getting near school age. He'd then said it would be a shame if we didn't get a proper education. When Mum agreed he put it to her that if we were to become

Catholics, the nuns at the Catholic school would take us in if he asked them.

I don't know if Mum already had a religion, but up until then she'd shown a particular dislike for Catholics. I had picked this up from comments she made on Sundays when, as she said, 'the Saturday night sinners roll up to the church to ask forgiveness and to impress their wives and little kiddies'.

But Father Gard, she told Aunty Glad, had worn her down. He'd spoken to the kindergarten teacher, Sister Teresa, and the head teacher at the primary school, Sister de Salles, and they had been enthusiastic, waiving fees and promising to help Mum keep us in uniforms.

Aunty Glad was scathing, also being not fond of Catholics. 'So you've sold them off to the Catholics, for a few pennies and some second-hand clothes,' she responded. But she was laughing when she said it, so I figured it couldn't be too bad—and I was deeply relieved to know that I'd not have to set foot into St Anne's again.

Aunty Glad assumed the role of our chief disciplinarian. She was a fearful figure and her annual visits were anticipated with dread by my sisters and I. Throughout the year, whenever we did anything naughty, Mum threatened us with Aunty Glad. Then Aunty Glad would arrive and, even though she'd only be at our house for a day or so at a time, she'd dispense doses of castor oil to whoever had been playing up. Holding us down on the floor or bed, kneeling on our flailing limbs, she'd force a dessertspoonful of the disgusting tasting stuff into our mouths. If any of us spluttered it back over her, she'd replace the dessertspoon with a tablespoon. Sometimes she'd dose us with senna tea, telling us 'naughtiness is caused by bowels not working properly. This will fix you up.' She inspected our hair for lice, which were a fairly common occurrence amongst children in those days, and if she found any, her method of dragging a fine comb through our tightly curled hair is one of the most vivid of my childhood memories. Leonie commiserated with Dellie and me, but she was the most fortunate as her short straight hair presented no resistance to the comb.

Aunty Glad was meaner to Dellie than to Leonie, because she was the youngest and therefore Mum's favourite, or to me, because I was so often ill. As a child I suffered from many serious diseases from which there was no protection or immunisation, including diphtheria, whooping cough, bronchitis and German measles. Despite my poorly disposition, Mum ensured that I also caught ordinary measles, mumps and chickenpox, as it was believed that children developed immunity through having these diseases as infants. Mothers deliberately exposed preschool-aged children to them so that they could have them 'over and done with' before starting school, and also so that we wouldn't have the much more serious complications which often accompany them if they strike in adulthood, as I was later to learn.

Because of these illnesses I spent a lot of time in bed. Our bedroom—when it wasn't being used for any other purpose—was directly next to the back verandah with a window that opened onto it. Whenever I was well enough but still recovering in bed, Mum, who did her lengthy bouts of ironing at the table up against the window, would have me recite the alphabet and, later, my times tables. So by the time I started school I already knew these things quite well. Another advantage of this was that when Aunty Glad or Nellie came to visit Mum, they'd be at the table, either talking to her while she continued her work or, with the ironing blanket removed, having their cups of tea. I'd wake from my feverish dozing to hear them talking, and eavesdrop until Mum popped her head through the window to see if I was awake. Even then I'd sometimes feign sleep because she had a habit of checking on me just as they were about to discuss something they thought really private. Occasionally I'd become so involved in their chats that I'd put my own chip in, which enraged Mum who would come in, slam the window closed, tweak my ear and tell me what happened to little girls like me who were sneaky and listened in on other people's conversations.

Also as a consequence of these diseases, I spent so many days in hospital that I lost count of them, and I was subjected to a lot of 'home therapies' because doctors often told Mum there were no cures for the things I had. Mum was a determined person in this regard, and either she or Aunty Glad administered treatments to me of the 'kill or cure' variety. When I had diphtheria Mum forced wads of kerosene-soaked rags into my throat, for example, and she would chip up a block of ice that was delivered to our house from the ice factory, fill a tin bathtub with the ice and water and plunge me into it whenever I developed a fever.

As well as these once-only diseases, I also had regular bouts of bronchitis, pneumonia and asthma. I was kept in darkened rooms, had Vicks rubbed on my chest, small camphor bags sewn to my singlets, and from as far back as I can remember, I was often made to sit at a tiny set of table and chairs with a towel draped over my head, inhaling eucalyptus fumes from a bowl of boiling water.

One night, during a period in which Mum had let out our bedroom to someone to subsidise her income, and we children were sleeping in a rough room constructed under the house, I developed a bad cold. Mum, exhausted from her day but not prepared to let me keep everyone awake with my coughing, brought a bowl of boiling eucalyptus water and towel to my bunk where I lay sleeping. She sat on a packing case and held the steaming bowl in one hand while positioning the towel over my head and the bowl with the other, then she promptly fell asleep.

I woke up screaming from the burning pain across my chest. Mum scooped me up in her arms and, yelling to everyone in the house that she was going, she ran out into the night carrying me. The hospital was a fair walk from our house by road, but Mum ignored the road and belted up a wild and rocky track over Melton Hill. She ran all the way.

When we arrived at the old casualty department, which was built from corrugated iron, Mum screamed and a nurse ran out to meet us. A young and inexperienced doctor came shortly, rubbed some thick sort of gel, similar to vaseline, on my chest and bound it on fast with sticking plaster; so tight I could barely breathe. Mum carried me home, she was crying all the way.

The doctor had told her to bring me back to casualty the next day when there'd be more experienced staff on duty to treat me. When we arrived and I'd been sat up on a table and looked at, the staff sent Mum outside. They tried to remove the plaster but it was stuck fast to my skin, and in the process my horribly bubbled skin was ripped. Then they filled a big tin full of tepid water, took my clothes off, cut across the plaster in places, and, lifting me into it, made me crouch down so the water came up to my neck.

After a while Mum's face appeared around the door, perhaps she distrusted them when they asked her to wait outside. When she saw me sitting in the tin, she pushed her way in and demanded to know what the nurse was doing to me. The nurse immediately went to get the doctor.

My arms hung over the sides of the tin, and I used them to push myself up a bit when the doctor spoke to me. Mum, the nurse and this doctor stood around me, quiet and staring, so I looked down at myself. Ugly strips and clumps of sticking plaster were hanging off me and taking my brown skin off with them. Underneath was a layer of bright pink and red, and I started to weep. So, too, did Mum and the nurse.

The doctor who had seen me the night before was called and we could hear him being soundly abused in the next room while the nurse was fixing me up with new dressing. This time I was given gauze, cotton wool and regular bandages tied loosely around my whole upper body, fashioned in a sort of thick singlet. Mum was told to keep me in a darkened room, as treatment for shock.

I survived all manner of injuries and illnesses, diseases and treatments—any of which could have killed me. But the effect of all these medical traumas was that I failed to thrive. By the time I was six years old, Dellie was taller and heavier than me. From then on, people often mistakenly believed her to be the eldest, and when we were out strangers would address their remarks and questions to her. Mum, however, continued to accord to me the responsibility—and some small measure of authority—which goes to the eldest child. Fortunately Dellie had an easygoing temperament and no real conflict stemmed from this in our early years, but I was forced to assert myself with some people in an effort to protect my sisters and maintain my 'oldest child' position.

Dellie's apparently laidback attitude was her way of dealing with the problems she and I faced as black children in an otherwise almost all-white environment. Leonie was not subjected to anything like the same amount of hostility, racism and rudeness which Dellie and I encountered.

One reason why people outside our family generally accepted me as spokesperson for us children was that Dellie was very shy. Another anecdote from our stock of family jokes centres on an episode which occurred when Mum sent Dellie, aged four, to the nearby shop when I was too sick to go. Dellie returned and told Mum she couldn't find the shop even though she'd accompanied me along the two short blocks many times.

'I told you to ask someone if you couldn't find it,' Mum said.

'I did ask someone, Mummy.'

'Who did you ask?'

'A man.'

'And what did he tell you?' Mum continued her questioning.

'He wouldn't tell me.'

'He wouldn't tell you?' Mum asked incredulously. 'Why wouldn't he tell you?'

'Well,' Dellie answered in her shy manner, 'I asked him under my breath.'

Dellie developed different ways of coping, or not coping, with the discomfort and stress in our lives. She'd say no when told to do errands and chores, whereas I was endlessly obliging and eager to please, and consequently she received many slaps and hidings. Even at four she would pit herself against Aunty Glad, spitting castor oil all over both herself and our aunt. She'd wrench the leather strap that was used to hit us out from Mum's or Aunty Glad's hand and run away with it. Her incontinence drew their wrath and an assortment of home remedies, all of which she defied. And she developed a series of uncontrollable tics— facial spasms during which her features would become distorted— that we all found distressing.

These tics took numerous forms and each would last a few weeks or months. For several weeks the tic would cause her jaw to jut forward violently every few min- utes, straining the thick cords in her neck. After a while, its form would change and instead her tongue would come whipping out of her mouth and straining to touch the bottom of her chin. For a few months we would live with this unhappy person who we were always telling, 'Stop pulling faces', and we would have to explain to strangers that she wasn't poking her tongue out at them; that she just couldn't help it. As suddenly as it had arrived, that tic would disappear and be replaced by another, which collapsed her face and caused it to jerk to the right or left. Sometimes, all the facial tics would disappear entirely, and instead Dellie would seize upon a piece of her hair and keep tugging at it until, a few strands at a time, her head developed a col- lection of bald spots.

Probably as a result of this, Dellie was quite with- drawn around people with whom she was not familiar.

When she was calm, her face was round, her cheeks plump, and she had stunning large dark eyes and full, shapely lips. People often passed remarks to Mum in front of us all on her beauty. With my smaller eyes frequently darkened by the deep shadows of my ailments, thin and often sunken features and cheek bones that stuck out of my face, Mum, while accepting the compliments on Dellie's beautiful features, would pat me on the head and reply, 'Yes, and this one's clever.' Rather than a compliment, however, in my early adult years my mother's words became a heavy cross to carry.

3

I was shaking with fear the day Mum took me down to the Catholic school. However, the Kindergarten was run by an elderly and very kindly woman, Sister Teresa, who shortly after offered to take Dellie as well. Mum was then able to put Leonie into the council creche and pursue a regular job.

She found work as a laundress at the Mater Hospital. When she first started, she was helping another older woman, but over time that woman retired and Mum took on the work single-handed. She'd rise at about three or four in the morning, rain, hail or shine, and cycle out to the hospital, which was miles away. By sunrise, the first loads of sheets were on the line and Mum would cycle home again. She'd then wake us, prepare our breakfast and lunches, and shepherd us off. She had a baby seat on the handlebars for Leonie and doubled Dellie on the rear carrier. I had to walk, although sometimes she'd put me on the seat and let me steer while she walked and pushed the lot of us along on the bike.

When we came out of kindy in the afternoon, Mum

would be standing there with Leonie already in her seat, and we'd go back up over the hills to our home. That was our routine. Mum would then have a nap (we'd already have had one on our little mats at kindy), and I'd watch the littlies play in the yard and handwash our clothes with soap in a galvanised bucket on the ground, ready for Mum to rinse and hang out when she woke up. This washing was really a great game for me because I'd spend most of the time blowing beautiful big soapy bubbles into the air through my fingers, to the delight of my sisters. As Townsville is in the tropics, work which involved playing water games was cooling and almost always a pleasure.

Even when Mum started work at the hospital, she continued her laundry work at home on weekends and after school, though not to the same extent as before. However, this still meant a lot of work for me, but work always made me feel happy. We didn't have a washing machine, and our laundry was only a lean-to attached to the house and therefore very exposed to the weather, but it never became really cold in Townsville, although in the rainy season there were often deluges and floods. Mum would lift the heavy sheets and shirts from the copper with a wooden poker and put them into one of the concrete tubs and cover them with water. Then she'd have me jump up and wash my feet in the empty tub before putting me in on the clothes to pound and thoroughly rinse the suds out of them. I'd stand up there, happy as a lark, with my skirt tucked into the bottom of my bloomers, stomping away in the water and having great fun.

Mum was always busy. When there wasn't paid work to do, she would sit at her treadle machine and make clothes for us, turning old and worn sheets into bloomers and cheap white flannelette into singlets. She sewed each of us a 'fancy' dress for the annual show, which was always held in winter. She made them from the same pattern, which was often discussed with me before being purchased, but varied the colours. One year she made smart A-line dresses, in navy and wine, with little white Peter Pan collars and cuffs. She also crotcheted, and we each had a lace frock which we were made to wear when she had to trot us out to government departments.

Mum's thrift extended to the yard and the kitchen. She grew snake beans, bananas and pumpkins, and we often lived off them. As well as mango trees, she had a row of pawpaw trees around the perimeter of the yard, the flowers of which she carefully fertilised in case the bees weren't as industrious as she needed them to be. We ate steamed green pawpaw as a rather tasteless but nutritious vegetable and diced ripe pawpaw for dessert.

After a year at kindy, I was deemed ready to go to St Joseph's primary school, which was in the same compound. Dellie was to remain at kindy for another year, so although I was nervous about moving off alone, the change made me feel older.

I wasn't at St Joseph's long before Mum became ill. She took me aside and told me that she would have to send us away for a while, and that I was going to have to look after Dellie. In conjunction with Father Gard and the nuns at the school, she had arranged for us to go to St Joseph's orphanage in Rockhampton.

She took us the five hundred miles by train and we were met at the station and taken into the countryside to a big imposing building on top of a hill. As we were being driven along, Dellie and I were anxious and upset, and the driver, another priest or a brother, told us that all the food we were going to eat at the orphan-age, which he called a school, was grown on the prop-erty by the people who lived there. From the car window I could see large tracts of land under cultiva-tion, just like in picture books I'd read, so I thought this new life would be exciting.

The staff at the hospital where Mum was to have her operation in Townsville had told her she could keep Leonie with her. Leonie was about two years old and her food was still supplemented by breastfeeding. However, Mum was visibly upset by having to leave us at the orphanage and kept promising to come back and get us. It hadn't crossed my mind that she wouldn't so I became confused when she kept repeating her promise to reassure us. I knew nothing about orphan-ages but had glimpsed older girls who were boarders at our school in Townsville and so assumed our lives would be something like theirs.

At the orphanage, Mum spent a little time with us in a parlour where she spoke to the nuns before being taken to Rockhampton to catch her train back to Townsville.

Mum had told me that while I was there I'd be able to meet a cousin of ours named Valda. We never knew we had any cousins, save for Aunty Glad's children. After watching Mum drive out of sight down the hill, and holding Dellie while we shed a few tears, I thought we'd then get to see this mysterious relative.

As soon as Mum left, we were taken out of the nice building which was the nun's quarters, and walked over to another part of the complex. A man working in the garden was called to take our suitcase away. There were no children about and I wondered where they were.

Probably working somewhere out in those fields, I thought, wrongly as it turned out.

Dellie was still crying loudly when the sister told us she was leaving us to play in their new recreation hall. This was a vast and very splendid, lowset building with glass windows. The nun opened the door with a key from her belt, pushed us inside and locked the door again. Except for a few wooden forms the hall was empty. I sat down and tried to distract Dellie from crying but there was nothing in the huge room to use for a game or diversion. The windows were all closed and I was unable to open them. At six years old, I wasn't very strong and bolts and catches were still a bit of a mystery to me. The hall became unbearably hot and by the time a nun came to fetch us eventually, I was upset too.

We were taken to another building to be processed, then we were given baths in a tub and our hair was washed and checked for lice. There were several nuns involved in this induction and they didn't really talk to us but about us, making comments about how thin I was but remarking that we were very clean. One nun ran her hand over my hair and said, 'Islanders. Put them in the Islanders dormitory.'

The dormitory building was large and double-storey. It had windows made of ply which could be held open by propping them up with sticks, but on that day they were all closed and the whole place was very dark. Our suitcase was waiting at the door and the nun and I hauled it up the narrow stairs. We were taken to two little bunks side by side, and I was told to put our pyjamas, soap and toothbrushes into small lockers which stood nearby. I was embarrassed when the nun rummaged in our suitcase because I wasn't used to anyone outside the family looking at our things. She sorted out some frocks, bloomers, singlets and socks and put them in the locker shelves. Everything else, she said, was to remain in the suitcase, and it would be locked up for us in the port room.

By the time we were taken to the dining room, another huge space with long wooden tables and forms on which to sit, I was exhausted and hungry, and Dellie was still crying. She was inconsolable and remained so for most of the time we were there. The dining hall was dim and empty when we arrived and we were made to sit at two separate tables. Dellie screamed louder and held out her little arms to me. I could do nothing except try to signal her with my face to be quieter.

The doors opened and hundreds of children, and a few adults, streamed in. No one was talking but the noise of so many shoes on the floor and the scratch and clash of forms being moved to and fro was thunderous. When everyone was seated, the room fell quiet for Grace which was said by a soft-voiced nun somewhere in the middle of the room. Otherwise, only Dellie's loud cries broke the silence. Big girls then began ferrying trays of food and jugs of milk and water into the room. Eventually a sister took Dellie outside and I was free to look around, observe and make comparisons between what I saw and things I'd seen before.

The boys and girls were seated in different sections, and there appeared to be far more girls than boys. There was a substantial number of people of colour, which was vastly different from my school in Townsville where Dellie and I were the only brown-skinned children. But everyone at my table was white apart from me, and they were as healthy and robust as any other group of children I'd ever seen. Seating was arranged so that at my end everyone was around the same age, and further along the room, the ages of the girls increased. Another difference between the children I had known in Townsville and these girls was their drabness. The Catholic girls at home came to school with their hair in neat plaits and matching ribbons, bows and slides in their hair. They wore pretty gold crosses and several had gold sleepers in their ears, tiny rings with their initials and many, even those too young to tell the time, wore handsome watches. From their pockets fluttered pretty handkerchiefs and they carried themselves with an air of being precious little people. These girls had neither that air nor those symbols of being cared about. Their hair wasn't brushed until it shone, and many of them were loath to smile because they had badly discoloured or chipped teeth.

I don't remember exactly how long we were at the orphanage, but it was several months, perhaps more than a year. Mum sent us Easter eggs, which the nuns made us share with other children, many of whom received no gifts, letters or visits the whole time we were there. No one came to visit Dellie and me either, but we'd get little letters from Mum which the nuns would read to us, small gifts on our birthday, such as lace hankies and toys, which they'd let us look at for a few minutes before putting them away in our locked suitcase, and colouring books, which were put in with the other colouring books in the classrooms.

Dellie and I spent our days apart, me in a grade room and Dellie in some sort of kindergarten. At night we slept side by side in our bunks. Dellie cried almost every night, but she wasn't alone. Frequently, the distressing sounds of many children weeping bitterly made it difficult for everyone to sleep, and sometimes the hopelessness and despair in their voices wakes me in the night to this very day.

Dellie got a hard time because of her incontinence. The nuns and other girls thought they could shame her into stopping, but they only managed to distress her. Then responsibility for her bed-wetting was put onto me, and I was expected to wake up and take her to the toilet when she wanted to go. The problem was that she didn't wake herself up, and the first thing I'd know about it was when I woke up to find her crying or laying quietly with big eyes and the covers pulled up tightly around her neck to prevent the acrid smell from permeating the dorm. The sister eventually put a bucket of water each night in the shower room and when I discovered the bed was wet, I had to get up and soak the sheets in the bucket. It was always pitch black when I had to do this, and I was frightened finding my way to the room in the dark and huddling over the bucket all by myself. Although it was taboo for girls to get into each other's beds, the nuns began to overlook it when I took Dellie into mine after these bed-wetting incidents.

Despite my early optimism, I didn't see much of cousin Valda and I learned nothing about her parents or how she was related to me. Although Valda had brown skin, her hair was straight, so she wasn't in the Islander line of the dorm. As well as the section for Islanders, there were separate areas for Aborigines, whites and others. I didn't know what an Islander was, so it didn't upset me for us to be where we were, or perhaps it was just that there were plenty of more urgent things to be upset about.

Overall, I was quite happy at the orphanage. It was a wonderful change from being the oldest and always carrying the responsibility at home. When other children called us names, such as 'abos', 'boongs', 'black gins' and 'niggers', the bigger girls took them on and fought them.

In the yard was a deep well with a handpump from which I loved to pump clear water that was always cold, and even though an occasional small green frog also came hurtling up with it, the water was the nicest I ever tasted. Other girls screamed and ran when the frogs came up, but I thought their colour was wonderful, and I'd carry them around in my pockets or in the front of my dress until some nun, attracted by girls carrying on and pointing at me, made me take them out.

The food was another high point for me. Although we were never actually starving at home and Mum was resourceful in the kitchen, we didn't have a lot of food. Mum would buy one apple or orange every day and cut it into four so that we'd each have a small piece for the vitamins it contained, and whatever she cooked we were obliged to eat. At the orphanage there was some small degree of choice, and while many of the other girls at my table whinged endlessly, I found the trays stacked high with thick slabs of freshly baked and crusty bread particularly inviting. Another favourite of mine was the very thick porridge that was served each morning, grown in the fields and ground up on the premises, and full of delicious little lumps to crunch. We'd swap food amongst ourselves and I often got through four or more bowls of porridge, while other girls ate my toast or bacon and eggs.

The deep distress of girls who felt themselves abandoned was upsetting to me, and there were others who teased them frightfully and cruelly about it. Whereas in my school in Townsville there was sometimes a bit of a fracas about the ownership of something, a toy or book perhaps, here there was relentless friction about whether or not one was loved or wanted. Sometimes I would hear them say, 'Your mother doesn't want you. You're here forever!' and the reply, 'Your mother doesn't want you either! No one in your family wants you. That's why you're here too!' Occasionally one of these nasty girls would direct their opening remark to me and Dellie. I'd take Dellie's hand and walk away with my head up boldly, but Dellie would always burst into tears. I never bothered to get into a fight about it, bolstered, no doubt, by the regular letters Mum sent us which continued to tell us she was still alive and that she'd be back for us.

Out of the blue, Aunty Glad turned up one day to collect us. Even Dellie was pleased to see her, though she showed it by bursting into tears. A taxi drew up outside, causing a great deal of excitement amongst all the girls because it wasn't a regular visiting day—which were often sad days anyway, because there were generally few visitors. When we all crowded up to the window of the classroom to peer through the slats to see who it was, I recognised Aunty Gladdie immediately. We were told to sit back at our desks and work, but my stomach began to churn and I couldn't settle down. At last, an older girl came running to tell the teacher to release me, and we both went to fetch Dellie.

We waited with Aunty Glad in the nun's parlour while our suitcase and the few items from our lockers were brought over and packed in front of us. I was so excited I forgot to mention some other things we had spread around elsewhere, such as our canvas games shoes which were stored in the recreation hall. When I remembered them in the taxi on the way back into

Rockhampton, Aunty Glad said not to worry, Mum would buy us some more.

I recall kneeling on the back seat of that taxi and looking through the rear window at the orphanage on the hill, surrounded by neat fields as it became smaller and smaller while we drove to the main road. I was torn between leaving my relatively carefree existence there and my desire to return to Mum and home. Aunty Glad had brought us each a package of embroidered boxed handkerchiefs edged with lace and a colourful little bracelet of beads to wear, and she had colouring books and pencils to keep us entertained during our long train ride home. I played with mine but Dellie looked out the window whenever she was awake, and she didn't seem to believe that we were going home until the train pulled up in Townsville. When she saw Mum waiting on the platform to meet us, she flung herself into her arms and cried some more.

Back at school, I was briefly the subject of rough teasing for having spent time in the orphanage. How my classmates learned about it, I've no idea. However, the fact that Dellie and I were from a poor family quickly took ascendancy in their taunts, as Catholic children, like others, are cruel. Sister de Salles was discreet about the things she gathered to give Mum—uniforms, hats and school insignia hatbands, sports uniforms—but still there were turned-up noses at the lunches we brought from home.

I was aware on some level that I was different from other children in a more basic way than just our clothes and what was in our lunch boxes, but it was a very low-level awareness. Children at our school were discouraged from name calling and punished if they were heard to do so. We were protected from children who attended the state school across the road from ours, who may have been inclined to be rude, by the presence of Mum who came in these early years to pick us up on her bike each day. There were no incidents on a daily basis and I was lulled into a false sense of security that my identity was the same as the other children around me. That was short lived.

One day some visitors came to the school, and we pupils were gathered in a circle to welcome them. After the greeting one woman in their party spoke very loudly, her eyes lighting up. 'How nice. Thank you. And *who* is that lovely little coloured girl?' she asked of the sister in charge of our class.

I looked around to see who she was talking about, and saw a sea of white faces, because one doesn't see one's own face in a crowd. Then I realised they were all looking at me. It was *me* she was talking about in that false tone of voice. *Me*, who was so different from the others that I could be picked out the minute anyone came through the door!

It was a revelatory moment and one which I've never forgotten. No matter that I wore the same uniform, did the same schoolwork, drank the same water and ate the same food, I was different and would always be different. In that flash of awareness, I realised that in my lifetime people would always see my colour first, no matter how good I was or how hard I worked, and that they'd attribute to me whatever feelings they had about people of colour.

Not long after this, Mum began waiting at the top of the first hill for us after school instead of coming all the way to the school gates. She'd watch as Dellie and I walked up the hill, to make sure we stayed on the dirt edge and didn't go on the road. Then she began waiting at Trembath's corner, and we'd have to cross two roads to meet her; and not long after she'd wait at our front gate. I was now fully in charge of our safety on the way to and from school. As it was a long way and often very hot in the mid-afternoon sun, Mum had been in the habit of buying us an icy-pole which cost a penny each at Hoopers' grocery store, which was a little over halfway home. She then made an arrangement with Mr Hooper to give us our icy-poles each day and put it in a book, and she'd pay at the end of the week.

There were periods when this system worked well, with Mum occasionally swooping down at unexpected places along the route to make sure we were sticking to all her rules. I didn't like us coming home alone, initially because we were often confronted by big dogs, which my sisters didn't mind much but I did. When I saw any dogs ahead of us on the road, I'd lead the way around the block to avoid them, and risk us all getting into trouble for being late. Mum told me to carry a big stick but it wasn't always easy to find one. As well, I was worried that any dog which was close enough to hit with a stick was already close enough to get me. I began loading my pockets up with stones, and leaving little piles of stones conveniently placed at handy spots along the way.

High on the hill behind the cathedral was the Townsville Migrant Hostel, where mainly English migrants were accommodated when they arrived. Children from the hostel went to the state school and, until they grew familiar with the area, they took very different roads from us. It wasn't long, however, before they worked out that the way we walked was a shorter and less arduous route.

Often a group of these migrant children walked

home together, and they took delight in calling us names. I'd lurk around the mango trees near our school until I saw them walking across the road at the top of the hill, because I always wanted them ahead of me so I could keep an eye on what they were doing. From behind, I could also regulate the distance between us because they were unlikely to run back along streets they had already negotiated. But when they dawdled it often made me and Dellie arrive home late from school, and then we were severely chastised.

Eventually, Leonie joined us, having completed her kindy and moved to St Joseph's primary. So there were three of us—against up to a dozen of the migrant children. I had two younger children in my care, one of whom had much shorter legs and was not keen to run even when trouble seemed imminent. I was nine, Dellie seven, and Leonie, five years old.

Then a mini war broke out. The migrant children were all very pale and often wore big cotton bonnets and straw hats to protect themselves from the sun. State school children wore ordinary day clothes to school, while Catholic school children wore navy uniforms and navy felt hats, so there was already a degree of rivalry between us on that basis. Most Catholic school children lived in the opposite directions to us, in North Ward or Belgian Gardens, and those whose parents didn't pick them up by car went home on the school bus or walked along the Strand. No bus came our way. Our colour added an additional dimension, as did the proximity of our house to where the migrant kids lived.

Migrant kids, joined by a handful of other state school kids, who lived more or less in our direction, began to wait at the top of the hill, calling us names and saying we were dirty, and arming themselves with stones to rain down on us. They were a raggedy band of ruffians, often with runny sores on their arms and legs from mosquito bites, against which they had no immunity. What they had in their favour was numbers.

When we reached the sanctuary of our front door, they'd sometimes come to the fence which overlooked our house and throw stones at our windows and onto our roof. If Mum came out, they'd scarper. From time to time, when she wasn't there, they'd yell abuse. 'We were brought over here to civilise you natives,' they'd scream, 'but you're just dirty black gins who don't deserve to live.' When I tried to complain to Mum and have her do something, she'd give me one of her three main lectures: ignore them, they're just stupid; turn the other cheek; and, this'll toughen you up for the real world.

My sisters were content to let me keep the roads safe for them and it was hard to get them to run whenever it was necessary, much less fight. Sometimes these altercations would increase because I wasn't prepared to accept insults. I'd tear up and threaten to push their words back down their throats. Although fist fights were rare, stoning us was common.

Mum was fond of relating an incident that occurred around then. Leonie wandered into the house first, and when she was followed at a distance by Dellie, Mum became concerned and asked Dellie where I was. Dellie, although bigger than me, answered disinterestedly, 'She's fighting. They're throwing stones at her again.'

Mum was horrified and asked Dellie why she wasn't back there helping me. 'Oh, she's winning,' came her reply.

I didn't always win, but I was always afraid. Several

times, well-aimed shots found their mark and I'd walk into the house with blood running down my face and clothes. Once, boys from a family named Ford who lived nearby stoned me and split my head open so badly I had to be rushed to hospital. Mum stormed over to their house, abused their mother and threatened that the next time they spoke a word to any of her children, she'd be back to cut their tongues out! Neither Mum nor I received any apology from their mother.

Another person who stoned me has since become a well-known writer for a Sydney newspaper. His mother, who became a friend and mentor to me when I was a young woman, was unaware of what he used to get up to on his way home from school, and would have been deeply distressed if I'd ever told her when I had the opportunity to do so. He was years older than me, so these fights were by no means equal even when they were one on one, which was rare.

The school began to let us out a few minutes early so that we could be up the hill and away before the state school children were released from their classes. Sometimes those minutes were too few, and I'd look around to see a crowd of children racing towards me. I'd quickly arm myself with stones or whatever I could pick up and tell my sisters to scoot along ahead of me. I'd walk backwards while they ran ahead, skittering my stones along the ground to keep our pursuers jumping so they'd have to slow down and my sisters could make good their escape. It was a strange way to grow up.

4

Two girls, Leila and Desma, spent so much time living with us that Mum tried to convince us they were our 'sisters' and have us treat them as such. Both were much older than me, and Desma was a few years older than Leila. Mum said they were orphans, but, although I believe they may have spent periods in orphanages and homes, Leila at least had a father who was there for her some of the time.

Leila's mother, or so Mum told Aunty Glad and me, had been a very beautiful woman who sold cosmetics and taught women how to use them. She had committed suicide when Leila was a little girl and living with her. Once, when she'd been drinking, she'd sent her small daughter to fetch Lysol from the bathroom and then drank it, dying a terrible and painful death in front of her child. Mum told me this to explain Leila's often bizarre behaviour. Leila always thought of herself as worthless, and that she'd poisoned her mother. A lot of things she did around me reflected these feelings.

Her father was a Finnish seaman who came to Townsville several times a year. His name was Mr Laaksonen;

we called him Laaka. He lived at Mrs Sullivan's house when he was in town, and was a hard worker and a good friend to Mum.

Mum described Desma as 'a child nobody wanted', but whether she was a true orphan or not, I have no idea. Neither girl was at our house all the time as they were in and out of other places. Many years later, one betrayed me and the other betrayed herself.

I don't recall Desma ever going to school with us, but Leila did so occasionally. She was a 'wild child' and showed us how to steal bottles of softdrink from Cobbs' factory which was on our way home. The bottles were stacked in boxes out in the factory yard in the sun and Leila told us we had to be careful because hot softdrink bottles explode easily. She showed me how she popped the caps on her teeth, a trick I never mastered, and had me scour the countryside looking for empty bottles to return to the factory for the cash refund, which she then spent on little packets of Ardath and Craven A cigarettes. I didn't mind that she kept most of the money because, being older and taller, while she was with us, the migrant hostel children didn't bother us.

As suddenly as she would appear, she'd disappear again, and there'd be whispered conferences between the adults about her and where she'd gone this time. Once, she spent a period at a home for wayward children in Brisbane. Mum kept threatening she'd send me there too, if she caught me going into the softdrink factory or being late home from school.

Dessie (Desma) and Leila, being older, were allowed privileges, such as wearing lipstick and shaving their legs, which I was not permitted. They also had boyfriends and talked and giggled a lot about them, and it made me feel very adult to be included occasionally in their conversations. In the main, I didn't understand what they were talking about and they'd banish me when I asked them to explain their jokes. They'd say I was 'such a baby' and send me off crying.

I only recall one of their boyfriends, a young man called Mervyn, who went to China on a ship and brought us back gifts. Mum received a beautiful china bottle of ginger in honey, which she kept for a long time, nibbling bits from it and sometimes sharing a few tastes with me. Then she treasured the empty bottle for its beauty and kept it on her dressing table. Mervyn told us about seamen from his ship finding dead bodies floating in a river in China. The crew was scandalised because when their captain got in touch with the local authorities he was asked if the bodies were of Asian or European appearance. When he replied that they were Asian, he was told to put them back in the river. Mervyn was one of the men who had to carry out that order, and he'd been very upset by the experience.

The opposite of today's fashions, the older girls became, the longer they were allowed to wear their skirts. Dellie and I were stuck with dresses that came to the middle of our knees, while Leila and Desma were allowed to wear theirs to a length which just showed a flash of ankle. They'd waltz around the house with their skirts swinging, singing pop tunes and teaching them to us. 'I've got a Lovely Bunch of Coconuts' and 'Yaba Dabba Dabba' were great favourites, and the expression they favoured most for styles, and men, which met their approval was 'Hubba hubba'.

Often neither of these girls was at home with us. Leila's father, however, continued his short calls, during which he'd build and repair things, such as our fences, and help Mum with heavy chores, like lopping overhanging branches from the mango trees, which banked up in his absence.

Mum obviously yearned to either have a man around the house or that I should have been a son. Although I was small and skinny, because of my personality she often made me fill this role.

I wasn't afraid of spiders or toads or other things that made Mum shudder and my sisters cry. We had all manner of boxes and suitcases left by people stored up under our house, where the space was narrow and cramped. Lots of small creatures lived up there too, but they never deterred me from crawling around amongst them, inspecting these forbidden treasure troves. I seemed to have no innate fear of insects, even spiders with long thin gangling legs climbing and swaying awkwardly around in their webs. I always remember groping around under the house as a real adventure. I'd go there with my heart beating quickly and loudly, and suddenly become conscious of the sound of my own breathing, the nerves in my ears alert and straining to hear my mother's footfalls on the wooden floor above my head. Any movement, the slightest squeaking of the floorboards, was likely to be a signal of her approach, of being caught, of being dragged away and hit. Quietly, so quietly, I'd creep forward, listening, and carefully ease open clasps which kept the cases closed. To touch something in the case—a brown hat with a piece of stiffened net attached to it, or a dress or coat across which I'd run my fingers lightly—my joy almost orgasmic.

Mum knew about my strange ways, and she'd say, 'Bring me a hammer and two short nails from those boxes under the house—the ones you're not allowed to touch!' Later, she said I could go there but to be careful, and I wasn't to take my sisters.

I made one of the boxes my own, and began storing up my own 'treasures': pieces of brightly coloured glass, a belt made of fabric and glue which I rescued from our rubbish bin, and other oddments. I always had my eye out for things to collect, combing through the piles, raking the dirt, and going through our own and our neighbours' rubbish bins. Mum laughed and called me a bower bird for always picking up shiny pieces and stashing them away. I didn't mind, I often found coins others had walked right over.

Mum nagged that I'd get bitten by something and die, or get tetanus from a rusty nail and die. I'd already been so close to dying during my illnesses that death seemed familiar to me. I felt I knew a lot about it already, and I wasn't afraid of it.

I don't recall exactly when my real lessons in the heavy stuff of birth and death actually started, apart from my own close tangos with death. I believe they started with the animals. We and all our neighbours always had a cat or two. If sterilisation or spaying was available, it wasn't something I ever heard anyone speak of in relation to small animals. I suspect from the coarse jokes I heard much later about 'prairie oysters' that sterilisation by any means was reserved for much bigger creatures.

Once, when I was about eight or nine, our cat had kittens, an event I witnessed until I became tired of the slowness of it all and walked away. Mum had prepared a box for the birth, placing it under a bed, the opening level with the edge of the bed. She hunted the cat when it got near its time and managed to coax it to begin its litter in the carton instead of in a basket of clean laundry, where it had birthed previously and obviously preferred.

I don't recall how many kittens the cat had in this litter. It's enough to say it was multiple births, because they were *always* multiple births.

I was asleep late that night when Mum came for me. She pulled on my dress and drew me out into the kitchen. This was something unusual—I was much more used to her shooing me off to bed in the evening when I didn't want to go than getting me up once I was asleep.

Laaka was sitting in the kitchen and he didn't look too happy. From the frown on his face I could tell he was being asked to do something that didn't meet with his approval. Mum's comment, 'Someone here has to know how to do it. Let her watch,' was not reassuring to me.

We all trooped down the steep back stairs, Laaka walking slowly on his long legs so I didn't have to hurry and perhaps trip on my shorter ones. Our laundry had no lights, but Laaka carried a torch. I was surprised to see there the box in which the cat had had her litter earlier that day, and even more surprised—given the lengths my mother had gone to set up a comfortable place for the delivery—to find the mother cat and kittens out in the night air.

The cat had cleaned the kittens. They scrambled blindly around her, eyes tightly closed, but still able by their sense of smell to find the way to her milk. Mum and Laaka each picked one up, rolled it onto its back in their palms to sort out males and females and to inspect its coat and colours. Eventually, they came to a decision about one of the kittens and it was put aside. Mum ran lightly and quietly back up the stairs and into the house while Laaka picked up the mother cat and the chosen kitten and followed her. He gently dropped the cat and kitten on their feet around the corner of the door and my mother abruptly closed it, and I could hear the bolt being slammed home, shutting off the light. Laaka came back and looked down at me in the moonlight. He shrugged. His English was poor at the time and he was unable to communicate very well with me.

Upstairs we could hear the cat scratching at the door, trying to get out, and soon we heard the sound of the window in the kitchen, which was over the laundry, being rattled noisily closed. It all felt a bit like a game to me, as we often closed the window when the cat was out sunning herself on the laundry roof, and she amused us by coming to the window and tapping on the glass to see if anyone would let her in, before easily stretching her sinewy body across from the roof to the stairs. Now the position was reversed, the cat inside and trying to get out. I knew she often moved into and out of the house through any and all of the windows, depending on her mood, so I was waiting to see how long it would take her to get back to us. Nothing else that was happening made any sense.

Laaka passed me the torch, indicating I was to keep it focused on the kittens. Squirming and nosing each other, and without control over their legs, they were more like fat grubs, yet to develop their kittenish appeal.

Laaka picked them up, put them into a soft cotton flour bag and dropped them into a kerosene tin which was more than half full of water. For me, the game of the mother cat trying to get back out to us was over. I was shocked. But Laaka worked quickly, using a stick to fully immerse the bag, which had billowed on the top of the water. Bubbles of air kept rising from the water, and Laaka frowned up at me as the light from the torch I was holding wavered and left him in the dark. As he took the torch from me, I thought I could see the shapes of the kittens' heads through the cloth on the top of the water, swimming and bobbing around. Laaka used the length of the torch to reach under the bench and retrieve one of the good sized rocks that were kept there. He used it to weight the bag to the bottom of the water, careful that none of the cloth was on the top. He put a flat wooden board right over the kerosene tin and another rock on top of that.

After he washed his hands in the cement laundry tub, we went upstairs, but Mum wouldn't let us in. The cat was still putting on a turn. I followed Laaka around the side of the house and we went in by the front door.

Mum asked me if I wanted a drink. I didn't. I felt sick. She whispered to me as she walked with me back to the bedroom I shared with my sisters that I wasn't to tell them anything. 'You're the oldest. You're the only one to know,' she said, transferring to my very young shoulders an awful weight not only of responsibility but also of silence.

It was never too hard for me to keep secrets from my sisters. As I was growing in knowledge, the things I told them often lacked meaning or importance for them. By the time they were old enough to be interested or to invite from me any confidences and secrets, I'd somehow, despite my youth, entered into a sort of conspiratorial pact with Mum and other adults about the true but uglier aspects of the world.

For example, it was always me who helped our mother keep Santa Claus alive. My reward was to be woken quietly after my sisters had at last fallen asleep, and together Mum and I would tiptoe around, doing the last minute wrapping, printing names on cards in neat block letters, and putting the gifts at the bottom of my sisters' beds or under a rough tree Mum had dragged in from outside. I helped keep the Tooth Fairy alive too, reminding my mother of who was to get the penny under their pillow when she, in her weariness, forgot. I always knew when it was Easter—Mum would creep into our bedroom and silently shake me awake, wanting a few of my tight curls to stick on the hen's eggs she had turned into our Easter treats. Occasionally, our Easter egg characters had cotton wool for hair as they nestled in their shoebox home, but Mum didn't believe in wasting money. She knew my hair would grow back, while cotton wool cost money. So much for the Easter Bunny.

Some weeks after the late-night episode of Laaka and the kittens, Mum again drew me aside. Mrs Scott's cat had had kittens. Mum asked me if I thought I could put them in a bucket of water, as Laaka was back at sea. I was already in the habit of doing lots of things for our neighbour Mrs Scott, such as running messages, and I thought her a kindly lady. She sometimes blessed me with pennies and threepenny pieces with which I could buy lollies. My mother said if I drowned the kittens, Mrs Scott would reward me.

At first I said no, but there was no walking away from Mum when she was talking to you. She kept insisting I should do it, and trying to impress me with a lot of reasons, all of which had to do with how it would be a great favour to Mrs Scott and how pleased she would be. When I continued to refuse, my mother put her face down to my level—which was always a sure sign things were getting serious—and asked me why not.

I told her straight. 'I don't want to get up in the dark. I'm frightened to come down here by myself. Why can't we wait until Laaka comes back and let him do it?'

I knew Laaka wasn't due for many months, but I didn't know why we couldn't wait. The kittens, it seemed to me, would have been able to enjoy a few months of life before it was all ended for them in the bottom of a bucket.

Mum laughed when she heard the cause of my fear, or at least the cause I was able to speak about. 'You don't have to do it at night. You can do it right now, if you want,' she said. I didn't want. I asked why she couldn't do it herself, and she reminded me that she didn't have the stomach or nerves for that sort of thing. I've no idea why she thought I did, except for her need for displacement.

Mum made me fetch a page from a notebook so that she could illustrate the point she wanted to make. Mrs Scott's cat had had six kittens, she told me, and they would all grow up into cats. She made me write '6' at the top of the page. Mrs Scott, an elderly widow, couldn't afford to feed six cats. Besides, cats aren't like people. Even if there were no other cats around—and of course there were, including our own cat and her kitten—Mrs Scott's cats would mate with each other and beget even more kittens. So, if half the new kittens were females, and in a few months time the female kittens all had more kittens, how many cats would be added to the world? With my pencil I came up with the answer, eighteen. 'That's on top of the cat she's got now, and the six others, so add all those in. The answer's not eighteen at all,' Mum said. 'Now, if even half the eighteen are female, and they all have six kittens, how many cats will Mrs Scott end up having to buy food for?'

The enormity of the problems posed by the cat population explosion which would come about if I didn't drown the kittens, became apparent to me. It would all be my fault. Mum made me feel worse by adding that Mrs Scott's cat would have another litter again in a few months, so how many would that be, and their kittens, and their kittens' kittens?

Mrs Scott was ready for me when I arrived. She'd tied the kittens into a cotton flour bag already, so I didn't have to see them. They were making squeaking noises from inside the bag, and I could see their bulky little sausage-like bodies heaving around and changing the shape of the bag. So I didn't look.

Mum told me I was to drown them in our laundry, not Mrs Scott's. When I brought them around the side of the house, Mum was indoors, giving my sisters some sort of treat to keep them inside and distracted while I 'got on with it'. I had to fill the kerosene tin up with a scoop because, even half filled with water, it would have been too heavy for me to lift out of the tub. I got everything ready, the bucket poised on the edge of the laundry floor so I could just tip it over on the ground when the time came to drain it.

I sat for a long time looking at the squirming bag, feeling sorry for the scraps of life that would never grow up and contribute to the big cat problem. I felt angry with God, who I'd been learning about in school and who had set this all up, and angry with my mother, who put the animal population problem onto me. I was aware of her weakness, and I knew I'd always have to be strong to look after her and do all the nasty things she wasn't able to do. I would do them to please her. I would do them because somebody had to do them.

Mum yelled from out of the kitchen window. 'Roberta'—when she was stressed she always said my full name and broke it into two separate syllables— have you finished that job yet?'

'I'm just doing it now.'

'Well, hurry up. The longer you leave it, the crueller you are.' I knew she was speaking in code, not mentioning exactly what it was I was doing, to maintain the secret between us.

I picked up the bag and dropped it into the water, using the stick to keep it submerged until most of the air was expelled. I lowered the rock into the water, careful not to crush the kittens with it, merely to catch and weigh down the fabric of the bag to keep them underwater.

I climbed up to the tubs and washed my hands before I went back upstairs. Mum raised her eyes quizzically at me, and offered me food and milk when I said the job was done, but I wasn't hungry. I began to wonder how long I was supposed to leave them there, and what I was to do with them once I emptied the bucket—things Laaka hadn't shown me.

Mum organised our games and chores indoors that afternoon, and when evening arrived, she said we were going for a walk into town. 'Town' was four blocks away, and we, and many other people, often strolled around when the heat of the day had subsided. Sometimes on these walks, if Mum could afford it, we would have the rare treat of an ice-cream, which cost two pence each, or an icy-pole—she could buy three for tuppence at the Greeks' store. I could feel an ice-cream due to me that evening.

I was sent down to empty the bucket but, with the rock in it, it was too heavy for me to tip over. Mum had to do it herself. My sisters peered at us from the top of the stairs, wanting to know what we were doing. 'Just fixing this bit of washing,' Mum replied to their nosy questions.

The bag began to dry out while Mum was getting us ready to go, and the shapes were discernible through the cloth. She had me wrap it in a bit of paper, then put it into an old hessian bag. We were taking it with us. In answer to my probing, she said we were going to throw the bag over the bridge into Ross River when it got dark. And what would happen to it then, I asked, visualising the dead, drying and rotting toads I had seen squashed on the roads, and wondering if dead kittens were anything like them. 'The sharks will probably swallow the bag for their lunch,' replied my mother, 'and if they don't, crocodiles will probably eat them.'

How many kittens I fed to how many sharks and crocodiles over the years, I don't know, I was unable to keep count. As word of my skill spread, old widows further afield were permitted to make use of my services. How much my mother received for loaning me out like this, or even whether she was paid at all, I still have no idea. Although I received ice-creams and other treats, the occasional chocolate bar and so on, my sisters had to get them too or, so my mother would warn me, they'd 'guess there's something going on'.

I came to understand that there are terrible secrets in this world, and that, for reasons which may have nothing really to do with the individuals, some people get to know about the secrets, and others don't. There were all these people who were much older than me, yet I was having to do their killing for them. I suppose my desire to please, to be helpful, and hopefully to be loved in return, extended to my mother, although I wasn't delighted about the nature of the efforts she expected of me. Having to 'do' for the old ladies, I didn't understand at all, but it seemed somehow to fit in with what I was learning at that time—that Mum and I were expected to do a lot of work for white people generally.

Mum's 'weak stomach' prevented her from doing all sorts of things which were then left to me. She wasn't happy to remove splinters or fragments of glass from kids' feet, or even her own. When I was too young to be trusted to strike a match, Mum would run the little flame over the tip of a sewing needle—'to sterilise it,' she said—and give it to me to pick out the splinters and pieces of glass from my own or my sisters' feet. Sometimes, while I was taking care of injuries, she busied herself with preparing a bread poultice—hot water poured over a thick crust—to whack onto the affected area to draw out any unseen fragments. Her bandages invariably fell off, she could never quite get the knack. She borrowed a book from the library for me to study how to tie up wounds, this was her way of coping.

After I'd been given the chore of preventing a local takeover by cats by drowning them, I was drafted in for the bloodier task of beheading poultry. To add to my little store of sparkling treasures, Mum gave me a tack hammer, a tomahawk and a good file.

I was never on first call for killing the chickens. Mum would search high and low to get some man to do it. Unlike the arrival of kittens, which would precipitate calls on my deadly skills at unexpected times, with poultry we usually knew in advance that someone would have to do the deed. There was always at least one bird killed at Christmas, often a rooster we'd been fattening for the occasion, but Easter, visits by Aunty Glad and her children, and other special events, also meant the preparation of a bird or two. I was to learn how to do it, and be prepared to knock off a head when no one else was available. I was to be Mother's 'good helper', doing another of the things she couldn't bring herself to do.

Mum would point out which bird she'd earmarked for the table that day, and usually their heads were knocked off first thing in the morning. It was a messy job and we had a chopping block in the backyard on which to do it. The block was also used to chop fuel for the fire, as we had a wood stove as well as a wood copper, and both were needed for the preparation of table birds.

When Mum was able to secure a man to behead the bird, she'd wiggle her eyebrows at me and tell me to, 'Sharpen the axe.' This was her sign that someone else was coming to do it, because the axe was too big, heavy and awkward for me to wield comfortably while holding the bird still on the block. When I was to do the job, she'd just ask me if my tomahawk was sharp. As the owner of the good file, though, I'd sit on the back stairs and carefully stroke to amazing sharpness the blade of the axe which was to be used to dispatch the bird as quickly and painlessly as possible. Horror stories abounded about beheading jobs that had been botched by blunt axes—chickens tearing around with their necks only half severed, others requiring three or four hacks with the axe to complete what should have been accomplished in one second. I prided myself that none of these sorts of things ever happened under my jurisdiction.

I learned to appreciate a fine axe, and to press my thumb on the side of a blade to test it for sharpness. 'Just because it's shiny doesn't mean it's sharp,' I was admonished.

When head was finally separated from bird, and the creature had stopped fluttering around with the jerky movements of its dying nervous system, it was hung from the line upside down for the blood to drain out. Once the bird was dead and still, Mum would reappear from wherever it was she'd hidden while the nasty bits were going on, and she'd take over.

After breakfast, it was time to light the copper and boil the water. The bird was plunged into scalding water, softening its feathers so they could be more easily plucked. Neighbourhood and family pets had to be kept at bay during this procedure, as there were also stories which did the rounds about how dogs and cats had taken off with the Sunday roast before it had even made it to the oven, leaving the family hungry.

When the bird's skin was completely clean and free from feathers, a stroke with Mum's specially sharpened knife around the nethers would open it up to be gutted. We sometimes killed 'old boilers' she'd pointed out for slaughter, but she would carry on loudly and accuse us of having made mistakes if the 'old boiler', when cut open, was actually carrying eggs.

A task Mum tried unsuccessfully to get me to do was to trim some of the hens' combs. We had Orpingtons, Rhode Island Reds, ducks and a few bantams. Some of the Orpington hens' combs grew so long that they drooped over one side of the poor chooks' faces, causing them to be blind on that side. I was sorry for them as their gait became awkward and they missed out on food they couldn't see. Mum sent me into the chook run with a pair of scissors and a sharp kitchen knife. When I inspected one bird closely I thought the comb, because of its red colour, was actually a blood centre and that, if cut, blood would squirt out all over me and the poor bird would probably die in my lap. I thought I'd do it if I could devise some way to cauterise the comb by using redhot wire to make the cut, but I was unable to work the bugs out of the plan, such as how to get wire which didn't break or melt when it was heated, and how to heat the wire *and* hold the chook still at the same time. I sat up on the rocks holding the old hen on my knees for so long that Dellie came up to join me. We agreed this was not a desirable job at all, and it didn't get done.

It was a great relief to me when Laaka stopped working on ships, got a job at the meatworks, and settled in permanently next door. He brought us two baby lambs which he'd saved at the abattoir, and we fed them from babies' bottles we bought for the purpose. His English improved and he laid out a big vegetable patch in front of both the houses. He even grew some tobacco and came in to dry it in our oven. He often came for dinner, and once I asked Mum why she didn't marry him so he could be our father. She said they didn't care about each other 'that way', that they were just friends.

Other Finnish seamen jumped ship and were taken in by old Mrs Sullivan. They got jobs at the meatworks too, and Mum arranged for me, now aged about ten, to give them lessons in English in return for pocket money. That was fun and I learned a smattering of Finnish. Mum said the government considered people from Finland to be desirable, hard working and good prospects for migrants, but the men couldn't get papers in Finland, so they hopped off the ship and hid in the country for a while before presenting themselves to the authorities. Then they got a fine and were allowed to stay because their ship had left and there was no way for them to return to Finland. Mum said I wasn't to talk about it at school.

With Laaka next door to look after our house, Mum took the opportunity to pay a return visit to her sister, our Aunty Glad. The four of us, Mum and us three girls, went to Brisbane by train. The trip took two nights and one day, and at Rockhampton Mum left the carriage to go up the street to buy fish and chips at a shop close to the station. I was to mind the littlies. When the passengers alighted the driver shunted the train up the line to take on water and coal, but I thought we were leaving without Mum. Panic stricken, I ran up and down the carriages, dragging my sisters by their arms, screaming and telling the guards they had to wait for her. Mum was very amused when the train pulled back into the station to pick up the passengers who'd alighted to buy food at the canteen and the guard told her what had happened. I wasn't, though, and felt that the whole trip would turn into a nightmare if Mum didn't give me more help by telling me what was going on.

We kids hadn't been thrilled by the idea of staying with Aunty Glad because she was so strict, but in her own house she was quite a different person, doing her best to prepare food with which we were familiar. At various times we'd met one or other of her children, but this was the first time we met them all together. Gerald and Patty were both older than me, Sandra about my own age, and Colleen was the youngest. Aunty Glad lived on a pension and rented out rooms in her South Brisbane house. She and Mum spent a lot of time catching up on the gossip about what was happening in the lives of other family members who, I learned, shunned Mum because her children were dark.

Aunty Glad and Mum took chairs into the backyard to talk so that we couldn't overhear their conversations, but sometimes they'd finish their chats while they were preparing meals, and I tuned in as often as I could. Aunty Glad chided Mum for not letting her kids 'mix with their own kind', and said she'd have the devil to pay later. I wondered who my own kind were, if they were not these cousins, her children, whom we were now growing to know.

One day Mum took us to meet another family, and there were many of them lined up at the door to welcome us. The adults spent the day upstairs talking and we were sent under the house to play with our cousin, Hiram. The house was close by the Brisbane Exhibition Grounds and the show was on, and show-goers could park their cars in the yard for a fee. This income was an important supplement to the family's funds.

Hiram's father was Jackie Ryan, champion Aboriginal boxer, and our mothers had been friends since they were young. I was surprised that I hadn't heard much about them before, but when we returned home, Mum showed me a snap of them together holding their small babies, who were myself and Hiram, up on a fence at the seaside. His mother had long, lustrous, wavy black hair and was very beautiful indeed.

Back in Townsville, Mum continued her work at the Mater Hospital laundry but also began doing occasional house-cleaning. This was strange because at home she did very little housework as she disliked domestic chores, other than cooking so we could all eat and washing, which she did for the money. Dellie and I, and even Leonie, all had to learn to use a broom and duster early. Mum had a long coir mat which ran the length of the hallway and we'd often be put to pick the dust and fluff off it with our fingers, a painful task. We didn't have luxuries like a vacuum cleaner, but then neither did we have carpets. Our floors were covered with congoleum over newspaper, and recovered when it became worn, until the congo covering was at least three or four layers thick.

Mum began keeping me home from school to accompany her on her house-cleaning missions. It was hard work on our hands and knees scrubbing floors and bathrooms, but Mum had given me a bike to ride conditionally and going cleaning was considered an appropriate occasion.

Unfortunately, around the same time Sister de Salles offered me the opportunity to be one of the Friday lunch girls. Students who wanted fish and chips on Fridays—and, being a Catholic school, that was just about everyone in the higher classes who could be entrusted not to lose their money—put their orders and cash in during the morning. At little lunch, two girls were dispatched to the fish shop to place the order, and we were given the nod by our teachers to leave class fifteen minutes before the regular lunchtime to pick up the lunches. The reward was the freedom, missing fifteen minutes of class, and lunch girls were each given a package of fish and chips for free from the store. Only girls with bikes were allowed to be lunch girls.

Friday was also the day most favoured by Mum for her house-cleaning. Mr Smith, a travelling salesman whose shirts Mum washed, was a bachelor who lived in a flat on the Strand and he often wanted it cleaned for when he came home on the weekends.

Sister de Salles didn't like the idea of me missing school to go cleaning houses, but Mum said, 'Sister de Salles doesn't pay the bills in this house, I do!' Although they were polite to one another, they both put pressure on each other through me. I was plagued by attacks of asthma and, curiously, they often occurred on Thursday nights, which I'd spend inhaling the fumes of crystals which were burnt on a little metal plate over a tiny lamp. Friday I'd get up and go house-cleaning or, if I was allowed, go to school and be lunch girl.

Sister de Salles made an impact on Mum, but the result was that Mum tried to coach me at home. Mum was an avid reader, a perfect speller, and knew all the times tables, but beyond that she could not be very helpful. She didn't know history or geography very well, apart from things she'd heard or learned about, such as World War II combat arenas. She didn't have the foggiest idea about algebra, and she was an opinionated woman who disputed almost everything we had to learn for social studies.

During my earliest years at school, our classrooms had been, to a significant extent, places of propaganda. We were often told simplistic things, such as 'Communism is a big black bear and it will come down from the north and get us if we're not careful.' As I knew we already lived in the north, in my mind the bear wouldn't have had far to go if it had wanted to get us. I often thought it might be lurking in the hills, getting ready to pounce. One day I'd shared this knowledge with Mum, and she hit the roof!

As well as setting me straight about how communism was just an idea, not a living animal, she told me the Catholics were too inclined to use threats of all kinds, including notions of hell and damnation, to get people to do what they wanted. I heard her tell Aunty Glad, during her next trip through Townsville, that the nuns were scaring kids with talk of big black bears and how angry she was about it.

So Mum's views of the world, and consequently of things we were taught in social studies, were somewhat at odds with the answers I was required to give in order to get high grades. I saw a coupon in a magazine offering, for a penny down, a set of books which would cover all the things I needed to know for school, so I sent it in with a penny.

Not long after, a salesman from Arthur Mee's Children's Encyclopedia Publishing Company turned up on our doorstep and told Mum I'd put the deposit down. Mum nearly choked. After she'd cooled down a bit, the man successfully worked out with her how I could have the books I wanted. He and his family only lived a short distance away on Melton Hill, and Mum began doing their laundry and housework until the encyclopedia was paid for. Even then he continued to offer her work. Naturally, I had to help.

St Joseph's provided me with sound basic literacy and numeracy skills, and having an encyclopedia in the house enabled me to pursue almost any subject I wanted. I felt the information was more neutral than offered either by the nuns or by Mum, and I loved the look and feel of the beautiful books as well as the bounty within them.

Mum began to worry about the amount of time I spent reading. She was a member of the local library and had been in the habit of letting me take out books on her card because I'd read all the children's books in which I had an interest and was beginning to work my way into some of the simple adult books. On top of this, I was also an avid comic reader with a fancy for the Phantom and other adventure stories, and I was active in a group of kids who were into swapping comics and cards from Stamina clothes.

Mum didn't like boys from school coming around to swap comics and tried to get us interested in other things. She made us join a children's theatrical group, but Dellie and I ended up standing around on the back of the stage in grass skirts as 'atmosphere' in plays in which white children got all the speaking roles, so that didn't last long.

Mum had paid off the house with money from her job and the extra she made from her work on the side. I was easily staying in the top three places in all exams at the school, and Sister de Salles told Mum I had the brains to do anything I wanted. I'd been sick so much that the most contact I'd had with anyone outside the family, apart from the nuns, was with doctors, and somehow in my mind the idea grew that it would be a wonderful thing to be a doctor and be able to help people when they were sick. It didn't occur to me that I'd never seen a Black doctor!

Mum began putting three pence a week into a special savings account, which she said was to go towards my costs when I went to university to do medicine. This was really a dream because there was no university in North Queensland. Still, whatever we decide to do as children is always abstract and nothing seems beyond the realm of possibility if you're determined.

Dellie was very athletic so Mum put her into Little Athletics. The club met a long way from where we lived and she wasn't allowed to go alone, of course, so that meant trying to interest me in athletics too. A couple of times a week, Dellie and I, and sometimes Leonie, caught a bus to Hermit Park for training. Dellie won consistently, but she didn't like training, and she'd often spend her bus fare on lollies so we couldn't go. At meets, she won all the cups for her age races and older, and they gave me a cup, 'Most Consistent Trier', for coming last in everything! I had weak ankles which kept getting wrenched out, but I thought if I tried hard enough I'd get over it and Mum would be pleased with me.

On one occasion, the Athletics Club organised a weekend meet with a club in Cairns, and Dellie was chosen to represent Townsville in her age group. Athletes were to be billeted and Dellie couldn't go alone so the club agreed to take me. The night before we left, Mum drew me aside and gave me a piece of paper with an address written on it. The address was meaningless to me, I'd never been to Cairns and there was no name on the paper. She said, 'If you or your sister want a drink of water or even if either of you is on fire, do *not* go into this house. You hear me?'

Her tone was frightening and not conducive to me asking any questions. Once more it was being demanded of me that I act on Mum's secrets without knowing what they were. Mum also gave me a plastic sheet and cotton sheeting to put on Dellie's bed so our hosts would not be inconvenienced.

We were placed with a very nice couple, both white of course, and I was terribly surprised to learn on our last day there that the man was a policeman. I'd have been surprised to have learned he was a banker, or any-thing, because I'd not really met or stayed at anyone's house like that. But a policeman?

Naturally, from the minute we arrived, I had my eye out for the street of my mother's note, which was burn-ing a hole in my pocket. My curiosity in those days was enormous. As it turned out, I didn't have long to wait because it was a main street. I couldn't believe my good fortune because it was the very street we drove along the next day in order to get to the sportsground. On the way back to our billet, I kept a very sharp eye out for the house number, but I was looking on the wrong side and missed it. I had one last chance as we were leaving the following day.

Next morning I counted the numbers down as we were driven along the street and the house came and went in my line of vision. It was highset, sitting in its own fairly large block of land, and in the corner of the block was a shop. I noticed from the sign that it was a hairdressers' shop, but that was all I could see. I wasn't in any position to ask our hosts to double around so I could look at it again.

I immediately and intensely hated whoever it was who lived there. What sort of people were they who wouldn't give two small girls a drink, or even water if they were on fire? The idea was like a thorn in my mind, and it would fester on for decades before the mystery would be solved, and even then, not completely.

5

With first the house and later the encyclopedias paid off, Mum looked around for another large purchase to make. She'd grown used to paying something off and liked the idea. So she went to Palings and bought a piano. The Taylor family, who lived in a very big, fancy house on the corner of our track and Hale Street, had a piano, and we'd often hear the daughter of the house, Pauline, practising of an afternoon. Mum couldn't play an instrument, so her choice surprised me, and she said she was going to send me to lessons. Like most children, I enjoyed singing and dancing and my sisters and I gave little concerts for Mum, Nellie or Maisie from time to time, but I hadn't thought of myself as particularly talented musically.

Mum said I needed 'another string in my bow' in case I wasn't able to get into medicine. That string was to be the piano. She told me that there was a 'coloured woman' who went all over the world playing piano, and that people were always happy to see her because she brought them joy with her wonderful music. Her name, she said, was Winifred Atwell. If I could only learn to play as well as Miss Atwell, Mum implied, people would like me and I'd be able to make a living.

I'd never heard of Miss Atwell or her music, but Mum went off and arranged for me to have music lessons after school with a woman who lived five blocks away. The woman, Mona Hinkle, who Mum said had also been a famous concert pianist before she married, was very strict and Mum told me how I should speak to her and how I should sit when I was at her house. The first time we went there, Mum came with me and the woman was very nice.

The second time I went alone, and she was okay. She showed me a few simple exercises and had me try to stretch my hand to cover eight keys, an octave. She said I was to do stretching exercises every day. The third time I went, I arrived early and could hear her yelling at the pupil before me and pounding her ruler. When it was my turn she was bad tempered with me, too, and sent me home early because, she said, I hadn't practised enough.

By the next week, I had several of the scales off pat, and sat down happily to play them. When I'd finished she said I had all the notes but needed to worry about time. She picked up the ruler and made me play the scales again, this time hitting the sharp edge of the ruler on my wrist as I played in time with some beat going on in her head. By the end of the lesson, my wrist was very sore.

A week later, my wrist was still sore but I wasn't game to tell Mum. Her expectations that I would become a world famous pianist, and the amount of money she was paying for the piano and lessons, put me in a bad position. So, instead of going to the music lesson, I left the house with my music book and hid in a telephone box just outside the Greeks' corner store until it was time to go home.

A few days later, Mum called me in, asked me a few questions about the lesson, then smacked my face for lying. She said she wouldn't pay for expensive lessons if I wouldn't go. I promised I'd go the next time. But at the end of that lesson, I knew I'd never go back again. The pain in my left wrist, where the teacher had tapped the time sharply, was so acute that I cried all the way home.

Mum was unsympathetic about my sore wrist and angry that I wouldn't go to my lessons. She went to the convent to discuss the problem with one of the nuns, who agreed with her that I should be trained in music. For a while I went over to the music rooms at St Patrick's College, which was in the same complex as the primary school. I learned very basic theory and more scales.

Over time, however, this arrangement didn't work out either, because it meant that my sisters had to walk home by themselves with me following an hour or so later. Mum came on her bike and walked home with them a few times. On top of this was the fact that I wasn't enjoying the lessons, and often had to hang around waiting for more favoured girls to finish before it was my turn.

When these music lessons didn't work out, Mum became terribly angry. Neither of my sisters showed any inclination to take up the piano, which didn't seem to bother Mum, but she flew into a rage from time to time, raining words and blows on my head, about the 'good money I have to keep paying out for this piano for you'—and what a bad child I was for being so lazy, idle and unwilling to go to lessons.

* * *

At the Roxy Theatre every Saturday morning, the local radio station hosted and broadcast a show called 'Juvenile Jamboree'. Children, talented or otherwise, could put their name on a list and be called on stage to perform. As part of my training for 'fame', when it came, Mum began to sign up Dellie and me to take part in it. At first, we recited short poems or sang short songs she had taught us. Singers were accompanied by a pianist who provided the backing for almost everything, from the complete song when she could, to strumming chords if she didn't know the tune. The program was broadcast live, full of kiddies' mistakes, tots bursting into tears on stage, and very flat voices along with the occasional pure voice, strung together by a very able host-announcer, who kept the show moving along even when nothing was happening.

Under pressure from Mum, I graduated from short songs to playing short piano pieces. Dellie still had to accompany me, and when I was called to the stage we would both go.

'And now, next on this morning's program, we have the very talented Patterson sisters! Yes, yes, come on up, girls . . . and my, listeners, they look very nice today. Everybody here seems to be wearing their new clothes . . . And what are you going to do for us this morning? . . . Wait a moment and I'll lower the microphone so you can speak into it.

'Well, girls, what are you going to do? Roberta, you're going to play a piece on the piano. Wonderful! And Dellie . . . what are you going to do? Oh, you're going to turn the pages for Roberta. Wonderful!

'Well, are we ready to start up now girls? . . . Okay,

let's hear it for the Patterson sisters! Oh, yes, a big hand now!'

My sisters' personalities were very different from my own. Dellie had height, grace and beauty, which I lacked, and she had long legs that enabled her to run quickly. However, she wasn't actually inclined to run, and would much rather saunter along enjoying fine things on the way. She was fun loving more than hard working, and generous—even though we didn't have much to be generous with.

Leonie was quite different again. At first I thought this was because she was the baby of the family and consequently was spoiled and didn't have to take on any responsibilities. But there was more. She was uncooperative, though not in the defiant manner which Dellie sometimes adopted, and very much inclined to be secretive. She was tight and played her cards close to her chest. When Mum gave us each two shillings to spend at the Townsville Show one year, Leonie came home with one and sixpence in her pocket. She'd begged food from us and sips from our softdrinks and whatever else she could cadge, skipping gaily along behind us, all the while quietly keeping her own money intact. Mum used to call her Ikey Mo, and say that she'd still have her first penny clutched in her fist when they buried her. Perhaps because of the age difference between us, Leonie was always more of a chore than a companion to me; she shared few of my interests and we spent very little time playing together during our childhood.

We had a big mango tree in the chook run, and its thick branches and low-hanging leaves shaded the area around the trunk where a tap had been installed and a

small cement duck pond had been built. When we were small, Dellie and I had played together, hoisting each other up amongst the boughs of the tree. But as we grew older, she wasn't so keen to continue these tomboy activities. While I couldn't run fast like Dellie, I was particularly supple and I enjoyed acrobatics and dangling upside down by my knees, ankles and feet. Mum said that I was always roosting in the mango tree like a fruit bat, and she wondered what I was doing up there alone so often.

While meditating in the mango tree was one of my favourite pastimes, I also liked to prowl around the perimeters of our territory. During daylight hours this could only entail Mum's turf, that is, our own fence up to the back of the chook run, along the top of the retaining wall to where it joined up with what we called 'old Mrs Sullivan's wall'. Then I'd run the length of that wall—poking my hand or face into cracks between the rocks where insects lived or where we spotted small snakes or lizards—before tracking down the cracked footpath to where I'd begun. Occasionally I'd add a reconnaissance of Mrs Scott's house, too.

Mrs Scott was dying, Mum told me, and when Edie was away it was my responsibility to sleep over at her house and look after her. There wasn't really much to do there, I just had to be on hand in case she died, but this idea was quite frightening to me. Mrs Scott snored and snuffled loudly all night, and I found comfort in her steady drone. When she broke her rhythm and woke up to use her commode or change her position, I'd sit bolt upright, tense at the silence.

During a normal week, most of my time was taken up with school, laundry work, running errands for Mum or Mrs Scott, homework, and looking after my sisters. There were other times, such as when the laundry was all hung out to dry and Mum was preparing our food or in that period between teatime at home and when I was expected at Mrs Scott's, when I was comparatively free to indulge my own whims. If I'd already made my compulsive rounds, I would take off across the road to run and climb over the stony shoulders of Castle Hill, bringing home chinkey apples, tamarinds, cascara beans and honeysuckle flowers from the cathedral bell-tower. So long as I brought something home and there was no outstanding work waiting for me to do, Mum didn't say much. She wasn't happy, however, with any plan to go out at night. She was worried about snakes, scorpions and poisonous spiders that lived up on the hill, and which she thought would get me.

But the little freedoms I managed to find for myself at night were bliss. I was unable, and unwilling even to try to convey to Mum the feeling of wonder, warmth and knowledge that somehow seeped out of the earth and into me through the pores of my skin whenever I lay flattened across the ground. The spiritual energy of rocks would course through my body and peace and stillness would flow into me. I couldn't tell Mum that I sometimes enjoyed the company of snakes and other creatures or that we had talks. I didn't have the trust which may have enabled me to share my secrets with her.

Poor old Mrs Sullivan died, and her house was put up for auction. Old Bert was moved out to live in another boarding house up the road somewhere. This situation made Mum very upset, she was used to living in the middle house between the two old ladies, Mrs Sullivan and Mrs Scott, and the three of them had fairly tight control over the dip. Our houses were huddled so close together that we would all cooperate with each other out of sheer necessity and proximity.

Suddenly, the possibility arose that newcomers with different ideas could move in and take over. Both Mrs Sullivan and Mrs Scott had become indebted to Mum in a variety of ways and over a long time, so the relationships which maintained stability in our block were badly skewed by this turn of events.

Mum and Laaka put their heads together and whispered away on the back verandah far into the night. Then Mum went down to see the bank manager. She told him how she, a widow with three little girls, would be at the mercy of strangers and possible child molesters if she was unable to take over Mrs Sullivan's house. Laaka, who lived there anyway, was standing by, ready to be Mum's first tenant, and he would continue to bring into the house Finnish seamen who wanted to jump ship and settle in Australia. Although, I doubt that Mum told the bank manager about this aspect of their plan.

The last outstanding problem was ensuring that the price didn't go so high that Mum couldn't afford it. The house had been neglected for years, and what with Mrs Sullivan's age, blindness, and Bert's foul habits, it wasn't the most salubrious of accommodations. Still, it was within walking distance of town, in a very quiet little backwater off of a main thoroughfare, so some people were sure to be interested.

On auction day, Mum had me sit at the piano while the auctioneer and prospective buyers arrived. I was to play all the vamp tunes she hated so much, and pound them out at full pitch. She said I could make as much noise as I liked, and my sisters were encouraged to sit near me and do likewise. After a while, she said we should run out and see who was coming to the auction. When we were too shy and just peeped out over our own verandah rail, she said she would give us three pence each if we made as much noise as possible. Then she pushed us out onto the stairs so that anyone considering buying the house could see that they would be living next to a houseful of noisy kids.

Mum was successful and bought the house for less than a thousand pounds.

No sooner had she bought it, though, than she began to panic about her ability to pay for it. Laaka's daughter was away doing nursing training and perhaps Mum worried that he might decide to live near her, and then Mum would be in the lurch.

A Young Women's Christian Association hostel was located on Denham Street. One day, Mum announced that she had been given a contract for the YWCA laundry, which entailed doing the work at our house plus getting the wash to and from the hostel.

Mum asked Laaka to build a very large cart with two long wooden handles and a crossbar in front. She said that I had to use it to collect the washing, but that Dellie and Leonie would both help me.

I'd trundle the cart down to the hostel on my way to school and, with Matron's permission, leave it partially concealed by the hydrangea bushes in the hostel's front garden. By the afternoon, Matron would have the cart filled with soiled laundry and I would bring it home. Sometimes my sisters helped, but at other times they did not and there was little I could do about it. The load often consisted of over a hundred sheets, plus pillow cases, towels, table cloths and table napkins. When the hostel had less guests, there was less work, but normally they had a full house. Rivers of sweat poured down my face and into my eyes as I dragged that metal-wheeled cart noisily along the road and up the hill. I used to think I must have done something wrong in my life already and that this was the penance.

Mum was elated by the enormous washloads and the cash the work brought in, with which she was able to pay off the mortgage. She'd had to put up our house as collateral, and this had made her nervous about how any economic downturn might affect us. She kept reminding me that she wasn't a young woman and didn't want to leave us without so much as a roof over our heads if she died. The YWCA contract almost killed both of us, although Mum lashed out and bought a hand wringer and an agitator, which fitted on top of the concrete tubs and was the forerunner to today's free-standing washing machines. She also had a gas copper installed, which was super because our wood copper had been out in the open, and when it was raining, it was very hard to fire it up. The gas copper sat neatly under cover by the side of the tubs with a penny meter mounted on the wall above it.

With the laundry, there was too much work to be done for Mum to worry about my piano lessons. When the acute pain in my wrist abated, I continued to experience discomfort. When we were sitting at the table one day, Mum looked down and said, 'What's that on your hand?'

A big knob, ugly and distorted, had grown on my wrist; it was a cyst which had turned into a ganglion. Through the nuns, Mum had made contact with Dr Ward, a Catholic medical practitioner whose surgery was not too far from our house, and she made me go there to see him. Dr Ward recommended surgery to remove the ganglion and said he'd do it under a local anaesthetic in his office. Mum accompanied me on the day, but she made me go in alone while she sat outside, because she didn't have the stomach to watch operations.

I was fascinated with the entire procedure, from first injection through to having my arm strapped up in a sling. There was a lot of pain, however, particularly later when my wrist throbbed and I had to take painkillers before I could get to sleep. But I fell in love with the idea of being able to perform operations, and my goal grew from studying ordinary medicine to surgery.

As well as the attraction I felt towards the mysteries which lay concealed under people's skins, I was also becoming aware of the increasingly abrasive nature of white people's relationships with me as I grew older, and I thought it would be better for my future if patients had to be anaesthetised while I operated on them to save their lives. I didn't want to save their lives *and* have to deal with their racism.

From the highest point on our side of the track we could see across three blocks to Flinders Street, in the centre of town. There was not much besides a few little cottages between the top of that hill and where the Townsville State High School was located. Across from the school was the Townsville Regional Electricity Board, where I was sent to pay bills once we had the power connected. On the next corner, directly across from the police station, was the ambulance centre, and both were one short block from the main street.

Once when we were walking home with Mum, a dark-skinned man was coming out of the ambulance centre. He was carrying a hessian sack which he put into a box in the front cabin of a little truck. The ambulance men were speaking to him so loudly that they seemed to want us to know that the man had a snake in his bag. Mum smiled at them and kept walking.

Around the corner, she explained that the man was Ram Chandra, an Indian who caught snakes and milked their venom so it could be made into antidote. Mum had read about him in the newspaper. I was instantly fascinated, and Ram Chandra seemed like someone after my own heart.

When I had time I'd run the three blocks to the ambulance centre just to inquire if the snake man had been around. The firemen and the ambulance officers may have been bored between their emergencies, because they were quite happy to sit and chat with passing children. The concrete driveway where the ambulances were parked was always smooth and cool underfoot, and Dellie and I had limped in there a few times to get help removing glass splinters from our feet.

From my perch at the top of the hill, I was also able to see Ram Chandra's truck when he parked alongside the ambulance centre. Then, quick as a flash, I'd be off down the hill. Mr Chandra once made the mistake of letting me help carry an end of a box he was taking into the centre, and from then on, as Mum said, I made a pest of myself.

I saw how Mr Chandra approached snakes, quickly pinning them to the ground with a stout stick, Y-shaped at one end, then gripping them fast just behind their heads. So I decided I'd pick one up too, when I next had the opportunity. But there's a difference between making such a decision and actually coming across a snake while carrying a stick of the right shape plus a thick hessian bag. Sometimes I'd have the bag and stick, and search for days for a snake, but to no avail. On other occasions, a very likely snake would be laying across my path, and I'd just be short of the stick and bag.

Once, in winter, after I had scrambled up the hill beside the cathedral, a snake and I, unbeknowns to each other, were both basking in the warmth of the sun's mid-morning rays when we spotted each other. It was a powerful moment. We fell into complete still-ness, each looking at the other's eyes and watching to see whether the other meant any harm. At the end of our careful mutual appraisal, I knew the snake was not a danger to me and continued to lay on the rock with-out fear. The snake, too, stayed curled on the rock for quite a while before slipping away into the grass. Although other smaller snakes, to Mum's mortification, sometimes slipped in and out of the retaining walls beside our house, this cathedral snake became my first real encounter. It was lucky that this didn't happen at home, because when Mum saw a snake she would have Laaka chase it, no matter what I said.

Classes at St Joseph's came out at different times. Junior classes finished at 3pm, more senior classes at 3.30. So when I was promoted, Dellie and Leonie had to walk home by themselves. Mum was so flush with cash by this time that she occasionally gave them coins so that they could catch a school bus to North Ward or the city and walk from there. Neither of these routes was really much shorter, but nor did they offer the privacy for racist attacks. As well, the city route was not quite so steep.

I wasn't very interested in catching the bus, so I found a way that suited me better. The views from the top of the road I chose were splendid and lots of little creatures lived along the way. The footpath was particularly steep, made up almost entirely of cement and rock stairs, which led past the maternity wing of Townsville General Hospital and through to the nurses' quarters. The difficulty of this route was one of its advantages as the likelihood of state school children coming this way was virtually nil, and their ability to wait in ambush for me, zilch.

At the top of the steep climb, a narrow road swept by past the top-floor entrance of the maternity hospital. The floors below were surrounded by verandahs which faced the sea in order to catch any cooling breeze. At the end of one verandah which I passed on my way home there would often be several black women, large in their pregnancy and wearing only night attire and bed jackets or robes.

'Psst. Psst,' I'd hear one of the women calling to me. They'd ask me to run errands across to the little store on the main road to get packets of biscuits or sometimes sweets, softdrink or chocolates. In summer they would ask me to bring them mangoes. The composition of the group was always changing as the women completed the three months each was obliged to spend— six weeks before and six weeks after giving birth—in this enforced loneliness.

'Who's your mummy?' some of the women asked.

'Mrs Patterson,' I'd reply.

'Oh, yeah. White one mummy, eh!' Then they would murmur and nudge each other about who might have given me up for adoption.

'And where are you from?' I'd ask them as I became bolder. I wasn't used to having conversations on an equal basis with adults, or very pregnant women.

Most were from Palm Island, and they would stretch their arms out wistfully to point where it was on the horizon. I couldn't see it, but many of the women told me they could. I met quite a number of women there who would, many years later, remember me in the capacity of their little messenger-girl.

Some of these women were only a few years older than me—although I didn't know this at the time. To my ten years, they were sixteen and seventeen, though many, of course, were much older, up to forty, I'd guess. The most noticeable thing about them was the deep sadness in their eyes and their general air of wretchedness and despair. Once I began to spend time chatting with them on my way home from school and trying to answer their questions, I began to badger Mum for information about our family.

For years I'd been overhearing Mum and Aunty Glad

carrying on their secret conversations on the back verandah, when they thought I was asleep. They'd used words I'd never heard of, such as 'throw-backs' and 'mulattoes', which confused me. When I asked Mum what 'throw-back' meant, she had slapped my face hard and called me a sneak.

I would occasionally try to pry information from her by a variety of methods. I would ask questions about her mother and father, which she refused to answer except to say that they were dead. 'Dead and buried,' she'd say to anything I asked. I'd inquired point blank a few times about my own father and received an assortment of answers. Once she told me he was from Fiji, another time that he was from Papua New Guinea. Then she said he was a war hero, and he was dead, and he'd been buried in Papua New Guinea. On another occasion, she answered shortly, 'Do you know what a Fuzzy-Wuzzy Angel is?' When I replied in the negative, she said, 'Well, get out of here until you do!'

I also asked her about our names. 'Where does my name, "Roberta", come from? How did you think to call me that?'

And at other times: 'How did you come to call Dellie "Delores"? Did you know someone called Delores? What about Leonie? Does her name have a meaning?'

Depending on Mum's mood, the answers I received ranged from plausible to bizarre.

'I called you Roberta after your father. His name was Robert and I added the "a".'

But I also heard: 'You were named Roberta after an opera. I heard it on the radio', and, 'You weren't named after anything, it was just a name I liked.'

Once when I pursued the reply that I'd been named after my father, I asked, 'That's nice, Mum. What was his last name?' She leaped up and whacked me. 'I know what you're doing, you sneaky girl,' she screamed.

Dellie, whose birth name was Delores, which Mum said was to be pronounced 'Del-or-aise', was named, according to Mum's story, after Our Lady of Sorrows. Given Mum's dislike of Catholics, which hadn't disappeared just because we went off to St Joseph's school each morning, it didn't ring true that she'd called her daughter after a Catholic figure, but I was in no position to argue. I began to suspect she'd read the name in a book and liked the sound of it.

Another time, Mum told me she'd named Leonie after her birth sign, Leo. I let it pass. Mum and I were the Leos in the family and Leonie, who was born in September, a Virgo. To contradict Mum was to invite trouble. Earlier, when Mum was having her screaming and swearing fits, both Aunty Glad and Nell had whispered to me, when Mum was mid-tantrum, that I should be considerate because she was having her 'change'. I recall wondering what she was likely to change into, but neither Aunty Glad or Nellie gave me any indication of what they meant. Mum's often violent moodiness remained, change or no change.

While all three of us girls had the surname 'Patterson', which again I was not allowed to ask about, Mum also gave Dellie and me a middle name, 'Barkley', and Leonie was given 'Mary'. Mum said she had taken Barkley from the tablelands of the same name, which were, at various times, either where she came from, or where she'd spent a lot of time, or where our father had come from or where she'd met him. Despite the inconsistency in her stories, it pleased me to know of some connection—until I learned that the name of the tablelands is not spelled the same way as she spelled our name. It didn't seem likely, given what a stickler she was for correct spelling, that she'd made an innocent mistake. I was profoundly disappointed.

So, one day I put together all the pieces I'd picked up over the years and tried to present them to Mum, to try to jolt her into giving me a more coherent picture of our family's background. Did I get a shock! I'd just started laying out some of the inconsistencies—Mum was sitting at her treadle machine—and she burst into tears. She said she was sick and tired of the government trying to take us off her, and why couldn't I just leave well enough alone? She continued that if I didn't stop giving her trouble by pestering for information that could only get us all put away, the government would take me and she'd let them have me. I didn't know whether to believe her or not.

From then on, she increased her efforts to create a credible history for us. She'd married, she said, an American soldier who was half Negro and half Cherokee Indian. She said that mixed marriages such as these often produced children who didn't look the same, and she pointed out brothers and sisters around the neighbourhood who didn't appear to share similar features or hair colouring. That, she said, was why Dellie and I looked one way, and Leonie looked another. It was because our father was of mixed blood. Dellie and I looked like half his family and Leonie looked like the other half.

She also said I'd been born in America, in a big house in Maryland, and didn't I remember how I used to run around and around with my hand on the shiny wooden pole at the bottom of the huge staircase? We had lived in that house with my father's mother, my grandmother. Mum described her as a very old black lady, a Negro, with grey hair and wrinkles.

This story was like an oasis to a person dying of thirst. I drank it all in and repeated it many times, to myself, my sisters and friends, and to welfare people who came around periodically. A few days after Mum had started the story, she continued it by saying that my father had been a hero in the war. She produced a sheet of paper which she said was a citation for his heroism and that it would be mine eventually, but in the meantime she'd keep it for me. It had nothing on it but a poorly typewritten tract, no insignia, no signature, just a small page of writing. Mum said she would put it in her trunk for me. Years later, after I'd seen a detective in a film compare print faces of typewritten ransom notes, I discovered the letters of the citation contained the same idiosyncrasies as the old manual typewriter Mum had given us. This, too, was disappointing, but so nicely did the story fit my deep need that I was able to explain the discrepancy away to myself.

One day when I was home in bed with asthma, I heard two men at the front door telling Mum that it would be in her children's best interest for them to be brought up by the government, and that she ought to let us go. Mum was speaking softly, trying to get them to keep their voices down because she knew I was only a few feet away in the back bedroom. But then I heard her yelling: 'You can't do that to a white woman. You're not dealing with some poor dumb Abo here!' When they left, I asked her what an 'Abo' was, but her rage had been stirred up by their visit and she ranted at me in her strongest language for the next half hour or so.

My fears—that being an 'Abo' was the worst thing one could be—had been mightily reinforced.

On other occasions, men in suits came around when Mum wasn't home, asking me or our neighbours questions: how many of us were living in the house? Did we have a bed each? How did Mummy make her money? We got a flogging from Mum if we went to the front door and answered questions or failed to call her immediately anyone knocked when she was home. Dellie and Leonie weren't allowed to answer questions. In Mum's absence, my sisters had to call me. Mum had coached me on a stock of answers with which to put people off, to get them to go away. I had to tell them that she would come down to their office, or ask them to go away and come back at a time when she'd be home.

I believed her story of our big house and family in America because I badly wanted it to be so. I wanted a story that would protect us, one in which my mother was not regarded as the local 'sinner' and her children could not be abused as bastards. Whatever her lifestyle may have been before she had us, there were no grounds for disrepute after, and I wanted a family history which reflected her goodness, her widowhood, and gave us a respectability in our town. That was all I wanted. Mum and I both worked very hard, earning our living, scrubbing people's houses and washing their dirty linen and clothes, and I understood we had to work for any material thing we got. But it seemed to me, from the shabby way people often spoke to us, that no matter how hard and long we worked, we would never earn their respect. Respect was something that flowed out of a family's history, and when Mum finally told me our wonderful story I wondered why she had kept it to herself all this time.

It didn't have to be true, and in a part of myself I knew that it was too good to be true. From time to time I tested Mum, asking her questions such as why we had come to Australia, to Townsville, to live. Her answer was that a lot of racists lived in Maryland and they didn't like children of mixed marriages. To my ten-year-old ears, this sounded like a good enough reply. From the way she talked, I thought Maryland was a little town, and I looked out for any mention of it in the American cowboy movies we sometimes saw at the theatre.

Perhaps Mum didn't notice, or didn't want to notice, that most of the white people who lived all around us in Townsville also didn't like children of mixed marriages, especially those who were poor.

The seating divisions in the local picture theatres were a good barometer of class. Children from my school, when they went to the theatre, sat up in the balcony, in the most expensive seats. Their parents bought their snacks from a snackbar which served only people sitting in the balcony, and the ladies' room which serviced that section had large mirrors and little stools on which to sit in order to repair makeup, quite unlike the spartan facilities available to those of us downstairs.

We were in another class and sat in the cheapest seats. We were lucky to have a few pennies with which to buy anything at interval, a sherbet or a drink between us. After the films we would always scramble about under the seats to collect the empty bottles left behind by the better classes, and redeem them for their cash deposits. In that way we'd try to ensure that we had enough money to go again the following week. As we grew older and Mum had a little loose change, she tried to stop us from collecting bottles, but our frugal habits were completely ingrained by then; to walk past an empty bottle was almost the same as walking past at least the equivalent of a dollar. Our coins were smaller but they bought a great deal more than today's money. As children we were given a shilling (ten cents in today's currency) to go to a film; admission tickets cost just nine pence each and most sweets were four or six for a penny.

It was at the picture theatres that I first began to meet other coloured kids—Mum had told us to refer to ourselves as 'coloured children' to stop other people from calling us 'niggers'—and was able to talk to them, because neither their parents nor my mother were there. We began to band together to work the theatres—collecting all the bottles and redeeming the deposits—and in the process, cut out poor white kids who wanted a share in the money.

Slowly, our familiarity grew. As we were leaving we'd call out, 'See you next Saturday,' and the other kids would reply, 'Yeah. Next Saturday.'

After a while I asked one child, 'Where d'ya live?', and got the reply, 'Garbutt. Where d'ya live?'

Garbutt sounded like a magical place because just about every coloured child I asked seemed to live there.

Laaka, who'd settled down and was employed in regular work for the railways, bought a truck. There weren't many vehicles in Townsville at that time and the roads were very safe, although you might not have thought so on Sundays when all the Catholics arrived at the cathedral for Mass.

Laaka's truck, like many other vehicles then, had to be cranked to start. It had a metal cabin and the entire back was built from planks of wood. For a few pounds, he also bought a small block of land on Black River, which was then regarded as a very long way out of town. I recall the first time he took us there to show us his purchase. Mum sat in the front of the truck with Leonie on her knee and a picnic basket on the seat, and Dellie and I slid around in the back and got splinters from the floorboards. Laaka later fixed a blanket for us to sit on if we were going anywhere, but on the first ride we were unaware of the hazards.

The idea of a trip was so exciting, and our family had been anticipating it for weeks. Apart from the journey to Cairns, we kids had only been to places which could be reached by the local bus service. Now we were going somewhere that we could walk around in the real bush, where we might see real animals—cows and horses— and I'd be able to climb up a real bush tree!

We left very early in the morning, just as the sun's first rays allowed us to see the road. The truck lights weren't strong enough for driving in darkness. The trip took hours, but our excitement kept us buoyant. We kids sang songs at the top of our voices. At long last, we pulled off the narrow bitumen strip onto a graded side road, and then onto an even smaller road. When we left that road we had to make our own track, because we were now on Laaka's little block.

Laaka carried everything we'd brought for our picnic to a clearing and Mum spread out a groundsheet on which to set it up. I was so delighted at the sight of the trees, all gums, that I announced loudly that I was going to climb one immediately. Everyone stopped what they were doing to watch me.

The one I chose was, naturally, the tallest tree around. It soared up into the air on its long thin and bare, but sturdy looking trunk, and had a few sparse boughs and leaves only at the very top. I had seen jungle films of people climbing trees of this shape, so I wrapped my arms and legs easily around the trunk and quickly worked my way almost to the top. I reached what I thought was the first of its boughs, scrambled over it and put my foot on it to get purchase. Suddenly, I was falling through the air towards the ground. The bough had been dead and had snapped off the tree at its fork. On the way down I heard Mum's shriek.

I lay on the ground for a moment, quite stunned and then, carefully moving each limb slowly at first to make sure it wasn't broken, I got to my feet. My knees were shaking like jelly from the shock. Laaka, Dellie and Leonie were standing wide-eyed, gazing at me in surprise, but Mum had her back to me and her spine was rigid with tension in her expectation that Laaka was about to tell her that I was dead, or my leg had been broken, or something. When I walked up behind her and said, 'My legs are wobbling,' Mum looked around in surprise at the sound of my voice, and let out a sharp gasp of relief.

She made me sit down and, as the water was just coming to the boil, she gave me the first cup of tea, sweet with a lot of condensed milk, 'to counter the shock,' she said.

My tree-climbing skills entered the family's store of jokes, and I was advised that it was better to keep my feet on the ground. This hiccup didn't deter me. No one in my family or circle of friends could climb faster or further than I. So what if tree-climbing freedom was bought with a few thrills and spills?

Over time, Laaka built a little lock-up, then a small shack on his block, and we were able to go there of a Saturday and return home on the Sunday. He installed an ingenious method of getting water up from the river to his place, which could be set up when he arrived and taken down and stored in the shed when he departed. He also made a light can, consisting of two cylinders, which I watched him solder together, one of which fitted upside inside the other, and from two tiny jets at the top some type of gas quietly spurted. When he put a match to this fitting, a small and steady flame burned for hours.

Weekends at Black River were fun for us kids, mainly because it was a change from where we were the rest of the time. Dellie and I ran along the stretch of river that was within eyesight of Laaka's block; the water was never deep when we were there, and often we had to dig a hole in the riverbed to reach damp sand. Leonie was small and neither interested nor allowed to accompany us on our explorations. At the far limit of where we were allowed to play, which wasn't very far, was a structure where a railway track crossed the river. No train ever came across it when we were there that I recall, but trains ran only infrequently at that time. We sometimes played on this bridge, dangling from its crossbars and dropping onto the sandy, and occasionally wet, riverbed below.

We were used to being the only people around there, so it came as a shock to me once, as we were making our way to the railway crossing, to look over and see other kids on the opposite bank. As soon as I got over my surprise I was happy, because they were dark coloured children, just like me and Dellie.

When they realised I'd seen them, they began to

shout at us. 'Go on, get out of here. What'd'ya think ya doin' here? Go on, get out!' There was a number of them and they swarmed down to the crossing where they quickly assumed proprietary positions, squatting in the angles of the bridge where the strutted arms were joined to the framework. On the way, and in case we thought they were joking, they'd pelted stones at us across the river—and very adept they were at it, too. They could make their pebbles skim and bounce on the water's surface, and although none of the stones reached our side of the river, I felt these weren't kids to get into a stone fight with.

We decided to leave when we saw them take over our favourite playing places. Neither Mum nor Laaka was interested in coming down and seeing these children, or in backing us up to get them to share instead of trying to scare us away. Instead, we could hear their jolly voices ring out as they laughed and played at our spot until it was time for us to go. After they'd spotted us there, we felt that these kids began to police the area quite regularly on the weekends, and much of the fun went out of going to Laaka's farm once they'd put an end to our total freedom. I met one of these 'unfriendly' children in Sydney, twenty years later, and we had a good laugh about our differing perspectives on these incidents, and we became friends after all that time.

On our way to Black River, we passed through the suburb of Garbutt, which was considered the absolute edge of Townsville, on the outbound northern road. Since discovering that the coloured children we met in town lived at Garbutt, my attraction to the area had grown. I was pleased to find out where it was, and now had only to work out how to get to and from the area by public transport.

My weekdays were busy with schoolwork, homework and helping Mum, and Garbutt was a long way away. Weekends were the only time I had even a small chance of going there, and, even so, I had dozens of other factors to juggle. Being the oldest, I was expected to go to the regular Saturday afternoon matinee with Dellie and Leonie, and look after them. Saturday would have been the best day to go because buses ran to and from Garbutt frequently, bringing shoppers into town, unlike Sundays.

When I finally made my first trip to Garbutt, it happened quite spontaneously. One morning, a girl I met regularly at the picture theatre walked into the Roxy Theatre where the 'Juvenile Jamboree' was being held. Her name was Jeannie Paterson. When it was time for me to take Dellie and Leonie home, we walked them to the crest where Stanley Street forked and watched them go the rest of the way alone before we ran off back down the hill. I knew that Mum would be livid but I'd told Dellie to tell her that I was going to visit at my friend's house for a while and would be back later in the afternoon.

We went by bus to Garbutt, and Jeannie showed me around the dismal and dusty suburb. Once the bus left the main road and began running up and down the Garbutt streets, the poverty of the area became obvious. Jeannie pointed out play areas along the way.

When we got out at her stop we found no one was at home at her house. So, we crossed over to a big field where children were playing rounders. People called to Jeannie and she waved, but we didn't join any of their groups. A pair of ten year olds don't go around making formal introductions, so we just lounged about and enjoyed ourselves, chatting through the afternoon. We went back to her house and found a box of Weetbix opened on the table, and we put a couple of them in our pockets for our lunch.

By mid-afternoon, I began to worry about getting back home before I ended up in *real* trouble from Mum. I was reluctant to leave because Jeannie had told me that she and her friends had forgone going to the city theatre as a good scary film was being shown that night at the Garbutt Picture Theatre, and nobody could afford to go to the pictures twice in the one day.

Jeannie sat with me at the bus stop, then I went back to town. I was afraid to go home because I knew I'd be in trouble, but eventually I crept in. Mum was strangely quiet, and I realised Dellie or Leonie had told her I'd run off with Jeannie. Later she took me aside.

'Where did you go?'

'You remember that girl who waved at me when you met us after the pictures two weeks ago? Well, I went to her house.'

'You went to Garbutt?'

'Yes. That's where she lives.'

'Well, let me tell you this, my girl. If you *ever* go to her house or to Garbutt again, you'll be eating your meals standing up for weeks, you hear me? I'll take the skin off your backside and you won't be able to sit down.'

It was no time to push my luck by asking why. Mum's face was rigid and I thought she was going to fly into a rage, but instead she just got up and left the room. I ran around tidying up the house, quiet as a mouse, trying to get back into her good books. For the next few weeks she watched me like a hawk and kept me so busy with work that there was no chance for me to 'think up mischief'.

Once I had found out how to get to Garbutt, though, there was no stopping me. I'd tell Mum I was going to visit a girl from my school, Althea Rankin, and then go by her house on my way to Garbutt. I was able to exploit the fact that we didn't have a phone, and Mum never used the public telephone herself—I took care of any phone business. So she was unable to check on my whereabouts by ringing Althea's house.

At Garbutt I'd watch kids playing rounders, but because I didn't live in the area and wasn't there when games started, I was generally not included in the teams. Instead, I'd sit on the wooden fence and watch.

An old man with ebony skin and short, soft grey hair on his head and face often came to sit with me. His clothes were tattered and he wore no shoes; the long thin bones in his feet were clearly etched in the light-coloured dust which clung to him all the way up past his ankles. Despite his age, his feet were extraordinarily flexible, and he used them in the same way another person might use their hands. He could pick up any object by stepping on it and curling his toes around it, and then, if he needed to, he'd bend his knee and pass the object up to his hand.

The first time he joined me, he told me the names of everyone playing on the field. He told me the names he knew them by and the 'whitefella' names by which they were called. Then he began to point out their features—one woman's high-pitched laugh, the almost tumbling awkward gait with which one stubby youth chased after the ball—and he attributed each of these features to the sound made or the stance adopted by different birds, fish and animals.

He drew animals in the dirt using a stick clutched between his toes, and showed the same dexterity as someone who drew with a pen in their hand. Anyone who attracted attention by their sound or antics on the field, he would depict on the ground their creature guise. His work was so fine and detailed—birds with their mouths wide open in protest, others engaged in a long-legged run with wings outstretched and flapping—that the totems of all the players became more familiar to me than many of the actual people, some of whom I never met or spoke to.

Years later, when I first saw a rock painting I recognised it as the same art—the depiction of familiar people doing familiar things being portrayed in the form of birds and other creatures.

'Who am I?' I asked the old man, after a couple of sessions when I'd grown comfortable chatting with him. He gazed away as if trying to decide whether to answer me or not, then he picked up the stick in his toes and drew in the dirt.

'You fella snake.' He spoke towards the ground as we both leaned against the fence and watched his foot drawing, as though it had a life of its own. 'Baby one, eh,' he added after a pause, a twinkle in his cloudy eyes.

I watched the coiled snake taking form in the soil. 'How come I'm a snake?' I wondered if he was referring to the fact that I was skinny and underweight.

'Um . . . snake. Anyone can see. Any fella wit' eyes, he can see. You very good snake,' he told me, smiling.

'Poisonous snake?' I thought of the lightning-fast snakes I'd seen in Ram Chandra's bags and boxes, and the idea of being so quick somehow appealed to me.

'Not very poison,' he replied, and I could feel him

watching me as I examined his finished representation. The old man had a habit of not looking at me when he was talking, rarely meeting my eyes with his own, and I'd become used to—though still conscious of—his sideways inspections of my reactions to the things he was teaching me in his game-playing way.

As I glanced up to see what he was thinking, from the corner of my eye I caught his dusty foot stretching out to cover the image. In one smooth action he wiped the picture out and the ground was again flat and bare.

'A bit deadly?' I was pushing, I wanted to hear something great about myself to hang onto.

'Yeah. Lil' bit deadly,' he said, as his quite unremarkable wrinkled face was briefly transformed by one of his rare smiles.

6

Along with her other jobs, Mum
and I continued to do the laundry for the YWCA hostel.
She inquired about the Association's activities and
found that it ran clubs for girls of different ages, in a
different location from the hostel. So, she enrolled
Dellie and me to go there on Saturday afternoons,
instead of going to the pictures.

Initially, we were heartbroken about this turn of
events. Our visit to the pictures had been our one big
weekly outing, and we were locked into the serials, such
as *Superman* and *The Lone Ranger*, which were shown
along with two films classified as suitable for children.
These constituted the standard dose of fantasy to
which we'd become accustomed, although we strongly
rejected the roles given to people with whom we
should have identified, such as Blacks, Indians and
women. In games we played after viewing these films,
neither Dellie nor I would agree to play Jane or the
natives carrying loads on their heads. Instead, we'd
both want the part of Tarzan, so that we could be
strong, beat on our chests and overcome adversity.

Such success depended on us being white and male—
but fantasy allows one to overlook these shortcomings.

Joining the YWCA turned out to be a good compromise. Instead of spending Saturday afternoons watching actors do exciting things, we began to learn to do
exciting things ourselves. Under the guidance of our
group leader, an energetic, sympathetic and fun-loving
woman, Fay Naylor, we learned how to knot ropes and
carry and use pocket knives. She organised camps to
Magnetic Island, where the YWCA had its own hut.

Dellie's bed-wetting was still a problem and we were
burdened with plastic sheeting and other paraphernalia
to deal with it. Fay, however, was the only person I ever
met who was considerate about this and relieved me of
the heavy feeling that caring for my sister was solely my
responsibility when we were away. She would let Dellie
sleep in a bunk near her and put me with the older girls
at the opposite end of the hut. It was such a relief.

At first we went on overnight camps, travelling to the
island by boat on Saturday morning and returning
Sunday, but during school holidays we went for a week
at a time. During fresh-water shortages, Fay taught us
how to wash ourselves in a single cupful of water when
we came back covered in salt and sand from a day on
the beaches. We sizzled sausages in pans around the
campfire and sang childish versions of bawdy ditties.
Each day, she marched us down the hill to use the facilities on the island, and had us vying with regular
tourists to get our turn with table-tennis and other
games equipment; ventures which substantially
increased our sense of self-esteem and social competi-
tiveness.

Fay was also the first white person I was able to
speak to about the racism we encountered in our daily

lives in the town, and over and above being open, sympathetic and caring enough to listen, she actively prevented race becoming an issue amongst the group of girls in her care. She was sensitive to slights we suffered from outsiders, such as when Dellie or I was left unserved at shops and kiosks on the island. She also—and without embarrassing us—ensured that we had our full YWCA uniforms, fitting us out from a store of bits and pieces which other girls had grown out of or left behind. Sometimes she even spent her own money so that we had the proper knives, pens and whistles required for our group's activities.

On one of these camps I became aware of how intensely many dogs didn't like me. I'd already had a few nasty nips from dogs on the mainland as we'd walked to and from school, but thought this was because when anything or anyone appeared threatening to us I was obliged to be the one at the front.

On the island, even in our big group, dogs singled me out and came straight for me. On several occasions other girls had to beat them off with sticks and it became something of a joke, though not to me, that dogs mistook my skinny legs for soup bones.

In Townsville I continued to see my friend Jeannie from time to time at the Juvenile Jamboree or in the streets shopping on Saturdays, but opportunities to visit Garbutt became rare.

One Saturday, the YWCA held a fete in the large yard behind the Meeting House. Planning and preparation took weeks and we were each assigned tasks for the day. I was to be Chief Cook, in charge of barbecuing sausages and serving them up on slices of bread with tomato sauce. I arrived early to help string decorations up in the trees and bushes, but after only a short time

I felt ill and was sent to lay down on a day bed in the office.

I had the most severe headache I'd ever experienced and fell into a deep sleep. Mum arrived and when she and Fay woke me, I stumbled down to the yard and stood behind my sausage stand, swaying. They took me back upstairs and made me stretch out again, and I lay there quietly crying as I could hear the happy sounds of the fete drifting in through the window.

I must have fallen asleep again because I suddenly saw several people in the room fretting over me. Then I was at home in my own bed without any memory of how I got there, apart from the fact that someone had picked me up from the YWCA day bed and carried me.

When I next woke, I was being trundled into the familiar environs of the children's ward at the Townsville General Hospital by a nurse, with a doctor and Mum walking briskly along beside me.

'She's burning up. Cold sponge, Nurse.'

The deep male voice jarred my head and every movement hurt me. My clothes were removed and the last thing I felt was the nurse plonking an ice-cold washer on me and whisking it over my chest and back, splashing my face and soaking the bed.

I was lying in a darkened room when next I opened my eyes again. I looked around cautiously to see if I could recognise where I was. A lamp stood on a bed-side locker and in its glow I saw a stand with tubes coming from it. The door opened and a nurse walked in. She noticed my eyes open and asked, 'Are you awake?'

'Where am I?'

'You're in hospital, in a private room.'

'Where's my mum?'

'I'll go and tell them you're awake and they'll send for her.' I closed my eyes to rest because I felt very weary. When I woke up, the overhead light was on and I could hear faint voices outside. The door opened and Mum's face peered around the corner. She looked shrunken and bent, much smaller than when I'd seen her last. I was shocked. She scuttled across the short distance between the door and the bed, and fell across the lower half the bed, crying and praying. I should have been surprised by her invocation of Christ, but I felt so dazed that nothing would have surprised me.

'Oh, thank God you're alive. Thank you, God.' She intoned the words like a chant. After a while she blew her nose and composed herself, sitting on the straight-backed chair the nurse had placed behind her. She sat patting my hand and saying words of sympathy and endearment.

'Oh, my poor darling. We didn't think you'd live. Oh, you poor little thing.'

I noticed suddenly how grey her hair was, and how gaunt she looked in the face. 'Where've you been?' I asked. She looked so haggard I thought she may have been in an accident.

Mum lifted up my hand and for the first time I saw that it was bandaged and a needle and tube were attached to it. The arm didn't look like mine—it was bare of any flesh and was just skin stretched over bones. The hand didn't feel like mine either, because I was unable to lift or control it, although I could feel Mum holding it up.

Mum was only there a few minutes before the nurse tapped her shoulder. When she stood up to go, her eyes didn't leave mine as she backed out of the room. I realised something serious must have happened to me but I was too tired to ask. Instead, I lapsed back into a cosy nap.

I spent the next few days sleeping and waking, not knowing when it was day or night because the curtains were always drawn and the room was kept in darkness. Over this time I pieced together part of the picture of what had happened to me, from brief conversations with nurses, augmented with details Mum told me on her daily visits. She was the only person allowed to come and see me, but she brought little notes and drawings which she'd coaxed my sisters into making for me.

I'd been in a coma for ten days. Local doctors had been unable to diagnose what was wrong with me. Two other children, admitted in the same condition, had both died.

Mum told me her version of events. 'They wouldn't let me stay at the hospital, the doctors sent me home and said they'd send an ambulance for me immediately if you took a turn for the worse, but I came back every afternoon at visiting hours,' she said. 'I came one afternoon to find a man leaning over you, wearing baggy old trousers and a dark coloured shirt, and he looked like the gardener. I thought he was molesting you, and I yelled at him to get away. A nurse came running and took me away. She told me he was a specialist, just in town for the day. He'd agreed to have a look at you and he'd found what was wrong with you. Meningitis. He was having you moved out of the ward and into the private area. He saved your life. A man who looked like a gardener saved your life!'

I never learned his name. He'd left instructions for my care, and the hospital had put a senior doctor in charge of looking after me. This doctor came in gingerly, accompanied by Mum, soon after I'd roused out of the coma. When he had checked my intravenous drip and the injection site, Mum pointed out scratches on his hands and arms and said that I'd attacked him one day when he came to give me one of the six lumbar punctures they'd taken. She said I must apologise to him, but he laughed the whole thing away and told me to just get well.

The day nurse assigned to me spent a lot of time looking at her face in a mirror which was hanging on the wall. She told me that she'd been given 'Privates' because she'd just had measles and, although she still had spots, which she kept inspecting, she wasn't contagious anymore.

One afternoon she brought in a sheet of paper and waved it at me.

'D'you know what this is?' she asked, laughing.

Well, of course I didn't, and I certainly wasn't strong enough yet to laugh with her. She brought it over and showed it to me.

'It's a death certificate. It's blank except for this bit on the bottom. The doctors thought you were going to die, and your mum would be too upset to sign it—so they got her to sign it when you were very sick so she wouldn't be made even more upset later.' She showed me Mum's signature. The nurse thought it was terribly funny, and said she'd been told to tear it up. She seemed to think of this as a mark of my improvement under her care. I didn't think of it that way, and burst into tears when she'd gone. How could my mother have signed it? How *could* she? I thought, rejecting her distress as a reason. Because of this, I harboured even deeper distrust of Mum's motives for many years.

For several days I continued to have trouble moving

my limbs, and I was on total bed care, fed by intravenous drips and my right leg was elevated on a pillow.
My leg had been hurt when the first intravenous drip,
which had been inserted in my ankle, had become
blocked in the vein above my knee and a nurse had
failed to look in until my leg had become badly
swollen. My skin was dark and wrinkled, like prune skin,
in a path from the inside of my lower thigh, down my
calf to the insertion site, and my leg was in pain all the
time and felt very sore to touch.

At some stage during the coma, I'd ripped a drip out
from my arm, which was also bandaged. When the
doctor checked on me, I begged to have the remaining
drip taken out. Because the fluid being pumped into
me looked like water, I cried that I'd drink the water
instead of having it go into my arm.

Without warning one afternoon, a trolley was trundled in and a wardsman lifted me onto it. The nurse
zipped around, putting my few belongings, drawings
and notes sent by my sisters, into a paper bag. She told
me the private room was needed for another patient
and I was being moved to the convalescent hospital. I
was afraid Mum wouldn't be able to find me when she
came but the nurse assured me that they would tell her
where I had gone.

The convalescent hospital was in the same complex,
but up a steep hill in a much older building. The wards-
men tried wheeling me there but the wheels were made
for flat surfaces and kept spinning out of control on the
broken path. Eventually, I was lifted into an ambulance
and driven the short distance. My nurse said that I'd
have a lovely time because there would be other children for me to play with. But when I arrived, I was put
into a very long and poorly lit dormitory ward, all by

myself. Through the wall I could occasionally hear children playing, but throughout my stay I didn't see any of them.

I was frightened in the ward. A sister came by shortly after my arrival and, to cheer me up, she said, 'We'll have your sea legs back for you in no time, and then we'll send you back to the island.' When she left, I cried until Mum came. I thought they were going to send me to Palm Island, where most of the expectant mothers I'd run messages for at the maternity ward lived. I recalled Mum telling me that the government had made several attempts to take us kids off her, and that they'd probably put us in a dormitory on Palm Island if that happened. It seemed that now, when I was so weak I couldn't even stand up much less fight them off, they were going to have their way. When Mum arrived I pleaded with her to take me home, but she said she was fearful I'd have a relapse and die. I thought I would surely die or be carried off by the welfare if she left me there. I would have cried that night, but instead I went for a journey inside myself in order to work out how best to handle this situation.

By the next day I had made a plan. I slid my legs down off the bed to run away, but they wouldn't hold me up. Then I couldn't get them back on the bed, and I ended up sinking slowly to the floor, still clutching the stiff sheets. Only a few nurses were working in this section of the hospital, so I lay on the ground for a long time before anyone found me.

Two people came in during the afternoon to try to talk to me, but I refused to cooperate. I wouldn't even answer them when they asked me my name. I was so distressed and had no other way to show it. That night, Mum visited me and she brought Dellie and Leonie.

They weren't allowed in but she had them look through a window and wave. It made me even more upset to see their freedom and to know that I had to stay there. A nurse had told Mum about the people who'd come to see me earlier and how I'd played up. Mum explained that it was their job to test me for brain damage, and the sooner I answered their questions, the sooner I'd be allowed to go home.

The next day the two people came again. I asked them if they were doctors but they said they weren't. They asked a lot of questions about things I'd learned at school and gave me a mental arithmetic test. However, when the woman gave me a book she wanted me to read from, I couldn't see the type clearly enough to read it. The man sat making notes. From the way Mum had spoken, I thought this examination was all I was being kept there for, so as they were walking away, I asked them if I could go now. The woman turned back and said, 'Oh, no. You'll be here at least three months.' A spear of pain went through my heart and I felt absolutely betrayed by everyone.

Late in the afternoon, an Asian man was brought into the ward. He arrived walking, accompanied by a nurse, and was made to put on pyjamas and get into a bed at the far end of the dormitory. On her way out, the nurse paused at my bed and told me that the man was Chinese, didn't speak English and was being kept there for quarantine.

In the evening when Mum came, she got very upset and went off to talk with the nurse. I was already frightened by being alone in that long gloomy ward, and the nurses had told me they couldn't hear me from their station. In fact, they left a pan on a chair beside my bed because my screams had previously gone unanswered

and I'd wet the bed. Now I was to be left in the dormitory with a strange man who had some disease which
needed quarantine, and I couldn't even speak to him,
nor could he speak to me.

That night, the nurse came by to administer my
evening medication and to turn off the lights. I
implored her to leave them on, and eventually she
agreed to leave a few on around me. No sooner had she
gone, however, than I realised that I was spot-lit but I
couldn't see what I needed to—that the man was staying in his bed and no other strangers were coming in
through the doors. I hoped the nurse would come back
so I could ask her to leave all the lights on as the present arrangement frightened me even more than being
in the dark. After a few hours, when she hadn't come
anywhere near the ward, I began to scream. I needed
some relief from the tension of fear, and I needed
to rest.

There was no response to my screams. In the
silences, when I was gathering my breath, I could hear
the Chinese man at his end of the room. He opened
and closed his locker and dragged a chair on the floor,
but I was much more frightened when the sounds
stopped and I didn't know what he was doing.

Realising that I would have to slide across the
ground like a grub in order to make my way out to
wherever the nurses spent their time, I slipped over the
edge of the bed and dropped to the floor. When I got as
far as the verandah I sat still for a few minutes to
recover my energy, and while I was there I heard firm
footsteps. I yelled out, 'Help, Nurse.' A man coming up
the path leading to the verandah saw me and went off
to find the nurses' station.

Nurse was very cross at being interrupted. She

carried me back to bed and she said she was going to settle me down 'once and for all'. She disappeared, then returned a few minutes later with a syringe in a kidney dish. I'd already had so many needles I looked like a pin cushion, and I felt that what was about to happen to me was grossly unfair. I tried to fight her off but she easily overpowered me, pinning me down by putting a pillow across my shoulders and leaning her bodyweight on it, while whipping up the hospital-issue nightgown I was wearing and sticking the needle into my scrawny buttocks.

When I woke the next morning, I knew there'd be no end to this torment unless I ended it myself. By then I was so stressed that nobody could speak to me and no one, apart from Mum, tried. I embarked on a terror campaign, turning myself around in the bed so my feet touched the wall and began drumming them loudly on the wall separating my ward from the children's polio rehabilitation ward. I swept my arm across the top of my locker, knocking everything off it, including a thermometer standing in a glass of sterilising fluid, onto the floor. After the nurse cleaned up the shards of broken glass and spilt mercury, and replaced the equipment, I broke them again. I worked the corners of the sheets from under the mattress and tore them from the bed, throwing them to the floor. This all required great effort and also caused me hardship. Mum came and told me that the staff were talking about keeping me constantly sedated. I said that they would have to fight me every time they tried, and she sighed. She knew I was a very determined child, and she had always regarded this as one of my strengths. Now she tried to convince me that it was self-destructive, but I didn't care. I decided that I'd have to show the staff that they should let me go home. I began by tra-la-la-ing loudly whenever a nurse spoke to me, so that I couldn't hear them.

When at last a nurse came to tell me that arrangements were being made to send me home, she grabbed my hands and yelled into my face to get my attention. I thought I heard her say, 'You're going home', but I couldn't trust my own ears. When she yelled it again, I was tra-la-ing a little more quietly in order to catch her words.

'Doctor spoke to your mother and she said she can handle you, so you're being allowed to go.' When she left I didn't feel victorious but lay huddled in my bed, crying at the pain of the ordeal I'd been put through. The nurse came back to pack my few things into a paper bag, and she said, 'Well, I thought you'd be happy now. What are you still crying for?'

There was nothing I could say.

A taxi brought Mum and me home. Neighbours came running out and helped her take me into the house. She could have carried me herself, however, because I was as light as a feather, and during the next few months she had to carry me many times. Nellie, her friend, had waited at the house to help Mum get me settled in. I was so happy to be home, but they were all looking at me sadly and shaking their heads.

Later, Mum had a serious talk with me. I was lying on her bed and she came in and sat by me. She said she was a bit sorry I'd come home early because she was having a room enclosed for me on the end of the verandah and had ordered furniture to be made especially for me, because the doctors had told her that I'd be confined to bed for a long time, perhaps as long as six months, and she wanted me to be comfortable. She said I'd been 'saved' because I was obviously meant to do something special with my life.

She also told me she'd had to lie to the hospital staff because she didn't like the way they were looking after me, and because she thought I may have ended up killing myself with the foolish things I'd been doing, if I had to stay there any longer. The truth was that she couldn't look after me in the way she had convinced them she could, because she couldn't stay home from work. Short of staying home, she said, she'd do everything else to help me, but I really had to look after myself from then on. I was so pleased to be back in my familiar environment that I would have agreed to anything.

Between Mum, Nellie and the neighbours, I had someone in the house with me most of the time for the next few days. They would prop pillows around me so I could sit up and feed myself from a tray, but my arm muscles were so wasted I could barely lift a spoon to my mouth. Every mealtime someone sat with me and gave me a pep talk because I had no appetite, but I had promised to eat. I choked on the food but, little by little, my capacity increased. My sisters came to the door and whinged at me for all the special attention I was getting, but they looked wide-eyed and somehow afraid of me and of the changes that had taken place in their lives because of my illness.

A lattice wall was built at the end of the verandah— I heard the hammering but wasn't able to see the progress. In time, the furniture was delivered and the day I was moved into the new room was regarded as quite an event. Nellie and some of the neighbours came to watch. I was carried to the door and we paused there so I could feast my eyes. The furniture was pastel pink, not a colour I particularly cared for but Mum must have thought it appropriate, and consisted of a single bed with a bedhead and a cupboard, which was half hanging space with drawers and mirror attached to one side. A doily and vase of flowers stood on the dressing table. Mum had sewn curtains and hung them across the latticework to afford me privacy, while the lattice-work allowed me to watch people coming and going and did not isolate me completely, as a solid wall would have done. The verandah was narrow and the room tiny, but it felt wonderful to have my own space.

My sisters, at ages ten and eight, were too young to appreciate the gravity of my condition or to understand the tension in the house. I heard Mum bellowing at them that they couldn't go to the pictures while their sister was close to death and I felt awful about being the cause of their getting into trouble. Nellie told me that throughout the time I'd spent in the coma, Mum had sat in the cane chair on the verandah every night, fully dressed with her handbag at her side at the ready, looking out for the ambulance the hospital had promised to send for her if my condition had worsened. The strain must have been enormous and the demands of my sisters caused an overload. So, Nellie took them out a few times to get them off Mum's hands.

Before long, I was bored stiff because there was nothing for me to do. Mum took me by taxi to an optometrist who fitted me with glasses. He felt that my eyes would strengthen and that my previous good vision would return over time. He lent me a pair of spectacles until I no longer needed them, and he charged us very little. I was pleased because Mum was having to work doubly hard now that I wasn't able to help her. Her almost complete dependence on me for so many years meant that neither of my sisters was as skilled and competent as I had become. I'd graduated to ironing, folding and packing long-sleeved starched shirts, and could take over the laundry when Mum wasn't feeling well.

I was happier once I had glasses as I was able to read. Mum told Dellie and Leonie to bring the encyclopedias into my room and, until my sisters began to complain that they needed them for their homework, the books stayed under my bed. Knowing I was going to be there for the long haul, I started at A and worked my way through to Z, reading the entire set. When Mum had to take them away for my sisters to use, I'd drop out of bed and crawl through the house on my hands and knees to get one, then push it ahead of me back to the bed. I usually returned it to the bookcase before Mum came home from work, but once I dropped off to sleep while I was reading. Mum discovered the book in my room and knew it hadn't been there when she left that morning. I received her 'both-barrels' lecture about how I'd have a relapse, but I had become used to that one by then.

Being lost in the encyclopedias was one of the most pleasant and rewarding experiences of my childhood. I drank them in, filling my mind with information, much of which I would never need, such as the gestation period of elephants and other animals, and some of which has been invaluable. I absorbed the illustrations, including photos of sculptures from all over the world, and fascinating data about people and their different ways of life, much of which was presented in racist and elitist ways by today's standards but which, nevertheless, left me with a yearning to travel and meet these people and see all these things for myself.

Some of the information I was able to put to use immediately, such as the details about nutrition. I began to understand cause and effect, and the different ways various foods affect different people, and to take these things into consideration in regard to my own health. I eliminated eggs from my diet because they were rich with albumen, which was regarded, at the time, as perhaps creating a predisposition towards asthma. I made this change much to Mum's annoyance since our hens were a plentiful source of eggs. I then cut out more foods and began experimenting with others. There wasn't a lot of scope available because my meals were prepared without any consultation with me, but when I'd worked out what I would and wouldn't eat and let it be known, if this food turned up on my plate I left it there.

I grew stronger although I was still very thin. One memorable day, two women, one a physiotherapist, came to help me to start walking again and to show Mum how I was to go about this. Mum had an old drop-side cot which she had put in the backyard for her two cattle dogs, Bluey and Delta, to sleep in. The women carried me into the backyard, put the dropside up, and propped me up by my elbows on the cot. Mum ran out to take my photo with the box brownie she kept for special occasions. The day is so clear in my mind, and I remember how wonderful it was to stand there at last with my feet on the ground, the sun beating down on my face and a light breeze blowing across my skin. It had been a very long time since I'd been able to do this. I recall how absolutely terrific I felt, but the memory I carry bears no relationship whatsoever to the photograph taken that day, in which I look like a starving child from a famine-ridden country.

The physio weighed me, and I clocked in at three stone six pounds (just under 22 kilograms). Mum wept on my bed when they'd gone, telling me I had to eat more. The women came for a short visit every few days, teaching me exercises to strengthen my muscles. They were amazed by the flexibility which I'd always had, as I could cross my ankles up behind my head and twist my arms around each other in the centre of my back to touch my head, but they wanted me to increase my physical strength. So, I began walking down the hall by holding onto the walls, then walking around the yard holding onto the fence, and soon I was walking almost as well as before. Mum said I could go back to school in the next year, which was still some months away.

I'd missed almost a year's schooling but I was determined that I would stay in my grade and sit the scholarship exam with the same girls who had always been in my class.

I'd already suffered enough embarrassments because Dellie was taller than me, and I didn't want to be put down into her class, because I felt there would then have been virtually nothing to make me stand out as the eldest. I also feared that people would then think I was dumb. I asked Dellie to bring me a list of the books my class was studying but she was unable to get it for me, so Mum went to the bookstore in town that stocked our school's requirements.

The nuns weren't happy about my decision to remain with my class but said they would give me a chance to show them whether I could catch up. By this time, my class had moved from St Joseph's Primary School to St Patrick's College. We wore long-sleeved uniforms with starched white cuffs and collars, ties and thick black stockings, even on the hottest summer days.

While I had been ill, I'd discovered that I could close my eyes and recall whole pages of the books I'd read that day and on previous days. I could also replay in my head popular songs and even classical music which I'd heard on the radio. When I returned to school I surprised myself with the degree of retentiveness I was able to bring to my lessons. Within a few months I'd caught up with the girls in my class and was permitted to proceed into the next grade and sit for the scholarship exams.

At the beginning of the school holidays I suffered another great trauma. Mum took Dellie shopping and she came home with half a dozen brassieres. Two years younger than me and already Dellie was wearing bras and I wasn't. Mum's response when I confronted her with the injustice of it all was, 'Well, you don't need them yet.' I didn't think Dellie needed them to cover up her little split peas either, but Mum said she had a bigger build than me and that her development was more prominent. When I continued to seek reassurances that my illnesses were not going to mark me all my life, Mum said cruel things. 'Wake up to yourself. You've got a figure like a snake, no hips and nothing at the top. In fact you go in where everybody else goes out! If I bought a bra for you we'd have to nail it on the right place with sticking plaster!'

I was wounded and no one seemed to understand my plight. At the age of thirteen, my classmates were turning into young women, hiding in the toilets and talking about their 'monthlies'. They were wearing jewellery and, on special occasions, perfume and pink lipstick. Of course, they all wore brassieres and many of them flaunted matching lacy underwear and suspender belts. My lucky sister was poised to join this group and

I was being left behind. I was so envious that, occasionally, I would crouch over and ask to be allowed to go home from school with cramps—just so my classmates would think that I, too, had reached menstruation and include me in their adult talk.

Since the physiotherapist's visit when she weighed me, Mum had been promising we could all go on a trip during the Christmas holidays if I would just eat enough to get to four and a half stone. I didn't exactly make it, but I was close enough for her to proceed with the plan. Dessie, by this time, had married a man named Reginald Mills. Reg was shorter than the willowy Dessie, of handsome appearance with jet-black hair and a small moustache. They'd taken a job running a property at Torrens Creek, which is along the Townsville—Mt Isa line. We went there by train, arrived at night and were met by Reg and Dessie to be taken in their truck another hundred or so miles to the property.

The minute I saw the place I loved it. The house was a big, old wooden two-storey structure, very open, with its own generator. There were a few horses, some cows for milk and a lot of sheep and kangaroos. The horses were ex-racehorses, and when Reg saddled them up he had to jump up on them and let them 'run their distance' before they'd settle down to being a station horse for the day. When the horses had tired from their fast run, Reg would put me on one of them and he and I would ride around to look at this and that. We had to check the windmill, which pumped up water, and various other things around the property that required monitoring and attention. He also let me trail along after him when he went to ride the boundary and check the fences. I think my last illness had caused Mum to become fatalistic about me, because she would look out warily at the horses and caution me about going on them, but she didn't stop me. My sisters didn't seem remotely interested in doing any of these things. We used to splash around in the old watertank, which was kept full of water for the horses to drink, when the heat became overpowering. But Dellie, in particular, was frightened to get into it. The water attracted bees, wasps and dragonflies, and my sisters were easily scared off by flying insects.

A creek which ran through the property had all but dried up, and only some waterholes were found along its course. These rapidly shrinking waterholes were packed with fish that were landlocked due to the drought. We would stand in the shallows and throw fish out onto the land with our hands, and we soon had as many as we could eat. If we stood still in the water, fish nipped us with their sharp little teeth.

There was a wind-up gramophone in the house, and I almost wore holes in the few records they had which I liked. We didn't have a gramophone at home and I'd never heard these particular songs before, but I'd wander around happily singing, 'She fought like a tiger for 'er honour, for 'er honour, for 'er honour', This was my favourite, along with 'These Foolish Things Remind Me of You', although I didn't have much of a clue what the words meant.

We stayed about ten days before Reg and Dessie drove us back into Torrens Creek to catch the train. The town consisted of one shop, which was more of a depot for picking up supplies sent up from the nearest major town, and one hotel. The train came through very late at night. To fill the time, the adults sat in the hotel and had a few drinks. They were all aware that I was unhappy to be leaving, and when Mum got a bit tipsy Dessie put it to her that I should be allowed to stay another two weeks, until Dessie herself would be coming down to Townsville for a dental appointment. Unbelievably, Mum said okay.

I had to scramble around and get some of my clothes out of the suitcases. We just rolled them up into a swag and put them in the truck. I couldn't trust my luck until I watched the train pull away, as I'd kept thinking Mum would come to her senses any moment and change her mind.

The next day I discovered that I hadn't managed to grab any bloomers, which meant that I only had the pair I was wearing. I was too shy to confide in Dessie and, besides, her clothes were too large for me, so the two weeks were spent in an agony of juggling between that pair and my swimming togs without anyone discovering my predicament.

This embarrassment was outweighed by all the terrific things we fitted into the time. On New Year's Eve, owners of the neighbouring station held a picture-show evening. We travelled the round trip of a hundred and twenty miles to their place to lay on the ground in their yard, watching a film flicker on a big bedsheet which they'd turned into a screen.

In the house, Dessie taught me to churn butter from the rich cream taken from the top of the milk, while in the yard Reg taught me to shoot and clean his rifle, and we went out on horseback looking for kangaroos. The first time we ran out of meat, Reg had me shoot a sheep from a flock wandering near the homestead. He threw it in the back of the truck to carry it a few hundred yards to a tree beside the house, where he winched it up to butcher it. Perhaps to put me off, he asked me if I'd slice it open. But he didn't know me very well, because I took the finely sharpened knife and had a go but was unable to make a cut through its fleece. When he saw I wasn't easily deterred, Reg showed me how to slit the carcass down the belly from neck to tail, identify the edible organs, and remove them before completely gutting it, then remove the sheepskin in one piece. Throughout the lesson, Dessie was yelling at him from inside the house where she was tending her small son, Neville, that he shouldn't have me doing things like that because Mum would have a fit if she found out. I didn't say anything about the kittens and chickens Mum had already made me kill because it seemed to me they had a different image of her than I did.

In the second week, Reg said he would have to ride out to a distant paddock to get another sheep, and he asked if I wanted to come for company. He told me not to wear the shorts I had on as we would probably have to walk in the bush. Mum had never allowed me to have long pants, because she said they weren't 'lady-like'. When I climbed into the truck Reg didn't notice I was still wearing the shorts.

Some miles from the house, Reg spotted a flock of sheep running through the trees and he drove as close to them as he could. They were disturbed by the motor, and we couldn't get near enough for a sure shot from the truck. He pulled up and began to sprint across the ground, with me in close pursuit. Bounding over a fallen tree trunk, I was just one step behind him when I felt a sting and looked down. A snake, seeming as startled as I felt, was staring back at me with a sad expression on its face. I didn't break stride but yelled, 'Reg, a snake's bit me.'

Reg reeled around and came running back towards me. I thought he would want to look at the bite mark, but instead I saw his fist come wickedly towards me, and next thing I was out like a light.

When I woke, I was in bed back at the house, my leg bandaged just above the knee. Reg and Dessie were hovering in the next room and when they saw I was awake, Reg came and sat beside me. I asked him what had happened and he told me he'd called the Flying Doctor, who'd come in and taken a piece out of my leg, so I'd be alright now. He said this in such a sly way, however, that I found it hard to believe him. I thought perhaps he had sliced into my leg and sucked the poison out himself, as all North Queenslanders were taught to do at the time, but Dessie stood in the doorway behind him, nodding at his explanation, and over the next few days they both stuck to this story. They told me that I shouldn't tell Mum because she'd be angry that she'd let me stay and might never let me come out to the station again. My leg was sore but nothing dramatic had happened to me, so I figured they were probably right and it was too trifling to bother Mum with. By the time Dessie and I were to return to Townsville I was walking as right as rain, and Mum didn't ask me about the band-aid, which by that time was all that was required to cover the small wound.

We had bigger problems to worry about when we arrived back. Dessie had developed a gum disease and had to have all her teeth removed. Instead of using a general anaesthetic, as they would probably do now, the staff at the dental hospital decided to take a quarter of her teeth out each day for four days. Every day, Dessie came home crying and in great pain. We kids were all frightened witless and undertook to brush our own teeth with more vigour than we'd ever shown before.

Dellie and I went back to the YWCA briefly, but we'd outgrown the Saturday afternoon juniors club and were expected to attend on Friday nights instead. I wasn't as happy there, and we no longer had Fay Naylor as our group leader, so I decided I wasn't going anymore.

Throughout the later years of primary school, we'd had class swimming. As Tobruk Memorial Pool is conveniently located almost directly across the street from the Catholic school, we had easy access. Mr Lawrence was the pool manager and his daughter, Kay Lawrence was a close friend in my class. Her older brother, Laurie, has since gone on to become an internationally famous swimming coach. Their family lived in an apartment above the pool.

At that time the Australian Olympic Swimming Team came north to do their winter training at Tobruk Pool. The whole town buzzed with excitement pending their arrival. It was not unusual to see Dawn Fraser or Lorraine Crapp, Ilsa or Jon Konrads walking down the street, and many people went to the pool early in the morning just to gaze at them through the chain-wire fence, swimming their laps. Forbes Carlisle was also there, walking up and down and consulting his stop watch.

I'd already demonstrated a propensity for swimming by winning a few races at our school carnivals, particularly in backstroke. Indeed, the doctors at the hospital had been suspicious that I may have picked up the meningitis virus from the swimming pool. Mum and I, however, had arrived at the conclusion that, because meningitis has a ten-day incubation period and I'd had my first polio immunisation exactly ten days before coming down with the disease, the immunisation had something to do with it. Although the doctors were loath to agree, because they might have regarded this as a slight on their profession, they did recommend that I not continue the polio immunisation program.

I'd read in the encyclopedia about the beneficial effects of swimming on lung capacity, and felt that this might be another excellent way to get on top of my asthma. Mum agreed. So, when I was well enough, I went back into the water and began chewing up the laps with all the other wannabees.

I had what I called 'inward looking feet', and Mum had always been worried about my stance. She had taken me to several doctors when I was younger to see if I needed an operation for pigeon-toes. Once she brought home a second-hand pair of surgical boots that some doctor had given her. They had irons attached which came up to my knees and were supposed to force my feet to grow outwards. I refused to wear them outside the house and eventually Mum returned them, so that a 'more grateful' child could benefit from them, she said. She later enrolled me in a ballet class to see if the outwards-pointing classical dance pose would assist my feet to look to the front, but again to no avail. Then a doctor told her there was nothing wrong with the bones in my legs, that some children stand pigeon-toed as a means of expressing embarrassment; advice which she ignored. After that, she stopped seeking a medical cure for my psychological distress.

When I announced that I was taking up swimming seriously, Mum nodded and said, 'With those big feet both pointing inwards, you won't have to wear flippers and you'll still swim fast. It might turn out to be the best sport for you after all.'

On my bicycle it was only minutes from our house to the pool, although it took a little longer to get home as it was uphill a lot of the way. I began to rise at five-thirty and slip out of the house to be at the pool by six, where I'd put in an hour or so before returning home for breakfast.

What with my studies, swimming, and a short stint with a gymnastics group where we learned tumbling and the basics of judo, time flew by very quickly and, in the main, fairly uneventfully. An extraordinary thing happened around the middle of the year, however, which was soon to have repercussions for my future. I was walking in the main street one day, as usual look-ing down—a habit left over from my bower-bird days—when I spotted a roll of money with a rubber-band around it lying right in my path. I picked it up, and when I realised how much was in the wad, I became frightened and started to shake. As I was on my way home, and had to walk past the police station, I handed the money in to the police. The constable on the desk took my name and address, and I was glad to be rid of my find.

In the evening there came a knock on the door, and Mum went to see who it was. I heard a man's voice, then Mum called me. A stranger in a white shirt and tie stood on the top step, and Mum asked curiously, 'Roberta, did you find a roll of money today?'

When I admitted that I had, she said that this gen-tleman had lost it. He didn't think he'd get it back but he had gone to the police station hopefully. Now he wanted to reward me for my honesty, and he handed

Mum twenty pounds. Mum ran around and told the neighbours how I had found over five hundred pounds and was so honest I'd taken it to the police station and hadn't even bothered to ask her. She told me to put the reward in my school bank account, where it more than doubled my meagre savings. Then I promptly forgot about the man.

At the end of the school year, girls began talking about what they planned to do during their holidays, with a few of us from the not well-to-do families deciding to put our names down for work at stores which hired additional staff over Christmas. I felt no one would hire me because there were no women of colour working in any store in Townsville at that time.

One day Mum pointed out an advertisement in the *Townsville Daily Bulletin*; a chemist store required a girl for a few weeks pre-Christmas work. She said to apply and to make sure the manager saw me. I was very intimidated by the idea, and hung around outside the shop for half an hour before gathering up the courage to walk through the door. I was told to ring or drop by the next day as the manager was making a decision that night.

I didn't want to be embarrassed by being told to my face that I didn't have the job, so at Mum's insistence, I made a call from the phone outside the Greeks' shop. I couldn't believe my ears when the woman who answered said I had the job. I ran home to tell Mum, who smiled knowingly.

'D'you know whose shop that is?' she asked. I didn't, of course. 'It belongs to the man whose roll of money you found, Mr Stuart Ritchie, and that's Ritchie's Chemist shop. I knew he'd want an honest girl to work for him, and he knew from his own experience that that was you.'

My job was to unpack boxes of gift perfumes and toiletry sets at the back of the store, dust them and put them around the counter for the sales staff to place on the shelves. I also ran errands all along the main street. Other store managers and salespeople were surprised to see me. They said, 'Hmm … you work for Mr Ritchie?' in ways which indicated to me that they were going to check this out with him before they gave me anything to take back to the store.

At lunchtime I walked around the other stores and looked at the merchandise—just as I saw other working women do. As I did so, I often heard people talking about me, 'the dark girl from the chemist shop'. Once Christmas was over, I had the rest of summer to spend at the pool.

When school resumed I had a major fight on my hands because the Queensland school system consisted of four years of high school after completing the scholarship exams, and this was to be my first year. I felt as if I was on the verge of realising my dream to study medicine and specialise in surgery, and that the experiences I'd had with animals and cutting up kangaroos and sheep were all leading in this direction. I'd carefully decided on the courses I would need to take— Latin, Chemistry, Biology, Physics, along with core subjects, such as English and Maths.

The nuns, however, had a different program mapped out for me. Although my scholarship marks were good enough to entitle me to go in any direction I chose, the nuns said I was to do Domestic Science subjects— sewing and cooking. Mum told me she didn't want me to be trained as a slave, and reminded me that she'd been putting little sums of money away so I could go to university if I was smart enough. But she wouldn't tell the nuns any such thing and expected me to make them change their minds. When they involved her at last, she tried to get us all to strike up a compromise— she told the nuns that she wanted me to take typing, bookkeeping and shorthand. I challenged her later about her change of mind, but she said it was obvious the nuns weren't going to give in, and that maybe my aspiration *was* a pipe dream. It was more likely, she thought now, that since I could be sickly all my life, I'd need a job where I used my head, such as clerical work, rather than my strength, as in heavy domestic work. I was very angry about this because it wasn't a job they were all talking about—it was my *life*.

Eventually, we entered into what was for me a very difficult arrangement. I would do the subjects they wanted me to study if they'd also agree that I could do the subjects *I* wanted to take. I had two years before I'd be required to sit for the Junior exams, and by that time it would be obvious which of the subjects I excelled in.

My life became frantic as I tried to juggle twelve subjects plus find time for swimming training. Only one nun at St Patrick's College, Sister Sebastian, tried to understand me. She, too, was asthmatic and we shared ideas about the causes and how to control it. Fortunately, she taught science subjects and was happy to meet me at the school at seven-thirty in the morning so that she could give me lessons in Chemistry, which was the only subject I couldn't manage to fit in during my regular schedule. Sister Sebastian had a great sense of fun, and we'd be bent laughing over our test tubes and bunsen burners; it was a wonderful start to the day. I took to carrying Vita-Brits with cheese and honey on them around in my school bag because I'd never know where I might be at mealtimes and I couldn't afford to lose weight.

A new member of staff was taken on at the Mater Hospital laundry. She had ideas Mum couldn't agree with, so Mum looked around for another job. The Central Hotel needed a laundress, and took her on. She started at six-thirty in the morning and finished theoretically at three-thirty, but she was free to go whenever she had completed her work. She lamented having to leave the hospital because she hated the smell of sour bar towels, which were used to soak up spilled beer. She said some people who took rooms at the hotel wet their beds as frequently as patients at the hospital, who couldn't help it, but that their beer-piss smelled worse. Most of all, she told me, she missed flying through the darkened streets on her bike, with the wind in her face, in the early hours of the morning. She had felt then as if the whole town somehow belonged to her because no one else was out at that hour. Even the dogs didn't stir, she said.

Mum hadn't renewed the YWCA laundry contract because rent from the lodgers in Mrs Sullivan's house was meeting the bank payments, and as long as she had the Central Hotel job she could afford to feed us. We still occasionally had to clean a house or apartment, but this was rare and we did them only on a Saturday. She retained a few of her favourite laundry clients who had used her services for many years. We did their clothes together and split the money according to which of us had done the most work. This way Mum helped me to earn pocket money, which I needed for admission to the swimming pool and to keep myself in Speedos.

During the first months back at school, I finally joined the ranks of the lucky girls who had their monthlies. Under pressure from me, Mum had talked to a doctor about my problem and been told that the most likely reason for my slow development was my weight and previous ill-health.

Once I started them though, I didn't like it. Mum bought us each a dozen small white barber's towels that we were to use, and which we were to wash out discreetly and hang on a special line concealed under the house, and then only overnight, so that no men would see them. Walking around with these thick wads between our legs was no fun at all, and I envied those girls at school whose parents could afford store-bought disposable pads.

At this time I became a member of the swimming club and began to participate in races. My wins attracted the attention of a trainer, who offered to train me for nothing. Mum came to the pool to meet him and didn't like him, but I couldn't afford another trainer and no one else offered. When I missed training for five days at a time, he told me to speak to some of the women from the Olympic team, but I was far too shy to approach them. Finally, he or one of the other trainers did so, and a few other young female swimmers and I were taken into the ladies' change rooms where the wonders of Tampax were explained to us. If we had any problems, the women said we were welcome to speak to them again.

When I told Mum she was horrified and said things like that cause cancer and illness, and that she wouldn't buy them for me. Her message was reinforced by Maisie, who was renting our front room, and by Nellie. Apart from buying us the towels, showing us on a table how to pin them, and giving us instructions about soaking and laundering them secretly, Mum had never spoken to us about this or any other sexual aspect of our lives. Instead, she had given me a slim book when I was about ten, called *The House Not Made With Hands*. It referred to the bodies of women as temples and how they should remain chaste, but offered no practical information or advice about what that meant or how we were to go about preserving ourselves from being defiled. Any other discussion had been delegated to Maisie.

Despite their admonitions, I bought tampons and figured out how to use them. After a while, Mum said that she had been thinking about the female Olympic swimmers and how they had to manage with their constant training and race dates, and said that 'they look healthy enough'. I felt that this was her way of telling me that she'd been groping around in my things and found my box of Tampax, and that as long as I only wore them when I was swimming, I would probably be alright.

Chatting casually one day, my swimming trainer mentioned an upcoming event, the Magnetic Island to Townsville Swim. I became fascinated with the idea of swimming so far, and I was intrigued with the cages that the participants were to use for protection from sharks. By this time I was swimming several miles a day, and I loved the meditative state long-distance swimmers go into which helps them overcome pain and exhaustion thresholds. I began to think that I could swim that distance, eight miles, and that I should start a program of training with that long swim as my aim. I was thrilled when my trainer told me that I had the stamina and just needed the strength, and that he'd help me develop a program with this goal in mind.

I began to spend every spare minute at the pool, doing a couple of miles before school—except when I had Chemistry classes with Sister Sebastian—and more laps after classes. Most nights I was back in the pool for a few hours before it closed at nine o'clock. On rare weekends I was invited to stay over with Kay and her family, who lived above the pool. This was fun but we were usually too exhausted to do much beyond talking about our homework before falling asleep. Laurie Lawrence often wasn't well and the family often seemed a bit stressed, but they always made me welcome.

Some Murri friends drew me aside and told me they weren't allowed in the pool, and one day I asked Mr Lawrence about this. He said they had sores and he couldn't let them in. From then on I watched to see if white people were allowed in if they had sores, and when I saw how many were admitted I found it deeply troubling. I brought this up with my trainer and he said, 'Yes, there's a lot of discrimination around.' I didn't know what the word meant and his meaning wasn't obvious from the dictionary definition when I looked it up, so I had to resort to asking Mum. She took a while to tell me that it was about being kept out of places because of skin colour or religion. She said that Jews were kept out of as many places as dark people were, and that they were white, so discrimination wasn't just about having dark skin. Her explanation made me more confused, but I didn't want to push the issue because I knew she'd get angry to learn I'd increased my circle of 'dark friends'. I didn't know any Jewish people, or, if I did, I didn't know that they were Jewish. Despite this incident, because of my personal association with them, for many years I regarded the Lawrences as being the least racist family I knew in Townsville.

7

Maisie and her husband, Fred, invited a guest to the house for dinner one night. Arthur became the classic 'guest who came for dinner' in that he never seemed to go home; he dropped in every day. At thirty-five years old, he had a little barber shop in town and still lived with his parents. Their house was just through the cutting (an overhead pass at the top of the hill), and he walked by our house on his way to and from work.

Mum and Maisie often discussed him—his drinking habits being of main concern. But Mum defended him, saying that 'anyone interested in picking up with a woman who has three kids can't be too bad!' The fact that he was almost twenty years younger than Mum may have added to his attraction. Also, he would peel notes off a great wad of cash he always carried in his pocket, and flash them at every opportunity.

Mum's attention to us kids became less intense when she took up with this man. His presence freed me up enormously as Mum no longer flew into a panic when I arrived home a few minutes late. Sometimes our meals were late because Mum was hanging out waiting for Arthur to join us. Then his mother started turning up, shouting over the top fence that his meal was ready at his own house. Once she threw a pile of his clothes over the fence, yelling, 'If you like it there so much, stay there!' Arthur eventually moved in with us, but he tried to keep the peace with his parents by going to their house for dinner from time to time. Nevertheless, the bickering continued.

Arthur refereed soccer matches on weekends, and Mum often went with him. I was shocked to see how differently she acted now there was a man in her life. She had brought us up to be quite independent, and to a large extent we were each in the habit of looking after ourselves. Suddenly, Mum was running after this man, offering him cups of tea, washing and ironing his clothes, and even taking him breakfast in bed. When he sat down at the table she would tell us that we had to wait on him. We weren't used to waiting on anyone, it was 'everybody do as much as they can for themselves' in our house. Dellie and I often aired our resentment at having to trot in and out with Arthur's dinner and his dirty plates. He would leave his cup wherever he was sitting and we were expected to go looking for it when we were doing the washing up.

Arthur was from Wales and spoke with a pronounced accent. He was about four and a half feet tall, with a stocky build despite his lack of height, and he tried to make up for his size by using a deep voice and acting like a bully.

He introduced several people from the United Kingdom into Mum's small circle of friends. A Scottish couple began coming by, and Mum and Arthur would also go to their house. They would eat and drink beer and get merry and sing. Everyone said that Arthur had a good voice, he particularly liked to sing 'Mona Lisa' and 'Barrow Boy'. My sisters and I would raise our eyebrows whenever he launched into his renditions, especially when we were trying to do our homework while a party was going on. Mum drank shandies and laughed a lot, but we kids were upset when we came out in the morning and had to clear away glasses of stale beer and clean up from the night before.

I had begun writing, mostly essays and poems, and continued to read as avidly as ever. Arthur regarded both these activities as a waste of time, but Mum, unbeknown to me, entered my name in the short story section of the local eisteddfod—then promptly forgot that she had done so. When I came in late one Sunday evening, Mum told me about the nomination and that the entry had had to be in by the previous Friday. An eisteddfod organiser had come by our house to tell her that my entry had not been received. Mum made me sit down, tired as I was, and write something for her to take in early the next morning on her way to work.

Our old house had a stove recess which had become very ricketty, and Arthur had made a big show of his carpentry skills by offering to fix it. He had peeled off the back wall, and then the sides, before realising he didn't have a clue what to do next. We pulled the stove from the recess and it stood in the middle of the kitchen, where we still had to use it, for a couple of months. Our kitchen wall, meanwhile, had a gaping hole in it. One day, heavy clouds gathered and at last Arthur was forced to do something before the rain poured in. Rather than repairing the recess, however, he hammered a sheet of tin across the hole, so that we had no stove recess at all.

As I sat at the kitchen table wondering what to write about, my eyes fell on the stove in the middle of the room. There was my story—a comedy. Unfortunately, I exceeded the permissible number of words and so didn't win in my section, but I did receive a Special Mention as a highly talented young writer. Arthur, meanwhile, was extremely unamused.

It was only a matter of time before a blow-up occurred between him and me. One evening, instead of Mum telling me to wait on him, Arthur told me himself. I brought his meal out and when he had finished, he got up and said, 'Clean up now.' I was doing my home-work at another small table and replied that I'd clean up when I was ready. He swore at me and turned red and blustery in the face. I stood up to stare him down.

'You'd like to hit me, wouldn't you?' I taunted.

'Yes, and I damned well will!'

'Well, if it'll make you feel big to hit me, go ahead.' I was still very small for my age, thirteen, and thin as a bean pole, and it had never occurred to me that a grown man would attack me. My ear rang and my eye smarted when he whacked me right across the face, nearly knocking my head off my shoulders.

In the moment I recovered, I saw in his eyes that he had lost control, they were bulging and straining in his head.

'Feel big now? Want to feel bigger? Hit me again if you have to?' He hit me on the other side of the head this time.

I spun on my heel and walked through the house, out the front door and down the lane. By the time I got to the Hale Street corner, I knew where I was going.

I went into the police station and told the officer on the counter what had happened. He was solicitous and said he could see the bright red marks on my face. He called a detective and they asked me if I wanted to make a complaint. I agreed, and gave them a signed statement.

When I went home nobody spoke to me and I went straight into my room. Dellie came and stood in the doorway, her shoulders hunched up with fear. She wanted to know if I was hurt. I told her not to worry, that I'd taken care of it, but I didn't let on what I'd done. I didn't want Mum or Arthur to get it out of her, so the best way was not to tell her.

At school a few days later, my teacher told me that I could leave early because my mother wanted to talk to me. Mum had come to the school on her bike so I collected mine and we went across to the Strand. She hadn't said a word so far, as the Sister had done all the talking at school.

'Roberta,' she said in her most serious voice, 'the police came to the house. Did you go there telling them our business?'

'What do you mean, *our* business? Where were you? It's not just "our business" when I've got to fight a grown man. He could have killed me. I don't mind having to fight off kids my own age but when I'm home I shouldn't have to fight men.'

'It's not "men". You're a big girl now and you have to begin to understand about these things. After all these years I've been alone and working to keep you kids, I have to worry about who's going to look after me in my old age. You're nearly grown up. Are *you* going to look after me for the rest of my life?'

I didn't know what awaited me in my life, so I wasn't prepared to make a commitment like this; one that I didn't understand anyway. 'I don't know,' I answered.

'Well, Arthur's prepared to look after me, and now the police want to put him in jail.'

'He deserves to go to jail.'

'I know. And he knows that now, too. He's promised he won't ever do it again.'

'That's not good enough. I don't understand why you want to spend the rest of your life with a drunk.'

'He's not a drunk. He's hard working. He's never missed a day's work in his life. And that's for me to decide, anyway.'

'It's for me to decide if I want someone punching me up for the rest of *my* life, and I don't. No one is ever going to hit me again.' Mum agreed. 'And no one is to hit Dellie or Leonie, either.'

'Yes, he knows that. I've told him if he ever so much as lays a hand on any of you kids again, he's out.'

I looked out at the ocean and remembered Mum running over the hill in the middle of the night carrying me, and now all she was wanting from me was to give Arthur another chance.

'What do you want me to do?' I asked finally.

'Sign a paper the police will give you saying you'll drop the charges.'

An uneasy truce came over the house. Arthur didn't bother me, and I didn't bother him. All the family, except for me, regularly went to watch him referee games. They also went off to watch Dellie competing at athletics carnivals, where she not only won her distance races but also excelled at high and long jumps.

Mum had always made us wear dresses or skirts and blouses, although in summer we were allowed to wear cotton shorts around the house. Jeans were becoming fashionable and I longed to have a pair, so I went without treats and saved my money in order to buy some for myself. I bought black jeans, which were the height of teen-fashion. Because of Mum's attitude to our wearing pants, however, I'd sometimes carry them out of the house in a bag and change into them further up the road.

The day Mum found them she flew into a rage, carried them at arm's length in front of her out of the house and down into the backyard, where she immediately lit a fire and burnt them in front of me. She said only tarts wore jeans, and that I'd only wear them over her dead body. Arthur and my sisters stood by and watched. I wept for weeks, and kept praying that I'd hurry and grow up so I could leave home and live my own life. I promised myself that when I was old enough I would listen to whatever music I liked when I liked, and own a whole wardrobe of jeans and slacks and pants. Mum's idea of how I should live and what I should wear was just so old-fashioned.

I was scheduled to swim in the North Queensland Swimming Carnival and was a certainty in the backstroke events, where I'd been turning in age-record times. Mum said that she would come to watch me, and on the night, she sent me off earlier on my bike to see the events that were on before mine. I suspected she wouldn't turn up, so instead of going in I went to sit on a cliff overlooking the swimming pool where I could watch both approaches. I could see everything that was going on and could hear the crowds yelling at the race finishes. Mum did not appear. Then I could hear the announcement of my first race, and they kept calling my name over the loudspeakers when I didn't come out to the starting block. I watched another girl win the race I should have won, and hung around to see her collecting her trophy. When I got home Mum's voice came out through their bedroom door.

'Is that you, Roberta? How did you do in your race?'

'Fine, Mum. Just fine.'

The rift in the relationship between Mum and me was becoming impregnable, and there seemed nothing I could do to change it. I regretted dropping the charges against Arthur because, although our previous relationship had been far from perfect, I had at least felt welcome in my own family. I grew withdrawn and absorbed myself in my swimming and school work. Sister Sebastian became my confidante and told me stories about her life in Ireland before she'd been sent by her order to work in Australia.

Mum's usual tiredness and her focus on Arthur meant that the needs of us girls were often overlooked. There was always food in the house and we received money for school, but in other ways her attention wasn't on us.

One afternoon as I was hanging out the washing, a heavy iron crowbar, which we used to impale cane toads which infested our yard, fell onto my foot. The pain was excruciating, but, once I'd got over the worst of it, I continued with the job until it was finished. By nightfall my right toe had become swollen and discoloured, but when I mentioned it to Mum she seemed uninterested.

I could barely get my school shoes on the next morning, and was grateful Mum always bought them one or two sizes too big, to give us 'growing room'. For the next few weeks I had to limp through my routine of work, school, swimming and errands. The day came when Mum wanted to send me on a message and I bailed up, explaining I was unable to run.

When Mum realised she'd have to go herself she told me to walk along with her. I was to go on to Dr Ward's surgery and she would join me there. Because my foot had been sore for so long, I imagined that Mum was making me go to the doctor's now in order to try to call what she thought was my bluff about my reluctance to do her bidding.

She was mightily surprised when Dr Ward told her that the X-ray showed the large joint of my toe had been smashed and was well on its way to knitting, but completely out of alignment. He recommended immediate surgery, to break the toe again and re-set it. I listened to the pros and cons, which included early arthritis if I let it go, but weighed that up against the experiences I'd already had in hospitals and decided against it. On the way home, Mum said she was most annoyed that she'd been embarrassed and made to look like a poor mother who was not interested in her children. I didn't reply. There were so many unhappy thoughts already swirling in my head.

My trainer had begun to notice how quiet and skittish I'd become around the pool, politely refusing to have my shoulders or calves massaged before races, and sitting by myself between events. I arrived alone and left alone, and, apart from the directions he gave me and my reports on how many laps I'd completed, I didn't speak to anyone. One Saturday he asked me if I would like to join him for a sandwich at his flat, which was directly over the road, and I declined. The next weekend he said that he had already made the sandwich and that I was to come with him and have it. I'd been warned not to go into any man's house alone if a woman wasn't there, so his order caused some conflict in my mind. Sensing this, he said he would leave the front door open and that we'd sit in the front room where any passers-by could see us.

He had created this opportunity to ask me questions about myself and about what he called my 'unhappiness'. When I didn't divulge much information, except with sharp and direct answers to his questions, he instead shared some advice—homilies and anecdotes—with me. Some made sense while others went completely over my head.

'If a person wants to appear clever when they're asked a question,' he said, 'they don't rush to give an answer, even if the question is quite silly. For instance, if someone asks what colour is the sky. The person who says, "Why, blue of course," is not the clever fellow. The one who pauses for a minute before answering is the person people will think of as smart—because he or she took the time to give the question their attention.'

By the time we returned to the pool I felt quite warm towards him. The next day he brought along his lunch and a chessboard, and in breaks between the miles of laps he began to teach me the game.

At school I chafed under the rules, many of which I began to regard as ridiculous, such as wearing long black stockings and ties in our sweltering heat. One day I wore short black socks instead, and was sent home to put stockings on. Another day I arrived at school and, looking down, realised I'd forgotten my tie. Our ties were pre-tied and attached to an elastic strip which went under our starched collars. Rather than go all the way home, which would have made me late for class, another student gave me a navy ribbon which I fashioned into a tie and put on. I was sent home anyway.

A few young people stayed at the boarding house

two doors up the hill from our house, and one morning as I was walking to school, a young man pulled up on his motorbike and called out to me.

'You're going to St Pat's? Hop on, I'm going right past there. I'll give you a lift.'

It was a relief not to have to carry my bag, heavy with books, all the way, and he dropped me off right in front of the school. As I walked up the path, the head teacher, Sister Joan, came out and directed me into her office. She said that if I ever came to school on a motorbike again, I'd be out, and that I was to sweep the classrooms and the exercise hall for two weeks as punishment.

I had never heard of any rule relating to how we were to come to school, so I felt the punishment didn't fit the crime and resented the fact that I'd fall behind with my swimming training, but I said nothing. Sister Joan was very formidable and it had been she who had insisted that I study Domestic Science. She had also apparently forgotten that I was not to sweep because dust particles often brought on my asthma attacks.

That afternoon, when I was alone, pushing the broom around the classroom, Sister Sebastian appeared and sprinkled water all over the floor to dampen the dust and prevent it from blowing up as I worked. When I finished, she called me to the window and we stood looking out at the sea.

'I dislike wearing this habit, too,' she said. 'It's not suitable for this climate.'

Sister Sebastian was tall and as thin as a straw, and her shoulders were perpetually hunched. Sometimes, if I stood close to her in the chemistry lab, I could hear her wheezing. 'The one thing I regret not having had a chance to do before I joined the order,' she told me conspiratorially, 'was have a ride on a motorbike. Now I am here for the rest of my life and will never have the opportunity. And, do you know, there are orders now in the south where women can wear shorter habits, and some of them even get around on scooters? Yes. If I were you, I would tell that young man to drop you off in the next street and then walk in the back way. That's what I'd do. Don't let them kill your spirit.'

The young man never asked me again, but I took on board the gist of what Sister Sebastian was telling me, and very much appreciated my friendship with her.

I'd heard tales from my friends who lived at Garbutt about the way they were treated at school, the few who still seemed to go. Jeannie spent her days looking after her brothers, sisters or cousins, and she told me that no one ever came to find out why she wasn't in class. When I told them I was planning to study medicine my friends smirked and whispered that I'd find out differently when I turned fourteen. I didn't believe them because my life was so different from theirs. My sisters and I continued to be the only coloured children at the Catholic school, and it seemed to me that we always had and were still receiving the same education as the white children, so I couldn't imagine that this would stop.

All the schools had holidays in May and August, as well as two-month breaks at the height of summer. My birthday fell during the August holidays, and on this year I turned fourteen. I'd forgotten the whispered comments of my friends when I rolled up on a Tuesday—Catholic Schools always started their terms on Tuesdays—for the final term of the first year of the two years of study before we were to sit for our Junior examinations.

During the first class a girl came in and said I was to report to Sister Joan in her office. Sister Sebastian was taking the class and her face looked stricken. I wondered what it was I may have done during the holidays that could warrant another lecture from Sister Joan. Sister Sebastian excused me and blessed herself when I walked out of the room.

Sister Joan told me that as I was fourteen now, I couldn't stay at the school any longer. She told me to go back to my classroom and collect my books and go home. This didn't seem a good time to accept her directions meekly, so I asked her why. She said I was bringing the school into discredit and disrepute. I asked her how. She replied that other parents had seen me coming to school on that motorbike. I had thought that this issue was over and done with because I'd served out my punishment, but she had other ideas, or perhaps she thought there'd been other rides since. Her face was flat and closed, and she said, 'Just get out of here and don't argue.'

As I was leaving the room she called me back, and I thought she had changed her mind. When I again stood in front of her large wooden desk, she opened a drawer and took out a set of rosary beads and a couple of holy pictures and handed them to me. 'Don't lose your faith,' she said, 'and may God bless you.'

My knees were shaking, so I went to the toilets where I had a good cry. I splashed my face with water then returned to the classroom. The class had finished and the room was empty. I scooped up the books from my desk and put them in my bag. I was moving slowly, hoping that Sister Sebastian would come back in and save me. This didn't happen.

I walked down the front path, crossed the road and

sat on a wooden bench on the Strand directly opposite the school. I sat there all day, where anyone who looked out the school windows could see my back, while I was facing out to the sea. I didn't turn around to look at them. I wondered what my mother would do now with the money she'd saved from all her hard work for my education. I had no idea how I could tell her what had happened. For that matter, I had no idea myself what had really happened, what was the real reason why I was expelled. I couldn't believe it was because of the motorbike incident, which had occurred during the previous term. I was in shock.

At three-thirty I met my sisters at our meeting place midway between the primary and secondary schools. We walked past the church where I had spent many hours as a primary student, cleaning the big brass vases and helping the nuns to arrange flowers for the altar and prepare the church for funerals and other religious ceremonies. It was the same church where I had been made a 'Holy Angel' and been given my red cloak to wear. I knew now that I'd never make it to be a 'Child of Mary' and wear the blue cloak, a status reserved for older girls.

Mum had given me money to go to Pelligrini's to get whatever new books we required for third term. We were to go into the city on the bus, but I promised my sisters they could use the bus fare to buy ice-creams if they walked. I didn't want to run into any of my classmates on the bus. I had no idea what I'd say if anyone were to ask me about my absence. I felt as if my whole world was coming apart and I had no contingency plan.

At home I said nothing, just went to my room to study, the same as usual. Next day I got up, dressed in my school uniform and went off on my bike and sat on the Strand all day. At three-thirty I went to the pool to train for a few hours. I repeated the whole thing the following day. By Friday, the shock and enormity of my predicament had begun to sink into my consciousness, and I realised I wouldn't be able to deceive Mum indefinitely. I decided I would have to run away from home in order to avoid telling her that I'd been expelled.

A young chap called Alan de Graf had arrived in Townsville and was boarding at Mrs Sullivan's old house. Mum had helped him to find work and to sort out a few problems he'd been having with the law. Alan had a major speech impediment, was poorly educated, his spelling was atrocious, but he was an excellent storyteller and avidly wrote all his stories down in terrible writing in a stack of exercise books. Through our appreciation of his stories, our family had formed a good relationship with him, and because of his own problems he was the only person I felt able to confide in about running away. Although he had very little money, he gave me all he had and, combined with the savings I'd drawn from my account that afternoon, I'd worked out that I would be able to catch a train to Brisbane and live for a while until I found a job.

On Friday nights, if we had done our homework and completed our chores all week without complaint, we were allowed to listen to 'Randy Stone', a serial which came on the radio at nine o'clock. Instead of doing my homework, I packed a few things into a bag, as I planned to leave as soon as everyone had gone to bed. The only person who picked up on my anxiety was Dellie, who occasionally displayed a sixth sense about knowing when I was going to do anything out of the ordinary.

I lay in bed, a bundle of nerves, waiting for the right

time to make my move. When at last the house was
quiet, I eased out of bed in the dark—and who should
be standing there but Dellie! She whispered threats
that she'd talk loudly if I didn't take her with me, so I
had to agree. She crept back through the house to pick
up her shoes and dress and a few other small things. I
wasn't happy about taking her with me. The Brisbane
train went through Townsville at 9.30 pm on its way
from Cairns, and I was going to have to hide in the hills
until the next train left the following evening. I knew
Dellie hated the hills because of the insects and
snakes, and the money Alan had given me would barely
cover two tickets and there would be none left over for
me to get a start in Brisbane. But there seemed no
alternative because Dellie wasn't about to let me go
and leave her at home.

At about midnight we tiptoed out of the house, and
didn't pass anyone we knew in the street. I had to
modify my plan to take Dellie into account, so instead
of going way up to the hills, we went to a quarry which
was not too far from the railway station. We climbed to
the rocks at the very top, where we couldn't be seen or
heard, and settled down to wait out the night and the
following day. By lunchtime we'd exhausted the few
supplies I'd manage to pack, so we had to go down to
a nearby store to get hamburgers. We decided that they
would last us until we had caught our train.

It was a very warm Queensland winter's day, and
after we'd eaten, we thought we'd better catch up on
the sleep we'd missed the previous night. So we curled
up on a large flat stone and put our heads down. Sometime later, I heard a sound and opened my eyes to find
a big black boot directly in my line of vision. Dark grey
trousers came into view as I looked up but the sun

blocked out the top half of the man's body. I heard him calling to someone.

'They're over here. They're both here.' And then to us, 'Come on you, get up. Come on, wake up. Time to go.'

Dellie was slower to wake. The man bent down and hauled us both to our feet.

I asked, suspiciously, 'Who are you?'

'Police. Come on, let's go.'

We were taken to the police station where several detectives sat around questioning us about why we had run away and where we thought we were going. I told them about being expelled from school, and one of them remembered me from my previous report about Arthur. They seemed sympathetic and told us that Mum had come down first thing in the morning to report us missing. We wondered how they'd found us but were too nervous to ask.

When they took us home in a police car, Mum already knew we were coming and was waiting for us on the verandah. She was angry and, stiff-lipped, she thanked the policeman who brought us in. Then she turned her wrath on us as soon as he had gone down the stairs. She called us sluts and accused us of having run away with boys, made us take off our clothes and examined our underwear; I had no idea what for.

When she finally exhausted her rage and was willing to listen for a minute, I told her what had happened at the school. That I'd run away so I wouldn't have to disappoint her, and that Dellie had just come with me because she had heard me getting ready to go. Mum calmed down a bit towards us when she heard this, but she set her face in a very hard expression which lasted for days. She wouldn't give us food that night, saying that we should be happy to starve at home since we'd been happy to starve in the quarry. On Sunday she made us work all day, finding all sorts of jobs for us to do. And she made us work separately, as she said that I was a troublemaker and I had led my sister into mischief.

On Monday, Mum told me to stay at home while she took Dellie and Leonie to school. She was away for a long time, and when she came back, Mum said that she'd been to see Sister Joan. She had told Mum that I'd been expelled because I had tattoos all over my back, and I was turning into a very rough sort of girl whom they didn't want at the school. She had said that I was a bad influence on the other girls, who were trying to be good Christians.

As she was leaving St Pat's, Mum had hurled the rosary beads and cards Sister Joan had given me down the hall and called Sister Joan a hypocrite, at the top of her voice.

After this, she had gone straight to the police, who'd promised to make their own inquiries of Sister Joan. Then she came home and ripped the shirt off my back. Mum said she knew that I didn't have tattoos, but Sister Joan had been so definite that she just had to check. I had no tattoos on my back or anywhere else, which Mum surely would have known if she had ever come with me to the swimming pool.

During the week the police reported to Mum that they'd been unable to influence Sister Joan, and that my expulsion had to stand. Mum sent me down to the state high school to see if I could be enrolled there. The headmaster told me to come back the next day. I was afraid to go there because I hadn't been to a coeducational school since third grade, but I knew it was my only hope. Next day the headmaster told me that I couldn't attend his school. When Mum spoke to him about his decision she was told that it was because my cousin, Betty, was there, and the headmaster had said that he understood that we ran wild together. Mum knew I hadn't even seen Betty for months and none of us had any idea what she might have been up to, but Mum had found it impossible to convince him otherwise. 'Tell her to come back and try next year,' he had said as she was leaving.

Although Betty was as fair-skinned as my mother, she was the only girl of 'colour' I'd seen attending that school. The headmaster had told Mum that he couldn't have 'the two of us' there. In her own way, Mum was as shocked as I was by this turn of events, and her impotence to help and protect me made her very gruff with me. As for my own feelings, I was reeling from the devastation of my life and the injustices that were happening to me. I'd still harboured the childish notion that mothers could somehow make things right, straighten out the world and save their children's rapidly collapsing dreams. When Mum was unable to do this, I felt betrayed. I could feel myself being pushed towards the wretchedness and despair of the Aboriginal women whose eyes I'd looked into at the maternity hospital, and I had to find some way to resist.

'What happens to me now?' I asked her, as there were no other high schools.

I was shocked when Mum said, 'Well, you're fourteen. You could get married.' For heaven's sake, I hardly even knew any boys and the ones I did were about fourteen or fifteen years old. Mum said Catholics like girls to marry early, and that in Spain and Italy many girls were married by fifteen. I had to remind her that I wasn't going to be a Catholic any longer because they were such hypocrites.

'You get a job then, that's what happens,' Mum said.

Over the next few weeks I scoured the employment column every day, but jobs in Townsville were generally advertised by word of mouth. Somebody always had a relative or knew of a friend looking for work. Because I'd been fixated on becoming a doctor, Mum told me to go up to the Townsville General Hospital and find out about becoming a nurse's aide, until I was old enough to take up training. I wasn't happy about this but it seemed like the next best thing. I was even less happy when I was told not to bother writing out an application—because dark girls couldn't train as nurses at their hospital.

I was beginning to despair when Mum brought in the newspaper and pointed out an ad for a store hand at the Town Hall newsagency, in Flinders Street. The shop was about three doors down from Stuart Ritchie's chemist shop, and Mum told me to ask Mr Ritchie if he would kindly give me a reference. He said he would be happy to, and that he'd walk down and tell Mr Foley personally how pleased he had been with my work.

My job at the newsagency was to unpack crates of books, comics and toys at the back of the store. Almost every morning, large crates were delivered and I had to count the items, tick them off against the invoice, make a note when orders were short, then dust the goods down and take them to the front of the store.

After I had been there a short while I would be asked occasionally to help out behind the counter during rush periods, and eventually I came to relieve staff on lunch breaks and sick days. Mr Foley was a good-natured man, well-known around the town, and he also lived 'through' the cutting that ran along our street.

When Sister Joan put me out of St Pat's, Mum had taken my sisters away too and enrolled them in state schools. She said she didn't want them mixing with hypocrites who were supposed to save souls but who instead threw souls out—if they were coloured—and into circumstances where they were likely to get lost.

Dellie began to run around with girls I didn't know, white girls from her new school, and we started to grow apart. My job meant that I was coming and going at different hours from her, and she and Leonie were doing things much more by themselves. I continued to put in a lot of time at the pool, but my trainer had told me that they had refused my application to enter the Townsville to Magnetic Island swim. I had to have a three-year clean bill of health after meningitis before they'd be prepared to take the risk. I suppose they didn't want me dying on the way. On weekends I was swimming twice the required distance in laps, so there was no chance that I'd exhaust myself with the effort, but the officials remained unconvinced.

Dessie and Reg Mills had moved back to Townsville and lived in a Housing Commission building at Garbutt with their growing family. Housing Commission dwellings were just old aeroplane hangars with rusting roofs and a fibro wall down the centre, which divided them in two. Their internal walls didn't reach the floor or roof, so privacy was minimal.

Reg drank a lot and several times he tried to molest me when he'd been drinking. Even when he hadn't been drinking, and when Dessie was out of earshot, he'd make suggestions that my breasts would grow if someone massaged them. The idea of showing any male the two tiny peas which had formed on my chest was laughable, so I made it my business to avoid being alone with him. Nevertheless, I often went to Dessie's place to escape being at home, and it was a base to hang around and from which to go places with my friends. From Dessie's house I was able to go to the Garbutt picture theatre without having to worry about how to get back to my home.

Mum said she would buy a car for Arthur and me; Mum didn't drive. She and Dessie had both told me their versions of how, before I was born, Dessie had run out into the street from between two parked cars when she saw Mum driving along in a car, and Mum had accidentally run over her. Mum hadn't driven since that day, and swore she would never drive again. Arthur didn't have a licence and I was too young to get one, but that didn't stop Mum. She bought an old Vanguard, and Arthur practised until he got his licence. She also coached him with the road rules.

Arthur was always telling stories about what a hero he'd been during the war, a rear gunner, and it seemed strange that he hadn't learned to drive during that time. Later, his mother and brother, Ivor, told Mum that Arthur had not been in the war at all. Ivor had been called up, but Arthur had been a barber in Wales—just as he was in Townsville.

Although Arthur could sign his name, make change for the price of his haircuts and other ordinary purchases, he was illiterate. Often, to our mirth, he had difficulty with words written and spoken. We had often cracked up hearing comments he made, such as when we wanted to go somewhere suddenly, he would say, 'If you'd told me earlier I'd have got myself repaired.'

With Mum's help, Arthur struggled to learn the rules of the road off by heart. Once he became a licensed driver he began to referee soccer games in the surrounding towns. Mum would always sit in the front seat of the car to read the road signs to him.

My sisters were made to go to the matches, and from time to time I'd agree to go too, as I was interested in exploring the nearby towns, such as Ayr, Homehill and Ingham. We went to Lucinda Point, near Ingham, which at the time consisted only of a long and beautiful deserted sandy beach with a pier running out into the water. I fell in love with it and schemed to go back there, to immerse myself in its magic.

I agreed to go to any soccer games that were scheduled for Ingham, but when we were almost there I'd set up some ploy designed to get them to drop me at Lucinda Point and pick me up after the game. Frequently it worked.

The main attractions for me there were the peace and beauty, and an old Black man, who lived somewhere nearby, whom I had met on our first visit to the beach. I had run along the dunes and suddenly stumbled into a big depression in the sand in which sat this old man and his dog. The dog leapt up to bark at me and the old man silenced him with some foreign-sounding words spoken in his very soft voice. The dog had slunk back behind the man, watching me, and I'd spoken briefly to the man and run off. But there was something about him and his aura which found their way into my dreams, and I longed to return to the Point.

The next time I convinced Mum and Arthur that I'd rather spend my time at Lucinda Point instead of watching sweaty men run around kicking a ball, I took along a towel and a sandwich. The beach stretched for miles and was devoid of any sign that anyone had ever been there; not even a footprint sullied the smooth golden sand. I was afraid to wander further up the beach again in case the dog was around. Instead, after a few splashes in the water, I lay on my back above the waterline, peacefully engrossed in an inspection of the red glow of the sun on the inside of my eyelids.

In a strange way I wasn't surprised when the old man's shadow suddenly cooled my feet and caused me to open my eyes and jump up into a sitting position to check out where the dog was.

'You again, eh,' he said. His dog stood behind him, watching me warily. I noticed the dog was old too, but I didn't trust strange dogs old or young. 'Where you from?'

'America,' I answered, hoping to impress him. He continued to look at me carefully and I was glad I'd pulled my shorts and top on over my togs because, although he wasn't looking at my body or legs, I curiously felt a bit immodest.

The old man made a clucking sound with his mouth and turned to walk away. It felt as if there was only him and me in the world and in that moment I became desperate for him not to leave.

'Don't you believe me?' I called at his back. He was wearing an old pair of pants rolled up almost to his knees, and his stick legs bore shiny scars on the skin of his calves.

'No.' He muttered more words I didn't understand, and I wasn't even sure that he was speaking to me. The sea rolled behind him, keeping up its own deep sounds, making his voice harder to hear. Then I realised he wasn't speaking in English.

'Well, I'm from Townsville.'

'You got no pidgin?'

I didn't know what this meant, so I just said no.

'I know your people.' My ears pricked up. 'Snake people from north.'

'D'ya want some of my sandwich?' I asked, trying to get him to sit down on the sand and talk to me for a while.

This was the first of several chats we had during that soccer season.

Over time, I learned that the old man lived alone in a shack nearby where, he said, he had everything he needed. He told me wondrous stories about crocodiles, which he said were plentiful in the rivers north, and of sharks and other creatures. At times he seemed angry that I didn't already know the stories he was telling me, and he complained that 'children today know nothing'.

Of 'my people', he had little to say, and didn't want to be drawn further on the question. He did tell me, however, that snake people have to look out for dogs because many breeds of dogs attack snakes. I was a bit amused by this because, in my mind, I had come to fancy myself as the taipan, the deadliest snake in Ram Chandra's collection, even though I would begin to tremble whenever I saw a dog. When I asked the old man if I was a taipan, he shook his head. 'No, not taipan. You fella snake fall on 'im and kill 'im, hug 'im to death.' I didn't see myself falling on any dog and hugging it to death, but then I hadn't yet heard about the huge pythons that live in the tropical rainforests and can throttle a bullock to death in their coils.

He said he 'watch the weather', and when I asked him if he had some sort of rain dance, he laughed. 'No need to ask for water 'round here,' he eventually replied. 'Everything green, that sugar cane, trees. Dance over there.' He indicated the land behind us, the west.

The old man could tell days in advance when a storm or a cyclone was going to hit, and he would walk up to higher land when he saw floods coming. He complained that no one wanted to know his secrets about how he saw the weather coming. When I offered to learn he startled me by leaning towards me and running his hand over my head, feeling the bristly short curls which Mum kept cropped close to my head. 'Sure you girl?' he asked. 'Only boy can learn. Humbug nephew.'

Arthur stopped going to Ingham because the players on one team held him upside down by his ankles when they won. Everything in his pockets fell onto the ground, money, keys, the lot. He and Mum talked about it all the way back to Townsville, while we kids rolled our eyes and giggled in the back seat.

Mum thought the players' joke was disrespectful, that they only did it because Arthur was so short, and she insisted he wasn't to go back until the club had apologised to him. Arthur said that the team had bought him drinks afterwards in the pub, while Mum had waited in the car. But she said this wasn't good enough, they had to know they'd done the wrong thing. Arthur wanted to let it rest because he liked feeling needed, and being a referee made him feel as if he had some authority over the big brawny players. He continued to referee in Townsville, Ayr and Homehill, and the following year he resumed driving to Ingham. By that time, however, I was no longer living at home.

The old man's words about 'my people' kept popping up in my dreams, pushing me to find out more about myself. So again I tackled my mother, this time taking another tack.

'Is there Aboriginal blood in our family?' I asked her one day, while I was holding a long piece of fabric clear of the floor as she sewed it.

'Every family that's been up here for more than two generations has got a touch of the tar,' she responded, quite absent-mindedly.

I was so stunned by her answer that I couldn't think of what to ask next. 'Almost every family,' she corrected herself.

'Well, why don't we ever say we're Aboriginal?'

'Because we're not! Don't start that business again, Roberta.' Mum was growing angry now and her attention was no longer distracted by the sewing. 'A touch of the tar doesn't make a person an Aborigine. Nobody in their right mind would want to be an Aborigine. You want to live in a bush hut? Then, say you're an Aborigine! You want to live worse than an animal?'

'But you're always saying I should be proud to be a coloured girl. When I ask you about where the colour comes from, you always talk about how rotten black people live, how they swing from trees and live in mud.'

I could feel another full-blown row about to erupt, and was relieved when Mum took a deep breath and went back to plying her needle and cranking her treadle.

At the next break, while she made her adjustments to the sewing, she continued. 'You're as good as a white person, and if you behave yourself properly, they'll treat you like a white person. You'll get the same opportunities, and the same chance to make a decent life for yourself. If you want to keep hanging around with the darkies at Garbutt, then you'll get pregnant and nothing will save you. You'll end up living in a bloody humpy and having a tribe of kids that the government'll take away from you. So you hear me straight, you're as good as a white person and you've got to act like a white person, or I won't be responsible for your fate. That's all I'm going to say on the matter.'

A glimmer of my mother's reality came through to me. Over time, although I was unable to articulate it, I began to realise that when Mum looked at us she didn't see us. She patted our long golden locks, stared into our deep blue eyes, and fixed us up in dresses and hair ribbons to match the peaches and cream complexions she saw on us. Who she saw when she looked in her own mirror, I had no idea. She sometimes said she was of Irish and Scottish descent and tinted her hair a reddish brown to keep whatever image she had of herself intact.

I came in from work one evening to find Mum in a state and she said that the police wanted to speak to me. I didn't have a clue what this might be about and was more puzzled than ever when she said she'd talk to me privately after dinner. She wanted to get Dellie and Leonie out of the way first.

When at last she sat down, her manner was extremely agitated. 'Tell me everything about that trainer of yours,' she ordered, and at first she wouldn't explain why she wanted to know. Her questioning flew in the face of the indifference she had previously displayed towards my swimming aspirations, and I began to feel I was suspected of something.

I told her the little I knew, which wasn't much. She asked me if he'd ever taken me to his flat. I admitted to the one visit and that we played chess—there was nothing more to tell.

'The police say he's been interfering with young girls,' Mum finally told me, 'and they want to talk to you to find out if you're a victim too.' I almost burst out laughing for a minute, because he had been kind to me but hardly interfering. 'I mean putting his hands in your swimming costume, or getting you to change your togs in front of him,' Mum snapped. I was confused because men weren't allowed into the ladies' change room.

'In his flat! Does he ask you to change in his flat?' Mum's voice began to rise. He didn't, of course, and I thought Mum was going to become angry because I had nothing to tell her, but eventually I was able to convince her.

When two detectives came to the door later, she explained that she'd questioned me herself and that I couldn't tell them anything. 'Roberta's undersized and underdeveloped for her age. She's a fast swimmer and good at diving, but she's nothing a grown man would take a fancy to,' I overheard her saying. 'She doesn't weigh more than four and half stone soaking wet.'

As I lay in bed that night I thought about this description , which seemed to carry with it the implication that I was seriously unattractive and no man would be interested in me. Mum's opinion appeared to be corroborated by the fact that, if my trainer had been making passes at some of the swimmers, he had certainly overlooked me.

At the time I was only training three nights a week and on weekends because, with the Magnetic Island Swim on hold, I had no goal beyond keeping up my speed and distance. I intended to discuss the police visit with my trainer the next day, but Mum wouldn't let me go to the pool. When I went on the weekend, he was no longer amongst the group of sun-tanned trainers and retirees playing chess on the grass behind the diving board. The front door of his flat, which he invariably kept open, was closed, and I never saw him again. My attempts to find out what had happened to him from Mum were met with pursed lips and mutterings that I shouldn't care what happens to 'dirty old lechers'. Under the circumstances, I felt it would have been inappropriate to ask anyone else. I remembered his kindness and thoughtfulness towards me, and I didn't want to make further trouble for him by behaving in a way that might have appeared as if we had been close. On the other hand, none of the other trainers seemed remotely interested in giving me any guidance, or even keeping score for me on the miles I swam at each training session, so I missed him sadly. I had to keep note of my own distances and try to watch my own speeds.

Mum's friend Nellie picked up with a bloke around this time. We were all very fond of Nellie; originally from what she called 'the UK', she was now getting on in years. Nellie had been a good friend to our family, passing us kids freshly baked biscuits and cakes as we passed Lowth's Hotel kitchen where she earned her living as their cook. Later, when she worked at the Mansfield Hotel, she would come on Sundays to take us, all dressed up in our best clothes, on bus rides around town and to have ice-cream sundaes and other treats at the Garden of Roses Cafe on our way home. When she retired, Mum arranged for her to board with old Mrs Scott, who was on her last legs, and this relieved me of the task of staying over at her house at night when Edie was out of town.

Nellie's man was much younger than her, and because she was a bit deaf he was able to slyly introduce her to strangers as his mother. She was glad to have male company and was generous to him, buying him clothes and a gold watch and leather wallet. He began to stand over her for money, and she started turning up with black eyes and bruises on her frail old arms and bony body. Eventually he assaulted her so badly that the police ran him out of town.

One night, the police came to our house to say that they had received a phone call from Dessie Mills, who was in some sort of trouble and wanted someone to go and get her. She had rung them because we didn't have a phone and the police station was just three blocks away from us. It was midnight and Mum didn't want to leave the house with Leonie and Dellie sleeping, so she woke me and asked me to go with Arthur to see what was the matter. Dessie had told the police she would be waiting at a phone box outside the post office a few blocks from her house. When we got there, we couldn't see her, so we circled around and found her house dark. We didn't know what sort of trouble the police had been referring to, and Arthur felt he couldn't just bowl up to the front door of her house as the children would be asleep. Back to the telephone box. As we were driving slowly past, for about the third or fourth time, I noticed something that looked like a sack in the grass. We stopped. I went over and yes, it was Dessie. Her clothes and hair were covered in blood, her eyes swelling to black, her face broken and bleeding. Reg had beaten her up.

On the station at Torrens Creek, they hadn't had alcohol in the house and it was a hundred miles to the nearest pub. But now that he was in town Reg had open slather at hotels and was either unwilling or unable to control his drinking. Beating up his wife had become a regular occurrence, which I had heard the adults whispering about, but this was the first time I'd been confronted with the hard evidence.

Dessie had passed out in the grass. I woke her up and helped her into the car. Reg was in the house so she didn't want to go back there. We drove her to our place and Mum came out to the car to help her in. I was sent back to bed, sick to my stomach with the scene I'd just witnessed. Reg had thrown a glass of beer at Dessie when she'd asked him to stop drinking and go to bed, so she smelled like the stale beer glasses we had had to clean up after Arthur's gatherings. But the deeper, richer smell of sticky blood was mingled in the rotten odour.

With my dream to become a surgeon apparently out of reach, and even nursing training appearing to be out of the question, I had begun to think seriously about what lay ahead for me. I wasn't able to come up with many options, but, slowly, what was becoming clear to me was a host of things I did not want to be. Like most convent-educated girls, I had even considered the sisterhood at various stages. However, I had been deterred by the nastiness of some nuns and the idea of having to live 'in peace and prayer' with women who had their own problems and preferred not to deal with them. I completely dismissed this idea when I was expelled from school. Also, I had run into one of my old classmates who had told me she'd heard that I was being ex-communicated anyway.

Now I decided that I would never marry because I didn't want any man beating me up. I hadn't thought much about men or marriage over the years. With no father or brothers in the house, we girls had never been very comfortable around men, and the idea of actually living with them was, if anything, a very remote concept. Arthur's appearance at our house had caused a lot of tensions, and I was particularly unnerved by the way my previously strong and independent mother had turned herself into a maid, happy to do his bidding and for no obvious reward. First, witnessing Nellie's experience of 'love' and then finding Dessie in the grass and learning that she had been beaten into this wretched state by the man who claimed to love her, the father of her children, completed my disillusionment.

I was still as skinny as a pole and small for my age, and it wasn't as if I had to beat men off with a stick. So the decision I made that night, to avoid men and marriage and not to leave myself vulnerable, wasn't much of a burden. At the same time, I was growing curious about these people—boys and men—and I noticed that it was not only their clothing that made them different from us, they behaved differently too.

Dessie went back to her husband, explaining to us that with small children there was little else she could do. Children, I thought then, too, were out. They chained women to situations where they could be beaten. When I next saw Reg he was his usual gregarious self, and it was hard to reconcile his sober state with the injuries I'd seen on his wife and the condition she'd been in when we found her.

'*Nemo me impune lacessit*,' I'd recite to myself from my studies in Latin. 'No one will attack me with impunity.' Not Arthur, not Mum, and not a husband.

Dessie often came over to our house and sat around talking with Mum, mostly about boring housekeeping matters but occasionally they had deeper conversations in which I was eager to participate.

We were chatting about nothing in particular one day when talk turned to childhood memories and how far back each of us could remember. Mum remembered ducks, and running around amongst them when a drake reared its head and was suddenly much taller than her. She remembered her fear. When it was my turn, I told them about my memory of being put on the petrol tank of a motorbike and being taken for a ride. Mum visibly paled and said, 'You can't remember that. Who told you that?'

'No one told me,' I insisted, 'I remember it. Who was it, Mum? Who took me on a ride?'

'Haven't you told her about Jimmy?' Dessie seemed to know about this person who had come to our house all those years ago, or perhaps she had even been there at the time. I was deeply curious and wanted to know more.

When Mum didn't reply, Dessie said, 'Well, you can't put it off forever. Someone's bound to tell her eventually and it would be better coming from you.'

Mum said that she would tell me later, but I said, 'No. I want to know now.' I knew that unless she told me immediately, while Dessie was there, she would put it off and get cross with me when I asked her next time.

So Mum said, 'You have a brother. His name is James. He grew up and left home, and I've no idea where he is. He doesn't write and he's only been home that one time since you were born.'

Here was another secret to be added to the store that Mum had kept from me. I realised then that there was a conspiracy of silence among Nellie, Aunty Glad, Dessie and Leila, and possibly our neighbours, who must have all known but had probably been told not to talk about our brother with us.

I was growing used to the fact that our whole family seemed to be based on secrets and deceit, and my sense of security in the idea of family was considerably undermined.

Dessie's best friend, Val Ludgator, often came around to visit us with Dessie and her kids.

One day, Val and another friend were shopping in the main street where a TB-screening van was parked. Because they weren't rushed for time and wanted to try out anything new, for a giggle the women stepped into the van and had their X-rays taken.

A few days later, Dessie came screaming into our house. Val had received notification that her X-ray had been unsatisfactory and had to go to the hospital to have another. Dessie accompanied her, both thinking the TB-van camera had been playing up. At the hospital the second X-ray was taken and they were told to wait until it was developed.

The doctor came and told Val she had tuberculosis and was being admitted to hospital immediately. She wasn't allowed to go home, even to get clothes or toothbrush, and she was scheduled for major surgery as soon as it could be arranged. Dessie was sent to tell her husband, Jim, and get her things, but because our house was closer, she came bursting in there first, very distressed.

The bakery where Val worked was closed immediately and within the next few days a huge plastic sheet was put over it and the entire building was fumigated. So, too, was the Ludgator's house. Everyone who had spent any time in Val's company, including Mum and us girls, was ordered to report to the hospital. Meanwhile, we heard that one of Val's lungs and most of the ribs on one side had been removed, and no one was allowed to see her.

Of all the tests taken, only mine was positive, so I had to go back for a series of X-rays. Long ago, Mum had decided that I was old enough to explain my own business to the doctors, so she always refused to take time off from work to accompany me to the hospital. Consequently, I had been treated quite poorly and often rudely by certain doctors. My file was very thick due to all the illnesses I'd suffered, and often the doctors didn't bother to plough their way through it before hustling me out of their offices.

Once, when I had gone to the casualty ward with an asthma attack, the doctor had tapped my file and asked me if I liked coming to the hospital. I didn't, of course, but I didn't know where else to go when I was gasping for breath and thought I was going to die.

My relationship with doctors grew worse after Val's episode when I was put on a list for regular compulsory TB X-rays. For days before each X-ray, I had to work out in my mind what to do if they tried to keep me in hospital and wanted to cut my lungs out. I received no feedback from these X-rays, just another appointment card setting out when I was next to present myself. Instead of weakening my resolve to become a surgeon, I determined to be a better and more caring doctor than the ones I was coming into contact with. Such were my dreams.

8

Mum became increasingly remote and inaccessible. She was away long hours at work, especially in the early morning, which was when Arthur and I would end up in all sorts of fights. He was often hungover and would want us to get out of his way in the bathroom, so that he could dress and go to work. But Dellie and Leonie also had to dress and go to school, and I had to be at work on time too.

Arthur resented the authority which I'd always had in the house when Mum was absent, and detested the way I'd jump in when he told either of my sisters to do other than what we had always done. He was forever saying, 'You keep out of this. Dellie (or Leonie) has to get out of the bathroom when I say so. I'm the one who has to go to work around here.'

For my part I resented his presence in many ways. I had learned from Mum that he didn't contribute to our upkeep or pay any of the bills generated by the household, and he had personal debts all over town. He spent a great deal of his money, as he always had, buying drinks and currying favour amongst the people who frequented the pool room where he had his barber shop. The idea that he could exercise the authority of a father-figure was laughable to me. He had no experience dealing with children or teenagers and had already demonstrated his ineptitude.

When my numerous pleas to Mum to sort this situation out fell on deaf ears, and after a particularly distressing argument with Arthur, I packed up and went to live at the YWCA hostel. I called in at the hostel one evening on my way home from work, spoke to the Matron, with whom I had a good relationship dating from when I used to pick up their laundry, and asked if I could be a boarder. I moved in the next day. When I told Mum I was leaving, she reminded me that she'd been out in the world working at the age of twelve, so she felt that I'd already had more home-life than she ever had.

There were no individual or shared rooms available at the Y, and even the dorms were full. The only places on offer were beds and lockers lined up along a wide hallway; a sort of enclosed verandah which ran crosswise through the middle of the hostel. Apart from the few items of clothing which I wore constantly—my work clothes and swimming costumes—the rest of my gear had to be kept in my suitcase and stored in the luggage room. The environment, with its strict regulations about our comings and going, set meal times and rules about washing and hanging out our clothes, was reminiscent of the orphanage and I felt safe there.

My board was three pounds seventeen and six a week, for which I received sleeping quarters, breakfast and a good meal at night during the week, with an additional light lunch available on weekends. My pay at the newsagency though, was only four pounds five shillings. This left me with seven and sixpence a week with which to buy lunch on work days, washing powder and soap, pay my entrance to the swimming pool, go to the pictures and, if necessary, buy clothes. Often I had to sneak a few slices of bread and marmalade from the breakfast table to eat at work, so the idea of having anything left over to save towards clothing was laughable.

Dellie, at this time, was still bed-wetting and getting into terrible trouble for it at home—Mum kept a thick off-cut of leather to flog her with. She rebelled by stealing sums of money anyone left around, and before I moved out she had been driving me crazy by wearing my clothes and putting them back into my cupboard and drawers dirty. When I was trying to get dressed to go to work, I would find that things I had planned to wear were gone or dirty, so it had been a real problem. Also, she was encountering the burden of racism at her school. Outside the house, Dellie was still shy about confronting people, so she was pushed around a fair bit.

I became alarmed when she came by the newsagency a few times in the middle of the day, with only feeble reasons for why she was not at school. She came in the company of a rather unkempt looking white girl, and I couldn't help but think they may have been up to mischief. One day after work, Dellie was waiting for me outside the shop and asked if I could give her some money. When I explained that I had barely enough to live on myself, she said she would be back the next day at lunchtime, then I was to point out things I wanted from the stores and she would get them for me.

Dellie didn't return, so I went alone to McKimmins and looked around at the plain black skirts and white shirts that were similar to those worn by women at my work. Although I yearned to own some fine things, different from the rough fabrics I'd bought at Woolworths with a loan from Mum so that I could start my job, I was relieved Dellie wasn't with me and that the decision of whether or not I'd become a receiver of stolen goods was staved off for another day.

The following afternoon, Mum came into the newsagency, told Mr Foley there was an emergency at home and asked him if he would let me leave an hour early. She was red-eyed with grief and he told me to go immediately. On the way up the street, Mum asked me if I knew that Dellie had been stealing or that she'd run away. I hadn't personally seen Dellie take anything so I said no to both questions.

We had to go to the police station where a detective was waiting to interview me. I told him the same thing I'd told Mum. He said he wanted to drop Mum off at her house and, with a uniformed officer in tow, go on to the Y and look through my belongings for stolen goods.

I felt wretched arriving at the Y with these two just as the other girls were beginning to arrive home from work. There was a front room where men sometimes came as visitors to sit and talk with the residents, but men walking through our living quarters was a most unusual sight, particularly police in uniform.

They examined the few items I had in my locker and hanging space, looked under my bed and asked me if that's all I had. I went to hunt up the key and get my suitcase out of the luggage room. It was dusty because it hadn't been opened since the first few days after I'd arrived. Satisfied that I had nothing to arouse their suspicions, I thought they'd leave me alone.

Instead, the detective said I was to come with him.

They drove me to Mum's house and had me wait in the car with the uniformed officer while the detective spoke again with Mum. Returning to the car, he said I could get out and he'd see me later.

Mum was even more distressed than before. When the police had first come to the house and told her about an incident which had happened the previous day involving Dellie and her friend, she'd been incredulous and had run in to look in Dellie's wardrobe. A stack of satin and sequinned frocks, glamorous dance outfits, bikinis and underwear had come tumbling down from the shelves. Mum had gone to pieces. When the police left the house she'd asked Leonie what she knew about this business, and Leonie had told her she knew nothing.

After the police had dropped Mum off on our way to the Y, she had gone out to the toilet in the backyard. The toilet bowl, Mum told me, was aglitter with jewellery, and she realised Leonie had thought she was disposing of her share of the goods by flushing them away. They were so heavy, though, that the water hadn't been able to carry them. Mum had fished them out with a stick and confronted Leonie. So by the time I returned they were both weeping.

Mum said that the detective was coming back after dinner and she wanted me to drive around with him to look at places where I thought Dellie might be holed up. Hoping that I might be able to coax Dellie to deal with the crisis instead of running away with the police in full pursuit, I agreed.

The detective arrived on his own. He said that two old bicycles had been taken from the railway yards and that he thought Dellie and her friend might be hiding somewhere on the edges of the town. I kept my eye out as we drove up and down some streets in town, then along the Strand, around Kissing Point and Belgian Gardens, and eventually he said we would drive to Cape Pallarenda to take a look.

Cape Pallarenda sat at the end of a road which ran past Happy Valley. There was only a store and a very few sparse dwellings in the area. By day, the Cape was a popular spot for people with cars as the road ran right beside the beach. At night, however, it was a Lover's Lane—quite desolate and deserted.

When the detective circled the car in front of the store, at the end of the road, I was relieved because there really wasn't anywhere for us to look. It was unlikely that Dellie would be hiding out in such rugged scrub, and I knew how much she disliked the spiders, snakes and small creatures that would live in it.

But not far back along the road, the detective pulled up, under the pretence of stopping to discuss where next we should look. He was a middle-aged man, tall, with brown hair, and he looked just like anyone's father. We had been parked there for only a few minutes before he started asking me personal questions about myself, such as how old I was and whether I had a boyfriend. The answers were fourteen and no. He then put his arm around my shoulders and began to pull me towards him, his hand on my knee and sliding up my leg. I stammered and stuttered because I didn't know what to say, but I pushed him away and moved along the bench seat until I was hard up against the car's door.

When he followed me across the seat, plunged his hand down the front of my blouse and tried to kiss me on the mouth, I was out of the car in a flash, running swiftly and quietly through the scrub. I bent low so that I would be harder to see in the fading light, and headed for a small grove of trees in the distance. I hid there in case he was searching for me, but he just stood near his car and called out. Staying low, I began to thread my way through the bush running parallel to the road. I didn't want to be seen but I didn't want to wander off into Happy Valley and get lost. Nightfall was rapidly approaching. I would have tried to get a lift from one of the few cars that passed, but with their headlights on I couldn't be sure that they weren't the detective's car until they had passed me.

It was a long run into town. I went the back way, through North Ward and over Melton Hill, in case he was sitting somewhere watching out for me. Coming down Hale Street I saw his car at the bottom of the laneway to Mum's house. I felt I was close enough to home to be safe, so I just walked past it. He was at the wheel, sitting and watching. When I reached Mum's front gate, he turned on the headlights, blinked them on and off a few times and drove away.

Mum was still in a state because Dellie hadn't been found, and I was disgusted to hear her talk about the detective in glowing terms. A family man with children of his own, she told me, prepared to give up his free time to look for her daughter. When I said that I had to go back to the Y, Mum tearfully begged me to 'give up this foolishness' and come home to help her with this crisis. I agreed, and Arthur said that he would fetch me the next day. He then drove me back to the Y and, for the last time, I fell asleep in the security of the hostel. As I drifted off, I worried about where Dellie was putting her head down that night.

Mum came to the newsagency the following day to tell me that Dellie and her friend had been sighted, headed for Ayr on bicycles, and that the police had detained them at Giru. They were being brought back to Townsville. The police had told Mum that she had lost control of Dellie, and that Dellie would be sent to a reform school.

Mum took the day off work to go to court, but she didn't tell me where she was going until it was all over. A heavy sadness descended on the house when Dellie was no longer there, and the tensions with Arthur that had prompted me to move out to the Y in the first place continued.

Dessie's husband Reg had become more predatory towards me and I only visited them when Dessie drove me there and brought me home. Still, they would visit Mum and Reg would make excuses to leave the conversation and come into my room. If I tried to walk out past him, he would grab me and maul the front of my dress, swooning his eyes as if with desire and pretending it was all a big joke. Mum tried to convince Dessie to leave him because of the beatings, but she would cry and ask who would look after her and the children. Also, she was pregnant again. I didn't know who would look after her either, so I felt it best to say nothing about Reg's constant and unwanted attention. I didn't want to be the one who broke up their home and left Dessie and the babies penniless.

I was very fond of Dessie and regarded her with greater affection than Leila, who didn't bother to maintain contact when she was away and was something of a phantom in our lives with her unscheduled comings and goings. Leila seemed to have a lot in her favour. She had graduated as a nursing sister, and people compared her looks favourably with the movie star, Jean Simmons. But there had always been an ominous side to her personality and we began to hear of her dismissals from various hospitals due to her suicide attempts. They weren't made public, Mum said, in order 'to protect the hospitals'. Leila would turn up with suitcases full of glamorous clothes and lay around gloomily for days before disappearing again.

Dessie, on the other hand, had remained closer to us. She and Reg had moved to Sydney for a while, and when they were living at Dee Why, her baby had become very ill. Completely broke, she had taken the baby in her arms and walked from Dee Why to Manly Hospital where they'd examined the infant but refused the child admission. On the way home the baby died in Dessie's arms. It was at this point that Mum had encouraged me to write to her, and for a long time I seemed to be almost her only friend. Even though I was much younger than Dessie, she would pour out her heart, grief and hopes to me in her letters. She must have been desperate to have been able to overlook the enthusiastic, but childish, letters she received in return. Now that she was back living in Townsville, I didn't want to wreck the marriage she clung to by dobbing in her husband, although I thought she was foolish for hanging in there when he beat her so badly. If she had known that he was also trying to seduce me and was making my life miserable, it may have been the last straw for her.

I still talked hopefully about finding a high school that would allow me to continue my studies so that I could do medicine. Mum said she'd help me to look for a nursing placement. I knew it wasn't the same, but it would help me to leave the increasingly difficult situation I was in at home.

I came in from work one day to find Mum happily waving a sheet of paper around and telling me she'd been successful. A hospital in Charters Towers was interested in having me train there.

I told Mum I'd go there on the long weekend to check out the hospital. My friends at Garbutt were also talking about an upcoming rodeo which was to be held in Charters Towers on the same weekend. Mum wasn't too happy about this, but Arthur was refereeing every weekend for the entire season, so there was no chance that they could take me.

To help me go, Mum gave me some money to supplement the savings I'd managed to accumulate since moving home. I rang ahead and booked a room at a hotel which Mum told me was respectable and she had Arthur drop me at the railway station.

From the hotel manager's expression I could tell he was surprised to see me, but I'd booked the room and arrived in a taxi from the station, so he couldn't very well turn me away. His wife came out of the bar to look at me before he showed me up to my room. The hotel was a typical country building, two storeys—the bar and dining room on the ground and accommodation above. My room was the last one along the long wooden balcony. I knew immediately that they thought I was a lowlife, so I was determined to keep my room looking neat and tidy for the three days I was to be there.

I walked up the street to the hospital, and then walked all the way around it, taking in the large lawns, tidy buildings and free-standing casualty department, separated from the main hospital by a sweeping driveway. I was afraid to go in, as Mum hadn't answered their letter yet and I shied away from the idea of bowling up to strange white people without some sort of letter of authority or explanation. Instead, I walked to the outskirts of town where the rodeo was being held, and spent the day watching people eat dust and many Aboriginal stockmen walk away with their pockets full of prize money. I didn't see any of my friends from Townsville and guessed they hadn't been able to scrape up the money to get there, after all.

In the evening, I sat on the verandah of the hotel, reading a novel while waiting for dinner. My reading was disturbed by heavy footsteps coming up the stairs and I looked up to see two detectives walking towards me. They asked me a lot of questions about why I was there, then they said they wanted to see my room. Everything was neat but they stripped the bed and rolled back the mattress to check if I had anything hidden under it, and they hauled my clothes out of the wardrobe onto the floor. I'd told them I was applying to be a nurse at the hospital and had come to look around, but they kept asking me if I was 'under the Act'. I had no idea what Act they were talking about. Eventually they shrugged, warned me not to bring men up to my room because they'd be watching me, and then left.

Apart from this incident, the weekend was quiet, even boring, and when I returned I asked Mum to write to the hospital and say I was willing. She was excited because, she said, the Matron, whose name was Moffitt, had been a sister at Townsville Hospital when I was born.

I hit the roof. What did she mean, 'when I was born'? Hadn't I been born in Maryland?

'Don't think you're too big for me to tan your arse for talking to me like that! Who do you think you are?' was the only response I could get from her.

Things moved very quickly once Mum wrote to Matron Moffitt. The hospital was short-staffed and they wanted me to come at once. I was to be a nurse's aide until the next induction, when I could begin regular training. I gave notice at the newsagency, and was pleased when Mr Foley said that if nursing didn't work out for me, he would be happy to have me back.

Arthur and Mum took the day off to drive me to Charters Towers and make sure I got settled in. When they left, I was nervous about this new situation, but my sense of relief at leaving Townsville was enormous.

At first, my work consisted of keeping the pan room sparkling clean, rolling bandages and putting things away. However, I soon discovered how desperately under-staffed they were when, the first week after my arrival, a nurse demonstrated how to wash patients and set up and dispense from a medicine tray, and these were added to my list of duties. About six weeks later I was shown how to give injections.

The hospital was small. The main building had two storeys, with three wards on the ground floor: men's, women's and children's medical, as well as the operating room and large kitchen. The second floor consisted of men's and women's surgical, with a line of private rooms running along the front. On the ground, a walk in one direction separated the nurses' quarters, and in another, the maternity section. The resident doctor's house stood at a distance, past maternity. Well-tended lawns and gardens created the effect of a cool oasis in the middle of an otherwise drab landscape.

Unlike big city hospitals, there was enough work to keep us moving at a steady pace all day, but we were rarely rushed. On some mornings no patients attended casualty, although this was rare.

Quite early in my training I was woken one night by knocking on my door. This was a surprise because, as a new member of staff, I was on day duty. An emergency had come in which required an operation. New staff, I was told, always had to attend an operation so that they could get used to it.

I was excited by the prospect and quickly dressed in one of my new white uniforms and starched caps. I had already met the resident doctor, a tall, youngish man who strode the hospital corridors with his eyes on the floor, rarely glancing up when he passed mere nurses. Another nurse's aide stood waiting outside the operating room, and she and I were shown how to scrub up before we were ushered in. The doctor was barely recognisable behind his mask. In the theatre, he chatted with the sister who was assisting him, patting knives and other surgical equipment into his hand as he asked for them. From time to time he glanced over in our direction, but otherwise our presence was barely acknowledged. A short time into the operation the other aide suddenly turned and left, and I was unsure whether I was supposed to follow her. No one told me to go, so I continued to stand there, fascinated by the mystery of things that lie just below the skin, and pulse, throb and slide around under surgeons' fingers.

The patient had been stabbed, or had managed to stab himself with some sharp object such as a stick, and splinters had to be fished out and torn tissues repaired. As operations go, this one was minor. On his way out, however, the doctor said, 'Well, congratulations, Nurse.' I learned later that, like the other nurse's aide who'd come in with me, most trainees and aides faint or become nauseated and leave at their first sight or smell of blood and the heavy fumes which permeate surgical theatres.

The doctor also ran the nurses' training programs, but by the time he formally called a class together, I had already been giving enemas, injections and other personal care duties for months. The only thing that was a shock to me on our training day was when he held up a huge syringe, which looked like a needle for a horse, and told us it was for lumbar punctures and was used to draw fluid from the spine. I came over sick and faint as I had had that cruel-looking instrument plunged into my backbone so many times when I'd had meningitis. When the doctor went into detail about the position patients had to adopt in order to insert a lumbar puncture—a squat kneeling position with their heads bent over the bed so their spines were fully extended—I got up and walked out of the room because I thought I was going to throw up.

After a couple of weeks of assisting a nurse on night duty in the men's medical ward, I was allocated the role of night nurse in this ward myself. I was also to keep an ear out for cars pulling into the hospital driveway, because there was no casualty nurse rostered at night.

The variety of experiences I encountered in the hospital was enormous. Unlike the larger hospitals where a trainee often spends months working on one aspect of nursing, in Charters Towers we were obliged to do everything that came along. In men's medical, most of our patients were elderly and many did not survive their hospital stay. Although I gradually learned how to attend the dead—to wash their bodies and pack their orifices to prevent seepage and leakage—my first mortality event occurred within weeks of my arrival. I was called upstairs to assist with some chore in the private patients' section. Here I was told that a woman had died and that I was to make sure she was presentable for the relations to view. I was apprehensive, and knowing looks and smirks passed between the nurses on the floor. When I opened the door another nurse was standing near the bed, and she immediately walked out, leaving me there alone.

The deceased was a thin, elderly white woman. She had been propped up on pillows, with one arm swept out and upwards towards the rail at the top of her bedstead, so that she looked curiously alive, as if she was just holding her breath. While I stood there, too scared by the unfamiliar presence of human death to stir, her arm began to move in a graceful arc. Still outstretched, it seemed to sail in the air, up and out. As it did so, the woman's torso also moved forward and I heard a sound emanate from her throat. I was out of that room in a flash, crying out and tearing down the corridor to tell the nurses they had made a mistake; that the patient was still alive. When I turned the corner at the nurses' station, they were all standing waiting for me, laughing.

The nurses who had arranged this awful prank thought it very funny, and told me I wasn't a good sport when I remained sullen. I was disturbed, not only for my own sake, but for the woman who had inhabited that body and who, even in death, had been used for an indignity.

I swore I'd never become so hardened and callous as these veteran nurses, but by the time I left I could feel myself moving in that direction. When I came over from the quarters to report for duty in the morning, retiring night nurses would make comments such as, 'I got old Mr Gardener through the night, but I don't expect to find him in his bed when I come back on shift this evening. If he stops breathing now, Nurse, it'll be up to you to pack him up.'

There were exceptions to the nurses' tough veneer, particularly when the patients concerned were young. A student from a nearly boys college had to have a testicle removed, and nurses in his ward walked around on the day of his surgery crying. Often they balanced the tensions and stresses of the job by making jokes, otherwise they would go crazy. As the frequent butt of their pranks, though, I rarely appreciated their humour. Generally, when I was called to the surgical wards, it was to have pranks or embarrassing situations put on me. No matter where I'd been rostered to work, I'd be sent for to do pre-surgical pubic shaves on men or teenage boys. As I hadn't seen a man's private area before I started at the hospital, I found these tasks excruciating, both for myself and for the patient. On one occasion I was told to make two-hourly checks on the swollen testicles of a young man suffering from the complications of adult mumps, to the acute embarrassment of us both.

Word of my, albeit reluctant, ability to do any task assigned to me soon spread and the fact that I hadn't keeled over in the operating theatre was also considered a plus. All nurses get a quota of dirty jobs involving bloody mess and unsavoury bodily waste, but in this small hospital there was a pecking order. As well as being on the bottom, I was young, coloured and seemingly able to tolerate whatever was thrown at me.

When patients died in the middle of the night, someone had to trundle them down the ill-lit path to the mortuary, which was located down by the back fence. For me this was a particularly scary job. I was once assigned to sit by a patient who, in the process of dying, developed a death rattle. His breathing would stop entirely for minutes and then suddenly, when it appeared that he was at last at peace, he would gasp and have a short period of rapid breathing. Over perhaps three or four minutes, this would slowly subside until he again stopped breathing. This was repeated for almost two hours, with his non-breathing periods becoming longer and longer. I sat beside him, timing his non-breathing intervals, and could only report that he'd irrevocably died when he hadn't gasped back to life once more for over five or six minutes. I found this experience extremely distressing, and I was unable to offer him any comfort if he did, indeed, regain any consciousness during this time. The last five minutes of waiting were interminable.

At various times, I was also called to assist in the operating theatre and in the mortuary. I occasionally relieved in the maternity ward too, when the sister had her meal break. The mysteries associated with birth and death became very familiar to me and I was awed by the wide variety of responses we, as humans, have to these experiences.

My wages for this work were small, but they were all mine. Our accommodation and food were included as part of the work conditions. With my first pay I put a deposit on two pairs of slacks, to pay off on layby, and I got them out the next fortnight. It was a small triumph over my mother's strictness.

At this time, Mum had put a payment down on a house in Norris Street, Hermit Park, and they moved there to get Leonie away from the old environment. Nellie and Laaka were overseeing the lodgers in the second of the Stanley Street cottages. Our own place was also rented out—to Koiki (Eddie) Mabo, whose name would become nationally famous in decades to

come, and his wife, Bonita, and they later became my
good friends. This income enabled Mum to pay off the
new house. It wasn't really new, but it was solid and
much more spacious than either of the tiny Stanley
Street houses. It was raised well off the ground and the
area beneath was surrounded by palings for privacy,
which doubled the space available.

When I had a rostered four-day weekend, and if I
could afford it, I would go down to Townsville. Trains
from Charters Towers to Townsville were infrequent so
these trips required careful planning. I was often the
only passenger on a goods train which stopped at Railway Estate at about 3 am. The area was always completely deserted at that hour, and I would have to walk
from there to Hermit Park carrying my suitcase. Mum
still had no phone, so there was no way I could contact
her to have Arthur come and pick me up.

To give myself something to do during my days off in
Charters Towers, I bought a drum kit. Generally, Matron
wouldn't let me practise as the night-shift nurses had
to be able to sleep if they wanted, and playing at night
was out of the question.

I also bought a horse, Nellie, from an old man who
had previously rented her to me on weekends. He was
going broke and had to sell her, so I purchased her for
twenty pounds, then paid him to keep her at his place
and look after her. The man was extremely happy with
this arrangement as he loved Nellie as much as I did.
On days off, I would ride around the outskirts of town.
Matron didn't like me tethering Nellie to the fence
beside the quarters, so this was another area in which
I fell foul of her.

Then a number of things happened which made my
life at the hospital quite unbearable. The day before my

birthday, I ran into Matron in the hall and she asked me to step into her office.

'Well, tomorrow's your big day, eh! Sixteen,' she said. She sat down behind her desk and began to pull out some papers. 'I want you to sign these forms and we'll get you registered as a trainee nurse instead of a nursing aide.'

I was startled and confused. 'But, I'm fifteen tomorrow.'

She looked up sharply and fixed me with her piercing eyes. 'You said on your application, here,' she pointed at the papers, and I could see my mother's handwriting, 'you said you were fifteen last year, and now you'll be sixteen.'

I took a deep breath. 'Mum wrote that letter, Matron. That's not my writing. She must have forgotten how old I am.'

In her own way, Matron had seemed quite fond of me, if that's the right word in these circumstances. For instance, the day after she had blown me up about the noise of my drums, she called me into her suite to have a cup of tea, a rare treat in itself, and she'd given me a gift of a rubber drum-practice pad which she had bought. She had also taken to gently ribbing me whenever a dance was being held in the Towers because she had found out I loved to dance. Then she would arrange the rosters so that older nurses worked and the few who liked to dance, including me, could attend. She would give me a smile and a nod as she posted the weekly rosters up on the notice board.

Had Mum forgotten my age? Or was she so keen to have me placed in a career that she was prepared to lie? I was never able to discover the truth.

After the revelation about my age, Matron's attitude

began to change. She seemed displeased that I was to spend another year as an aide. I was blamed for things I hadn't done, and for not doing things when I'd not been told to do them. My duties became more onerous but I was still not registered as a trainee nurse.

There was very little social life in Charters Towers for a young girl. There were just two milk bars, only one of which had a juke box, and a theatre which screened pictures on Friday and Saturday nights. The ratio of females to males was seven to one, as the men left to work on surrounding properties and boys were encouraged to find work in larger towns. So the nurses swooned over any available man.

I was asked out once by a young coloured boy, a ringer who'd come in from one of the surrounding stations. He had swarthy skin and piercing blue eyes. I thought all my dreams had come at once. He took me to the picture theatre, bought me a ticket and said he'd join me later. At interval he reappeared from a hotel across the street and bought me a softdrink. After the pictures he walked me back to the quarters, or I walked and he staggered, and he said he would be back in Charters Towers in two months, did I want to go out again?

On another occasion, I was asked out by a white boy who lived in the town. He, too, took me to the pictures and we had a milkshake at the milk bar on the way back to the quarters. The next day I received phone calls from three different girls who each warned me to stay away from their boyfriend. These two dates were the sum total of my interaction with the local lads in Charters Towers.

Because of the cost and difficulties involved in going down to Townsville, a friend came up one weekend and drove me down on the back of his motorbike. As we were riding on a narrow country road we passed Matron's car speeding towards Charters Towers. We passed so quickly I didn't recognise her car until I looked around, yet she saw me.

When I returned after the weekend, she pulled me up on the staircase in front of other nurses.

'Nurse,' she said, 'my nurses *do not* ride pillion on motorbikes. A few years ago a nurse was killed on a motorbike. You will not get on the back of a motorbike again.'

The cost of buying a car was prohibitive and I was too young to have a licence, so I bought a small second-hand motorbike. I imagined that Matron was implying a lack of faith in the ability of men on bikes, not of me riding one myself. Mum had bought a Birina motor which she'd had fitted to the back wheel of her pushbike, turning it into a motorcycle, and I saw very little difference between her motorised transport and my own. Matron, however, thought otherwise, and she was on my case every time I turned around.

I had received several urgent notes from Mum, thick with underlining, telling me that she was in trouble with the Income Tax Department. Renting out the two little cottages in Stanley Street meant that her tax returns had become too complicated.

Mum had never used a telephone, she always wrote. So when I was called to the phone in the nurses' quarters and heard my mother's voice at the other end of the line, I knew immediately this must mean trouble. She begged and pleaded with me to leave Charters Towers and come back and help her to work our her taxation problem. She said they would probably put her in

jail otherwise. Because of his illiteracy, Arthur was of no help at all.

I went to Townsville on my next weekend off, but when I saw the size of the task I knew it would take me a few weeks to sort it all out. As I'd griped about how meanly I was being treated by Matron, and that I had been wrongly accused of things, Mum convinced me to leave the hospital. She said that they hadn't signed me up as a trainee and therefore my work wouldn't be counted towards my goal. By then I had come to realise that my real goal, to study medicine and specialise in surgery, would never be achieved through emptying bedpans and bathing the elderly and frail. Or by chasing naked male patients from the Broughton Hall Psychiatric Hospital who ran out into the grounds in the middle of the night. So I didn't need too much pressure. Mum said that she would help me to find another job in Townsville when I had taken care of her business. I handed Matron my notice, went to the stable and told the old man I was leaving and that he could either have Nellie as a gift or re-sell her, and prepared to move back home.

With the little bookkeeping I'd mastered at St Pat's, I managed to get Mum's affairs in order. I developed a simple way for her to keep track of her banking and showed her how to keep a receipt book so that she would stay on top of things. Then I hopped on a train and went to Rockhampton to see what was happening there, if any jobs were to be had, and to get away from the rows which had already started up again between Arthur and me.

I had been in Rockhampton for only three hours, having booked into the People's Palace and gone for a walk, when the police stopped me and asked if I had a permit to be off the reserve. When I told them I didn't live on a reserve, they didn't believe me and marched me back to the People's Palace so they could search my suitcase. They found two American one dollar bills and a few coins which Mum had given me, probably to strengthen her story about how we'd come from there, and a set of balanced feathered darts. I had bought them after learning to play in the pool room when I was waiting for Arthur to close up his barber shop and drive us home. The police said that they suspected these things were stolen and, even though it was evening, made me pack my bag and accompany them to the police station.

When I ran them the story about Mum being white and how we'd all come from America when I was a baby, I saw looks of shock and disbelief on their faces. They made me wait while they rang Townsville police and asked them to go out and interview Mum. Fortunately, I had a book on psychology in my bag, as I was intent on learning things and very much into escapism through reading, so I settled down to fill in the time while they were detaining me. But when another two officers came in and saw me reading they began to make rude comments about me to the men who had stopped me, such as 'Where did you pick up this smart-arse?', until glowers from the other police silenced them.

Eventually, they all gathered around me and began to ask more questions. Earlier I had been asked only questions requiring monosyllable replies and Mum's address, and they'd taken my story as a complete fabrication, easily disproved by a phone call to Townsville. Now I had the opportunity to explain that I'd gone to St Pat's College—without telling them I'd been expelled, of course—and had just completed a year at Charters Towers Base Hospital.

I could tell they were very impressed—*if* it was all true. They were waiting on word from Townsville to verify it. Otherwise, they said, it was back to the reserve for me. I wondered which reserve they'd send me to, and fervently hoped Mum would back up my story.

About midnight, a call came through, after which I was informed that the theft they'd hoped to charge me with was dropped, but that a policeman was taking me back to Townsville the next day, because at fifteen I was still under age. When they said they were making up a bed on a desk in an office, and that I had to sleep there, I remembered the last time I had been in close proximity to a detective, and became very afraid.

Despite my fears, I fell asleep immediately. As officers changed shifts, the door was opened several times and the room was flooded with light, waking me, and there would be three or four men, detectives and uniformed officers standing there looking at me. On one occasion I heard a male voice say, 'Pretty scrawny, isn't she?' before the door closed again. I slept fully dressed.

Early next morning I was woken and told to have a

wash in the staff washroom. An officer stood outside the door so that no one else would enter. A strong odour of stale urine hung in the air, lightly covered by a whiff of a commercial disinfectant. My recent experience at the hospital had made me acutely aware of these sorts of things and I was anxious not to pick up any germs. Then I was given a stale sandwich and cup of tea before being taken to the railway station in a police car. As we left the police station the officer who was to travel with me said he was going to put me in handcuffs. After I'd promised not to try to run away— I wasn't going anywhere without my suitcase—he had agreed that they might not be necessary. Another officer laughed and said I was so skinny the handcuffs would probably just have fallen off anyway.

People waiting for the train who saw me arriving in a police car and being escorted by a uniformed officer acted as though I'd been arrested for murder. They stared and conspicuously called their children to stand close beside them, in case I struck out at any moment. When we boarded the train, the officer took the outside seat and made me sit near the window. As we got underway, however, he became more friendly and told me that getting a trip to Townsville was a real windfall for him. He bought food in the dining car for me, and disappeared somewhere for almost the entire journey.

When we arrived, Mum was waiting at the station. I hadn't told her I was going to Rockhampton, so she was mighty cross, but she also realised that I had spent most of the last eighteen months living by myself and being my own boss. In another year or so, she said, I'd be able to do as I liked, but in the meantime I was to understand that the police would just bring me back if I kept wandering off by myself.

That week I found an advertisement in the *Townsville Daily Bulletin* for female machine operators to work in a cardboard factory, so I applied. My first job there was to fold cartons after a more experienced worker had stitched them together with large metal staples. I soon moved on to the stapling machines myself and became their fastest hand. When the factory received major orders I was always asked to work overtime. I could make those machines zing with speed and it took two folders to keep up with my output. After I'd mastered the process I became bored, but I was still the fastest person on the floor. I began to work only on Mondays, Wednesdays and Fridays, but I was often asked to come in on Saturdays on double time.

After work I'd go dancing, which I loved, until the early hours. On my free days I took up swimming training again and rode my motorbikes. I now owned a BSA and a Norton, which I'd ride over hills and trails. I still wasn't old enough to get a licence, so I was very circumspect about riding in the street.

My work became so routine that I lived just to dance and swim. There were a number of us dark girls who went to almost every dance and we'd enter jive competitions and win. These dances were held in halls around the town, and people often came with their children. Early in the night the children would be up on the floor dancing too, and everyone danced with everybody else, young, old, and in between. As the evening wore on,. children were put down to sleep behind the long forms against the walls. Then the serious dancing would begin and we young bloods would shimmy, shake, and rock and roll. We'd spend days making ourselves special dance clothes, modelled, of course, on pictures in the latest magazines. Bill Haley reigned supreme. With

Renata Pryor as my partner, we won a competition at the Norgate one night, and established ourselves as the Queens of Rock in the town.

From time to time, I went to rodeos and began entering their competitions. I won the Ladies' Calf-riding, but the prize was a cask of beer. Tradition had it that winners turn their cask on for their friends in the evening when the riding is out of the way. However, as the legal drinking age was twenty-one, which was still years away for me, I wasn't even game to tell Mum that I'd won. I just let the other rodeo participants and their friends drink it.

Mum constantly harped at me to find a boyfriend, get married and settle down. It was her big dream for all us girls. She said she was keen to pass responsibility for us over to husbands. Also, she wished that each of us would have three daughters, thereby receiving our punishment for the trials she said we had put her through. When I pointed out that I was only a teenager and happy to just keep on dancing and working for a while, she would bring up the names of two girls with whom I'd gone to school who had married at the age of fifteen, as though they were perfect examples for me to follow.

On several occasions, Mum's nagging turned into flaring arguments. I was supporting myself and I didn't want to hear about how some man could take me 'away from all this'. From what I'd seen, women weren't taken away from anything except their freedom. Mum, herself, started work at dawn and she contributed to Arthur's upkeep by paying all the bills and buying him cars, not the reverse. Dessie's money, too, went to pay the household bills, and she and many other women I knew were expected to be punching bags for their husbands' frustrations and inadequacies. The rows often ended with Mum striking me across the face, then breaking down and apologising. 'I only want to see you happy,' she'd say tearfully, as though marriage was synonymous with happiness.

Val Ludgator was out of hospital and Dessie, Val and I used to rocket around in Dessie's big station wagon, the three of us sitting on the bench seat in the front and Dessie's children piled in the back. Sometimes we only had the little children with us, and at other times, Neville and Teresa, her two oldest, kept an eye on them at home and we'd go out by ourselves. Dessie had opened a book exchange, which I thought was a wonderful idea, and I happily relieved her at work from time to time because it gave me access to as many books as I could read. I was always wandering around with a bag of books in case I had a spare moment in which to do a bit of reading.

One afternoon, the three of us were driving west down Flinders Street, heading towards my house, with Dessie at the wheel, Val on my left, and me squeezed in between them, as usual. The footpaths along the street approaching the Causeway were deserted, and I was gazing out at nothing in particular. Then I heard a deep voice say, 'That place is going to burn down tonight,' which immediately drew my attention, and I turned and saw that we were passing an old timber hotel on our right. Then I looked quickly at Dessie and Val to see which of them had spoken, and realised that they were both looking at me. The moment was so eerie that not one of us said anything about it. We didn't question each other, but I was sure they thought it was me who had made the statement when I knew I hadn't said anything at all.

That night, the hotel burnt down. Dessie came over

to the house in the morning to tell us about the big fire in the main street, but she didn't mention anything about what we'd heard in the car.

A few weeks later we were again sailing along the same street, and again my mind was pretty much blank, when I was shocked to hear the voice repeat the exact same words. 'That place is going to burn down tonight.' I didn't bother to look around for the building the voice was referring to, because I realised the voice had come from my own throat. I clapped my hands over my mouth and began to protest, 'I didn't say that. I didn't say that,' but Dessie and Val just looked at me strangely and then at each other.

Very early the next morning, I was woken by voices on the front verandah. Arthur had heard a knock at the door and, followed by Mum, opened it to find two policemen standing there. I could hear him answering their questions: that Dessie and Val had brought me home at five-thirty, that I'd been in all evening, and that I was asleep in my bed and, no, they wouldn't wake me. Mum's voice, softer but somehow more shrill, kept insisting that the police tell her why they were being questioned. Not long after, I had almost gone back to sleep when my bedroom door opened and I knew Mum was peering in through the darkness to check that I was still there.

When I got up Mum had already left for the six o'clock start at the Central Hotel. Arthur greeted me with the news that another building had burnt down in Flinders Street, and that the police had come to find out if I had done it. I didn't bother to feign surprise because somehow I knew that the building had burnt, but I had no way to say that I already knew without people thinking that I was either guilty or crazy.

I made up my mind then that I was not to allow my mind to wander into a trance. I'd already become used to experiencing a fairly high level of kinetic energy around myself. I had often been afraid to go to sleep for fear of what I might dream or do. Sometimes I would wake up in the morning to find that during my sleep I had gone through my drawers and piled all my belongings up in the middle of the room, or written a poem, or made bizarre diary entries. I marked this down to sleep-walking and told no one about it, because I wanted to be normal. I didn't feel abnormal but I often wished these sorts of inexplicable things would stop happening around me and to me.

I didn't know who had reported the prediction to the police. Although it could have been either Dessie or Val, or even somebody they may have inadvertently told, I began to suspect Val; mainly because I wanted so badly to trust Dessie. However, I could not bring myself to ask either of them outright, so I told myself the voice itself, and therefore the predictions, were my problem and that I'd have to deal with it.

When Dellie came back from the Catholic home for girls in Brisbane, she was very sedate. She wore a corset, gloves and stockings, which we'd never even thought of wearing before, and which I still couldn't countenance. She was aloof and in many ways seemed much older than when she'd left. We still enjoyed talking about the latest music and dance styles together, but the distance and experience had created a different head space for her which I found impossible to penetrate. She was no longer just my little sister. Even though we were nowhere near as close as before, sharing secrets and discussing every little item of gossip as though our lives depended on it, we trimmed our hair exactly alike and bought identical lipsticks and trinkets to heighten the similarity between us.

Mum and Arthur made life very difficult for her, and I wasn't surprised when she ran off again. Nor was I surprised when Mum asked me to go looking for her, even though it was immediately apparent that Dellie had left Townsville and headed south. Although I was still not yet seventeen, Mum promised to speak to the police if they picked me up on my travels. I decided to have a quick look in Rockhampton, then go on to Brisbane and stay with Aunty Glad.

I'd been given a third motorbike, a Harley-Davidson, by a gypsy who was leaving Australia to return to Europe. Being of swarthy complexion, he had also been subjected to a lot of racism by the police and people generally in North Queensland. I'd met him at a few motorbike meets where he and I were the only two left out of proceedings, he because he was dark and I because I was dark and female. We were only casually acquainted, and although he thought his bike was too big for me, when I kicked it over and rode it around the block, he had said I could have it because he didn't have any more time to waste trying to sell it.

The bike had been warm already when I kicked it over, and I was never able to start it again from cold. Mum, initially upset when I brought home such a big bike, used to look out the kitchen window and laugh as I took running leaps onto the pedal in my efforts to kick it over. The pedal would just rise up powerfully again and hurl me onto the ground. I thought, however, if I went off on any of the bikes, the police would be bound to stop me so I sold the lot off cheaply and left Townsville by train.

9

When I arrived in Rockhampton this time, I had a very different mind-set. Earlier I'd been scouting, merely looking around to see what was happening, and I felt it may have been my casual attitude which had attracted police attention. Now I was focussed on what I had to do. Before I left Townsville, Mum had told me that the police had been to see her again, as they, too, were looking for Dellie over something to do with her travelling companion.

I left my suitcase in the luggage room at the railway station and bowled right up to the front desk of the police station. When I walked in, every head snapped up and turned towards me. It was obvious they thought I was Dellie. Two officers came to stand near me, menacingly; probably waiting to grab me in case I turned to run. I didn't recognise any of them from my earlier escapade and it seemed apparent that none recognised me. Perhaps the staff had changed, I thought, or maybe this was a different shift.

'I understand you're looking for my sister,' I said,

with much more confidence than I actually felt, 'and I want to know if you've found her yet.'

'And who are you?' asked one of the men who was standing by my side.

'I thought I just told you. I'm Dellie's sister.'

'Well, you answer to her description. How do we know you're not her?'

'You think she'd be crazy enough to walk in here, knowing you're looking for her? She's also about five inches taller than me.'

Some remained suspicious and there was a lot of eye contact and raised eyebrows being passed between them all.

I leaned across the counter towards the officer who appeared to be in charge of public inquiries, groped in my bag and pulled out my pocket diary. I held it firmly in case any of them made a grab for it, and showed the officer the cover on which I had long ago written my name—Roberta Patterson.

'Of course you can't read it,' I told the startled officer, as I fluttered through the pages to the entries I'd made in the train, 'but you can see here on this page that I caught the Sunlander down last night, this was my seat number, and as I was on the train and it's just left, I can't also be Dellie coming down by car.'

The atmosphere in the room relaxed a bit, and a few police even went back to their work. Finally, one of them took it upon himself to tell me that Dellie and her companion were thought to have passed through Rockhampton and were on their way to Brisbane. Roadblocks were expected to pick them up at any minute. I was told that, wherever she was stopped, Dellie would be taken to Brisbane. With this information, I thanked the policemen and left.

The next Sunlander wasn't due until the next day, and I felt an urgency about my mission, so I didn't want to wait. I collected my case, made some inquiries, pulled a cap tight on my head and walked out to a truckstop service station on the Pacific Highway to try to get a lift. Mum would have hit the roof, I knew, but this was an emergency. The cap, I felt, disguised me and, being so thin and wearing jeans and a jacket, I thought I'd pass for a boy.

I had a choice of trucks as, being late afternoon, truckies were preparing for their night haul to Brisbane. I picked a driver with a severe limp—in case of trouble. As it was, he chattered all the way about his wife and the funny things his kids said and did, and only when we were on the outskirts of Brisbane did he tell me that the cap hadn't fooled anyone. I was glad to have chosen a decent family man because stories I'd heard about truckies had made me very apprehensive, and only my anxiety about Dellie's precarious position had enabled me to surmount my fear.

I had no idea how I'd go about trying to save her because I didn't know the process or what she'd be charged with, but I did know that I would fight harder for Dellie's freedom than I felt our mother ever had.

I went to Aunty Glad's house in South Brisbane. She'd received a letter from Mum telling her that I might be coming, so she wasn't surprised to see me. She had a full house and I had to sleep on the lounge. Aunty Glad was a chain-smoker who sat up most of the night watching television, doing crosswords and reading, so catching up on the sleep I'd missed during the past three nights wasn't really possible. We still didn't have television in Townsville, and I found the droning sound of voices squawking from the box quite off-putting.

I went to Central Police Station on the day of my arrival, where I learned that Dellie had been apprehended almost as soon as I'd walked out of Rockhampton Police Station. She'd been booked, although no one told me on what charges, and was already on her way back to Townsville under police escort. I was shattered and felt my trip had been in vain.

Aunty Glad told me that there was nothing I, or anyone, could do now. She invited me to stay and work in Brisbane until I heard from Mum and decided what I wanted to do.

I looked for casual work because I didn't want to get locked into anything, and I had heard that the Golden Circle cannery at Northgate employed women and girls on day labour. This sounded ideal, being hired every morning and paid every afternoon, but it also meant getting up at 5 am, leaving the house in the dark to catch the tram to the city, then transferring to a train to Northgate. The work, trimming the remaining eyes from mechanically skinned pineapples, was wet and sticky, and workers were issued with thick rubber aprons, boots and gloves. The big shiny knives the women worked with were kept constantly sharpened by men, who also did most of the cleaner and more attractive jobs around the factory.

There were often other coloured women and girls working in the factory, and we automatically began to seek out each other's company.

When I was out shopping one Saturday, a young white lad who worked in a store began chatting with me. He invited me to join him and his friends to see a theatrical performance the next weekend and we arranged a time for him to come to the house to collect me. I was so happy—here I was, in Brisbane, and being asked out to, of all places, the theatre. At last I felt that my life was going to be like those people I'd watched in the movies and read about in books—being taken to wonderful places on the arm of handsome escorts. Aunty Glad, almost an exact replica of my mother as far as her attitudes on boyfriends and marriage were concerned, was ecstatic and during the week helped me to buy the perfect clothes for this date. When he tapped on the door, Aunty Glad almost knocked me to the floor in her rush to greet him. She said she wanted to establish in his mind that I wasn't an orphan and had family to whom he'd be answerable.

He didn't have a car, so we walked down to the tram stop, laughing at the transparency of Aunty Glad's concern. When we arrived at the theatre, I could see by the people dressed in their fancy clothes who were sweeping by into the foyer and standing around on the street, that this was a major production. His friends, none of whom I knew, were standing in a group and their surprise to see him arrive with a coloured girl was evident, though not unpleasant. Introductions were made and we waited outside for the last couple in the party to arrive.

Two detectives, who were as obvious as if they wore signs, came to stand on the kerb, and after a few minutes I could feel them staring at me.

'Hey, you!' Everyone else turned around but I pretended not to hear, until I felt a hand on my arm and I was being pulled away. I was livid at being embarrassed in this way, but there seemed to be nothing I could do. By now, everyone was staring at me and the police, and there were knowing nudges and querulous looks, some of distaste, being passed around amongst them. The detective took me over to the edge of the kerb.

'Where's your pass?'

'What pass?'

'Don't give me that shit. Where's your pass—or are you a runaway?'

I frankly didn't have a clue what I was being asked for, and since I wanted the excruciating humiliation to be over, I offered to get the theatre tickets from my date to show them.

'Are you under the Act? What reserve are you from?'

'I don't live on a reserve. I don't know what Act you're talking about. You'd better leave me alone because my mother's white.'

It worked almost like magic. With little further ado, I was allowed to rejoin my new friend, although I got an intimidating finger-wagging and narrowed-eye stare loaded with meaning from the detective as I walked away.

The atmosphere in the group had changed and even my date stood a little further away from me when I returned. The girls all wore neat frocks and the men white shirts and ties. I had a lot of time to examine them because, after I shrugged and said, 'Oh, nothing really,' to their question about what the police wanted with me, I was left completely out of the conversation.

I remember nothing of the show, which was my first theatrical event in Brisbane and one which I'd been very excited to attend. Throughout the performance my mind churned over everything except what was taking place before my eyes. At interval I didn't even bother to join the group as they went out for drinks and sweets; I thought I'd let them have a chance to talk about me if they wanted. By the time they had slipped back into their seats for the resumption of the show, I'd already decided I couldn't risk being so embarrassed, so I wouldn't see any of them again.

It was probably lucky I made that decision when I did, because I would have been terribly hurt by their coolness later. My date saw me back to Aunty Glad's house and opened the gate to see me inside the yard. He said pleasantly enough, 'I'll see you again.' But as he walked back down the street, I knew that we both understood that our first date was also our last.

I kept my pains to myself, not sharing them with Aunty Glad or my cousins, or even with my best friend, Josie, who I'd met at Golden Circle.

Josie was an intuitive soul, a dark girl like myself and about my own age, who also loved to dance. She had introduced me to the Railway Institute, a wooden dance hall in the centre of town, where the entry fee was well within our means. Live bands played all the music, and the only thing on everybody's mind was to dance themselves to exhaustion before the place closed at eleven-thirty.

Josie lived at Chermside, which was much closer to Golden Circle than where I had to travel from, in a house shared by an Aboriginal family who informally took in some women lodgers. I'd been by her place a few times after work and when she said they would all welcome me if I wanted to move in with them, I jumped at the chance.

To say Aunty Glad was displeased is an understatement. She thought moving into a Black household was tantamount to treachery and a snub to all the things Mum had tried to make me become over the years, that is, white. But she was also aware that we could walk from Chermside to the Golden Circle cannery in the same time it took me to get the tram into the city before even beginning the train journey to the factory.

Living in the Chermside household was a good experience, everyone maintained their autonomy, yet there was a lot of cooperation. We all put in money for the rent and those who could, carried the price of the food. The family kept us all supplied with staples, such as breakfast foods, bread, sugar and milk. Outside of that, anyone was welcome to cook for everybody else. Somehow, it all worked well, even though there was no such thing as a formal roster.

Work at the factory became irregular. We sometimes went there early to stand in the crowd of hopefuls, and were turned away. Josie and I began to worry about our money. We heard that the Brisbane Exhibition was hiring people to work in booths during the show, so we went in and put our names down. However, only I was taken on.

My employers ran a big show of variety entertainment, with a band, knife thrower, acrobat and clowns. We were all required to live-in for the length of the exhibition, so I borrowed a small bag and packed the few clothes I thought I'd need. My job was to do anything I could: run errands, help the artists prepare, stand by to pass them any items they required from behind stage. The owners had two long caravans, one that they lived in, the other was for some of the more permanent employees. A camping tent with folding beds, sleeping bags and blankets, provided shelter for the casual female employees. The four or five young men and boys who were working with us as casuals, wrapped themselves up in canvas off-cuts for warmth and slept in a corner of the big top. The lifestyle wasn't very flash.

The atmosphere generated an air of excitement, and each morning I scurried around the exhibition-ground, buying milk and sandwiches for the casual staff. The place was rife with dogs, but they were chained up close to the doors of the caravans they were kept to guard. As long as I stayed on main paths, and didn't try to take shortcuts by passing between tents and kiosks, I was safe from them.

By about ten-thirty or eleven each morning, the performers were all painted, costumed and ready to go. A man would climb up on the ledge high above the front opening to the big top and beat on his drum. During the day he was sometimes joined by other musicians, who'd give the crowd a small taste of what they would experience if they paid their money to walk through the door. A girl or woman in heavy makeup and fish-net stockings would also make an appearance, seeming to promise titillation as part of the show.

The hours were long, from eleven to eleven each day (although on slow weekday evenings we often didn't work so late), and the pay was good, even though we were docked for food. Most of the casuals had been travelling with the show and were fairly friendly with each other, sometimes going off to have a drink together after work. I didn't accompany them as I was still under age.

The best part of this job, though, was that they carried a seven-foot carpet snake, Satan, as part of the repertoire. Anyone who wasn't afraid of him would drape him across their shoulders or wind him around their waist to walk with him in the pre-show parade. He didn't play a formal part in the program but added a feeling of adventure and mystique to the line-up. Otherwise, Satan lived in a sack, at least until I arrived.

Then he moved in with me and would happily coil himself around me while I slept, in an effort to keep himself warm. Snakes like warmth but they have no innate heating ability, which is why they're regarded as being cold-blooded. I found they're only cold if they're left out in the cold. It was comforting, too, to know he was by me when I occasionally heard footsteps stumbling around near the tent late at night when I was there alone.

During the show week I celebrated my seventeenth birthday. Celebrated is hardly the appropriate word. I told my employer and his wife gave me a couple of hours off during the slow part of the afternoon, so I tore over to Aunty Glad's and we had a cup of tea and slices of a cake she had bought for me. However, she wasted no time on good wishes but launched straight into a lecture on how I should be careful and look after myself. She also gave me the letters Mum had sent down for me, including one with a ten shilling note in it to buy a birthday present for myself. Oddly, these letters contained much the same advice as Aunty Glad's lecture, some parts were actually word for word. I figured Mum had written the same letters to Aunty Glad, so that she could tell me what to do, just in case I wasn't taking her written words on board. That evening, some of the staff took me to a nearby milk bar, which was also a hangout for many of the local deaf and dumb youths from the area. They loved to play the jukebox and could dance to the vibrations if not the sound. We all had Cokes and sundaes to toast my coming of age. Seventeen was the age of consent, though not, at that time, the eligible age to vote or to enter a hotel, even if the person was white.

I took stock of myself on my birthday. I'd been

earning my own living for more than three years. I hadn't starved but I had not saved much either. My goal to be a surgeon was as far away as ever. Still, I was enjoying life and, particularly, my freedom to dance. The band playing at the big top had let me sit in as drummer a few times, which was extremely exciting. I hadn't grown all that much, being about five foot two or three tall, and constantly struggling to reach six stone in weight. But I felt healthy and energetic, and thought that I wasn't doing too badly for someone with the barriers and limitations I'd faced.

When the Exhibition was over, I went back to Chermside. Josie and I scooted into town on Friday night and tore up the dance floor at the Institute. A few times we had considered going to Cloudland, but the expense and our lack of what we regarded as suitable clothes prevented us.

I've never been much of a singer, but in Townsville I'd put together a few songs I could have a go with; ones which didn't require a range of notes. I could pull out a note and sit on it, whether it be soprano or alto, but found it impossible to guide my voice from one note to another. Consequently, my repertoire consisted of one-note songs such as 'Johnny Be Good' and 'Bony Marony', which needed a good memory rather than vocal skills.

Josie and I were very excited when the Institute dance organisers announced a talent quest, with prizes of tickets to appear in some capacity on Brian Henderson's 'Bandstand'. We rehearsed so much I'm sure the other people in the house got tired of us, but not one of them said so. Instead, they'd sing along and clap, and watch us preening and selecting postures and gestures with which to win the competition.

On the big night, the hall was filled with strange men in suits, beautifully groomed, and a whole host of people, would-be performers who, we thought, had never set foot inside the Institute before. Musical instruments and several sets of drum kits blocked off a fair bit of the dance floor, and the casual and fun atmosphere we were used to had been replaced with an air of severe competition and judgement.

We were wearing our best dance clothes, which we had spent an agonising week selecting. I had on a pair of black trousers with a silver thread through the fabric, loose for movement but pegged in at the ankle, a pure white, long-sleeve poloneck sweater, which I thought made me appear 'elfin'—even though it was far too hot to wear comfortably under stage lights, flat, black patent-leather shoes, all the better to dance in, and flu-orescent socks which were all the rage, and the better to be noticed in. Josie was similarly attired in her own version of the very latest 'look'.

We were almost put off by the change in the feeling of the place, and if I'd been alone, I doubt very much that I'd have mustered the nerve to go ahead with the registration. Josie, however, said she'd register us both, so I stood against the wall watching musicians and technical people rush around the stage completing their preparations. When she returned, she passed me a ticket with a number on it and said I'd be first.

'First! I'm first?' My stomach did a full loop in dread.

'No, silly. First out of you 'n' me.' My relief was tangible.

We didn't want to get our gear soiled by perspiration before our turn on stage, so we picked a good spot just to watch. As the night wore on, Josie and I kept each other's nerves steady and our enthusiasm high by giggling and earnestly, though dismissively, discussing everyone else's performance. In the breaks we stepped outside to escape the heat which built up under all those lights.

Suddenly, we heard my number being called. I pranced up on stage, shoved onto it with a good-luck push from Josie. One of the regular back-up groups had already agreed that they would play for me, so it took no time at all for me to be up there behind the microphone. Nervous? I would have been if I'd actually looked at anyone in the audience. Instead, I pinned my gaze on some spot at the back of the hall in the 'true Hollywood' style we'd rehearsed, and belted out 'Johnny Be Good'. At the first short vocal break which was filled by the musicians, I even remembered to shake my legs, stamp around and shimmy a bit to encourage the audience into the mood of the piece.

It was all over in a flash. I took my bow to enthusiastic applause, and was surprised on my way to the steps to be called back to do another number. I grinned out at Josie who was waving her arms in the air with joy. We'd rehearsed for just such an event and I slid quickly into 'Bony Marony'.

I was back in Josie's arms—she was hugging me so tight—and the next act was on stage, before I realised that it was supposed to be Josie's turn. The minute I realised, she knew it, and placing her hands on my shoulders she admitted that she hadn't put her own name in at all. But her elation at how well I had been received swept away any pangs of disappointment almost before I had time to feel them.

It was late now as the more professional acts had played earlier in the evening. The air was charged with tension while we waited to learn the results of the competition. Some of the guys in suits from the television station had already departed, leaving their instructions with the minions who had to wait until the end.

Josie and I were over the moon when my name was amongst those called to the stage to collect Participant Tickets to 'Bandstand'. I was handed two large, crisp white cardboard tickets, and I quickly shoved one at Josie. With such a coup, we knew we were too excited just to get on a tram and go quietly home to sleep, so I was more than agreeable when Josie suggested we go to a midnight movie at a city theatre.

When we arrived, it was a bit disappointing because there was only a thin crowd. I'd expected midnight shows in Brisbane to attract the same large crowds as the very occasional midnight screenings did in Townsville. Josie, at least, knew by sight a couple of the other patrons and she gave them a wave as we made our way towards the front of the theatre. I noticed everyone else in the theatre was white, but this had no great significance because almost every theatre around the country drew white or predominantly white audiences.

The film was engrossing, and I was transported into the essence of the story until my concentration was interrupted by a young man, who came to sit beside Josie and spoke to her in urgent, hushed tones. I couldn't hear what they were saying, so I was concentrating on the film when Josie shook my arm and asked me to give her all the cash I had on me. Her boyfriend had been arrested and had sent his friend out to scout up bail. This was all a bit of a mystery to me, as Josie hadn't mentioned having a steady boyfriend in all the weeks I'd known her. As I passed her my money she told me she was going to bail him out and that she'd be back before the film was over so that the four of us, including the man who was with her now, would go back to Chermside as he had offered us a lift.

I was unhappy about being left alone in the theatre. Glancing around nervously, I noticed that, as she left, Josie stopped at the group of people to whom she had waved earlier. They seemed to be contributing to the bail fund. I watched the film but without the intent concentration of before as I kept feeling the minutes tick by without Josie reappearing. I thought this was a let-down when we were supposed to be celebrating.

When the lights came up at the film's end, I looked about anxiously to see if Josie had returned, but this was wishful thinking.

I followed the small crowd outside and by the time I reached the footpath most of them had disappeared into the night. I stood around for a short while, despairing of Josie's promised return, sorting through my options. Without cash, I couldn't jump into a taxi, and even if I'd still had the few pounds I'd so trustingly given away, they wouldn't have been enough for a cab-fare all the way to Chermside. It was so late that there were no trams running and the early morning trams wouldn't begin for hours. The idea of sitting alone on a tramstop during the wee hours was frightening. And the thought of walking through the city, across the bridge and over to Aunty Glad's house was also scary, not to mention having to rouse her when she wasn't even expecting me. And Josie—I didn't have a clue which police station she'd gone to or what her boyfriend's name was, and I wasn't keen to wander around the streets from one station to another looking for her. The truth was—I was stuck.

I was grateful to see that a few of the people Josie

had spoken to were still hanging about, perhaps also hoping that she'd return to make some arrangement about returning the money they'd put up for bail. They looked reasonably well-dressed and quiet, so I saw no good reason to be afraid when one of them walked over and spoke to me.

'She didn't come back, eh? D'you know where she went?' His voice was polite, friendly, and he didn't come across as if he was trying to chat me up or anything.

'Sort of, but I don't know if she's still there. She's been gone a very long time.'

'These things take time, they can keep you hanging around for hours. D'you want a lift home?'

I was concerned about accepting a lift from a stranger, but there were girls standing with the group, so I supposed there would be at least two cars, or maybe we were all to go in a couple of taxis.

'Which way are you going?' I asked.

'There's a few of us, so we'll have to go all over. We'll drop you wherever you have to go.'

'Well, thanks very much. I was beginning to wonder how I was going to get home.'

A car drew up slowly on the other side of the street and as it did so, the man said, 'There's our car now. Let's go.' He was smiling, and his face looked pleasant.

As we crossed the street, some of the other people in the group peeled off and walked towards the next corner. When we reached the car I noticed that there was a man behind the wheel, and the man who'd offered me the lift opened the back kerbside door for me to get in. He got in the back as well, and then two other men broke away from the few people who remained on the footpath. One sat in the front seat and the other in the back alongside the man who was sitting next to me. The car started up immediately without a word being said, and for a moment I was filled with panic and apprehension.

'Where to, ma'am?' came a voice from the front.

'Chermside. I'm going to Chermside.' We were approaching the first corner on the main street through Brisbane, so I added, 'We turn to the right here.'

The car quickly turned to the left and I looked through the back window, stunned. 'We're going the wrong way. Oh, please put me down here. We're going the wrong way.'

No one seemed to take any notice, they acted as if they were deaf or I hadn't spoken at all. I was glad to be sitting on the kerbside door, and even though the car was gathering speed, I grabbed the handle to jump out.

I saw the shoulder of the dark-haired man sitting in the front passenger seat swivel, and the next thing I knew, his closed fist flew through the air and landed on the side of my face. My brain rocked in my head and I tried to shake it to clear the fuzziness. As my eyes began to regain focus I could see his fist coming again but it was travelling too fast. I saw what was coming but was unable to move out of its path.

When I came to, I was slumped in the seat and the car was speeding through the night. No one spoke. I lay still for a moment while I collected my thoughts, my eyes barely open so that no one would notice my consciousness. A very occasional street light shone briefly into the car, so I figured we were somewhere on the outskirts of the city, but where, I had no idea. It seemed to me it was now or never, even though the car was moving quickly, so I snaked out my hand to the door, yanked the handle up and slid myself across the seat all in one movement.

The man who had offered me the lift grabbed at me, stopping my movement, and the one in the front turned and thumped my head once more.

My next recall was of the car travelling more slowly, moving across very bumpy ground, and hitting pot-holes along the way. My mind was awake at last, but I couldn't get my body to respond, to make any move-ment at all. Then headlights from a car behind us played across the inside roof of the car, and I hoped beyond hope that it was the police, that they'd noticed this car and were following it. Still no one spoke.

Just as suddenly, it seemed, we'd stopped. Car doors were opened, the door beside me clicked open, and I was dragged out by rough hands on my good white sweater.

I was pushed around the rear of the vehicle, and I noticed that there was not one, but two, other cars parked there with their doors open and men pouring out of them.

I was pushed up against a timber wall, then the rough hands let me go. The dark-haired man who'd been sitting in the passenger seat stood directly in front of me. He had cold eyes and his face looked very grim.

'Are you going to give it up?' he asked.

'What? Give what up?' I was confused and I didn't know what he was asking me.

He reached out his hand at waist level and ripped at the top of my trousers. The fabric, reinforced with silver thread, was strong and resisted his effort to tear it. He was standing very close, so I brought up my leg and delivered him a direct blow to his testicles. He bent over in pain but uttered not one sound.

I looked around in desperation. I was surrounded by what appeared to be a sea of white male faces. Some stood in the back, with brown bottles in their hands, and I realised they were drinking beer. A very tall, blond man, strikingly handsome, stood near the front, and I could make out his features very clearly. He walked towards me, stood to the right of the man doubled over in front of me and, foolishly, I thought he was coming to save me.

'Here, don't panic. Give me your hands.' I mistook his expression for kindness, or maybe I was so desperate that my mind only saw what it wanted to see. I held out my hands to him. He took them, one in each of his large hands, and wrenched them up, pinning them to the wall on either side of me. The man who was doubled over stood up, and I realised that the tall man was holding me still so that this dark-haired monster could punch me again. His angry face and fist were the last things I saw.

I came to lying on the ground in the dark, inside a shed, and there seemed to be men moving all around. A sharp stone was digging into my back but I was unable to lift myself off it. A voice said, 'Wait,' and in the moment before I passed out again, I felt a bristled face brush roughly against my lower stomach and strong sharp teeth bite a piece out of my flesh. The pain was so severe that for a second I thought I was being stabbed, and then blackness overtook me.

I was in the middle of a nightmare. I could feel someone dragging me along the ground by one foot. My other leg became twisted beneath me until someone else pulled it free. My head was bouncing over dirt and stones. I heard a moan escape from my lips.

'Christ,' said a voice, and I looked up and saw in the moonlight shining brightly through the open doorway, that the man I'd kicked in the groin was standing at the door. I knew immediately that it was his voice. 'She's still alive.'

The sharp sound of his boots on the ground assailed my ears. When I opened my eyes again, I saw his thick boot, his kick, coming directly towards my eyes, and there wasn't a damned thing I could do to move out of its way.

I awoke to silence. My entire body felt pain, but there was no single source of it. I was naked and cold, chilled. I crawled around on the ground and my hand struck, thank the heavens, my black trousers. I pulled them on. Then I saw the outline of my sweater in a corner as my eyes became accustomed to the dark. Moonlight still streamed through an opening in the wall where perhaps there'd once been a window. My bra and white T-shirt were with my sweater, and nearby I found my shoes. I pulled them all on. I patted around in the dark, hoping to find my underpants and socks. The cold and damp were making me feel clammy. I walked out of the shed and examined everything I had in my pockets, taking stock of what little had been left with me. I had a slim wallet, empty but for coins, and a few other small bits and pieces. I'd been carrying nothing of much value, and now I had even less. Moonlight bounced off a large white card as I pulled it from my pocket. In big letters I read 'Invitation' and 'Bandstand'. It felt as though I was handling something from years ago, not just a few short hours earlier.

I looked around. The shed was in a large field. I followed the car tracks in the moonlight and came to a fence, which I walked through to where the track joined another, more frequently used, roadway. I was unsure of which direction to take. A long way off in the distance I saw a pair of carlights pass at right angles to the track on which I was standing, I set off in that direction.

I passed a driveway, just a break in a fence, and could see the silhouette of a homestead in the distance. Then I could hear dogs barking, they had probably heard me stumbling along or picked up my scent on the wind. I was too afraid of them to chance walking up the driveway to get help.

The track stopped at a T-junction where it met a narrow bitumen strip. No other car had passed, and I had no idea in which direction Brisbane lay. I was feeling very sick in my stomach, and while walking I'd become aware of a severe pain in my abdomen. I sat down beside the road to wait for more carlights to appear, but I lapsed once more into unconsciousness.

A droning sound woke me and I realised a car was coming, but it was still a long way off. I remembered the pain and slid my hand down the front of my pants. My fingers touched a gaping wound and when I pulled them out they were covered in blood. The car, when it came close enough, was a small milk van. I staggered onto the road and it stopped. I asked the driver which way was the road to Brisbane. He told me it was in the direction he was faced, but that he was turning off the road at the next corner and was unable to give me a lift. He was making his deliveries. Another car, he said, should be along very soon, and it would be better for me to try my luck with that one.

I sat back down beside the road. After a while I

thought the world was moving, the trees seemed to be going up and down, and then I realised that it was me, I was swaying even while sitting down.

I had no watch, no idea of the time, but, in shock, I had no sense of urgency. Utter tiredness overwhelmed me. When more headlights appeared, I stood up again and walked onto the road. The driver either didn't see until late or he was afraid to stop, because he started to veer around me. Then he drew to a halt. I asked if he was going to Brisbane, and he said, yes, named a suburb I'd never heard of, and I asked him if he'd give me a lift.

I climbed into the cabin and sat huddled near the door. The warm air from his heater began to thaw my frozen limbs. I could feel localised sore spots on my legs and body. I touched my fingers to my head and found my entire face swollen. I sobbed quietly in the dark so as not to alarm the driver.

He drove slowly, and the sun was coming up when he pulled up at the vegetable farm which was his home. We were somewhere high up, but still in the town. He swung out of the truck and said if I waited a while, he'd give me a lift to a railway station. He spoke with an accent, European, perhaps Italian or Greek, I thought.

The truck was parked in front of a very large shed or storehouse. When he'd gone back up the walkway to the house on the block, some workers came out of the shed and peered at me sitting in the cabin. Eventually, one of them came over and asked me if I'd have sex with him for money. He indicated the bunch of workers who stood, eager and hopeful, in the doorway of the building. I was too exhausted even to be shocked. When he'd gone back, no doubt to relay my unwilling response, I slid across the seat and looked at my face in the rear-vision mirror. I couldn't look as bad as I felt, I thought, if these men don't notice how beaten up I am. A crust of dried blood lay across the top of my swollen nose, and my eyes were clotted. Every inch of my head and hair was covered in a film of dirt. Tracks from my tears had created a sort of pattern in the dark shadows beneath my eyes. I looked down at my clothes. My good white sweater was filthy. It looked as if I'd been rolling in mud.

The owner returned and said he would drive me to wherever I wanted to go. When I said Chermside he just nodded and we set off. The sun was well up now and I noticed on his clock that the time was moving towards 8 am. I thanked him without much enthusiasm when he dropped me right outside the house where I was living.

When I walked in I went straight to the bed, and stared up at the ceiling. One of the other girls with whom I shared the room jumped up and ran out to fetch the woman of the house. She came in and very kindly and gently asked me what had happened, and was upset when I could only shake my head.

She had another girl run a bath for me and helped me to take my clothes off and climb into it. She was very distressed by the dark bruises that seemed to cover my body and by the places on my abdomen where, she thought, I'd been bitten by some sort of animal. How right she was!

When I was alone, soaking in the bath, tears again overwhelmed me, turning into great sobs. I could sense the anxiety in the house over my grief and my appearance. I didn't see Josie and I hadn't asked if she was home. There seemed no point, no point in asking or saying anything.

The woman of the house came into the bathroom

with a cup. She said it was a drink of gin, and it would help me in case I 'needed to lose, well, you know'. I accepted her act of kindness but couldn't drink it. Apart from the sherry Mum had tried to force me to drink as some sort of appetite stimulant when I'd been ill and underweight, I didn't drink and this didn't seem a good time to start.

When I got out of the bath I wrapped myself up and lay on my bed. Sleep was a million miles away. I could hear everyone out in the sitting room discussing me. They were afraid I might want to go to the police.

I was brought many warm cups of milky tea, slices of bread spread thickly with peanut paste—which everyone in the house knew was my absolute favourite food—and bowls of soup. I had no appetite, I drank and ate nothing. I lay in the shadowed room for days, not really sleeping, not really awake. From time to time my mind raced through a list of things I ought to do: get up, go to work, wash my filthy clothes, pack, move out, and even get ready to attend 'Bandstand'. Then my mind would float away to nothingness once more.

Fragments of conversations floated in to me now and then, people in the sitting room, in the kitchen, outside in the hall. The tension in the house was tangible, but I couldn't rouse myself to take any of it in. I felt no urgency to do anything but lay there quietly in the half dark.

How many days passed? I have no idea. Three? Four? Then I woke and gingerly sat up on the side of the bed. I noticed that the other bed in the room had been slept in, and obviously the routine of the household had continued without my being aware of it.

Soon a girl came to the door and saw me sitting up. She rushed away and came back with another cup of warm tea. When I took it from her, my hands shook and when I lifted it to my lips I found them flaky and stuck together. I could see the pity in her eyes, and tears flowing down her face as she tried to help me.

I had a shower and stood under the hot water for a long time; refusing to look down at myself, wishing the water could wash away the atrocities that sat out there on the edge of my mind. I felt that if I tried hard enough, I could push them even further away, and it would be as though they had never happened.

I learned that Josie had gone back to the mission, and the fear that my presence would attract police attention was paramount in everyone's mind. An Aboriginal household was a target for the police anyway, and they didn't need me around to give the police justification for their unwanted attention.

As soon as I was able, I packed my things and walked down to catch a tram. I had a few pounds from my savings, my rent money had been returned to me, and everyone in the house felt so badly about what was happening that they had given me the little money they had.

I got off the tram in the Valley, bought a copy of the *Courier-Mail*, and sat on a street bench to read the accommodation section. I found two advertisements for 'share accommodation for working female lodgers' at nearby New Farm. I rang one and heard that the room had gone, the other was still available. I picked up my suitcase and set off on foot to find the address.

I was exhausted by the time I arrived. One of the residents showed me around—shared kitchen, shared bathroom with a coin heater, shower and bath—and gave me a chair in the hall so I could sit and wait for the manager, who had gone up the street.

The manager asked me a few cursory questions, and in the dimly lit hall she didn't notice my swollen face or bruises. I paid her two weeks' rent in advance and was taken to a room off the main hallway which contained two single beds separated by a night table, and two small cupboards. The room was curtained and clean, the sheets on my bed crisp and fresh.

The manager told me where to find the government employment agency and said that there was a lot of work available, I'd get a job, no worry.

When I informed the agency of the type of work I'd been doing in the north, nursing aide and specialist machine operator, they placed me in a job in a sugar packaging company. At the factory, a small group of women gathered around the funnel of a chute all day, taking the bags which the machine had automatically filled with sugar, and adding or removing a few grains to standardise the contents before doubling the tops over to seal them. The work was boring and without challenge, there was no chance of variation or advancement, and the constant exposure to fine dust from the sugar made me wheezy.

I went back to the employment agency. My next position was at P. J. Firth, another company which made cartons, though much smaller ones than the large meat-packing boxes I had been making in Townsville. The building was two storeys, narrow and pokey, without much access to natural light and poorly ventilated. The employers were kindly though dour, as were the employees, and it seemed that they'd all been working there together, quietly and efficiently earning their wages, for decades.

I lived on hamburgers from a takeaway store nearby, and in my free time I sat in New Farm Park and

ploughed my way through piles of novels and magazines. I found a book exchange, which kept the cost of
my addiction to escapism within my means.

I'd been at Firth's for a few weeks and they were
happy with my work when, one Monday, during our
morning-tea break I became faint and fell on the stairs.
No real damage was done but the manager was concerned that I'd lost my balance, and insisted I get a
medical check-up before I returned to my stapling
machine. He rang the hospital and told them I was
coming.

The wind was crisp but the sunlight was brilliant as
I walked through the Valley to the hospital. My blood
pressure and urine tests were taken and I was told to
return the next afternoon for the results. As I couldn't
go back to work without a health certificate, I took my
book to the park the next morning and soaked up the
sun, while indulging my passion for fantasy.

As I walked back to the hospital, however, I began to
shake. I had no idea why I was so distressed and out of
control. I could barely walk along the footpath putting
one foot in front of the other, and I tripped on the kerb
as I went. The stairs which led up to casualty seemed to
be several storeys high, and by the time I arrived my
heart was beating savagely and I was badly out of
breath. Perhaps I really *was* sick, I thought.

I had a long wait, and many people who arrived after
me were seen before me. My concentration had disappeared and I was unable to focus on reading. I felt like
an observer at a film, watching people come and go,
and I had no thoughts at all apart from registering what
was occurring in front of my eyes.

A tall, white-smocked doctor with a stethoscope
slung around his neck came in and called my name.

He ushered me into a room, and I looked around and saw the usual charts and cut-away body pictures on the walls, a filing cabinet, phone, files and sterilising thermometer on his desk. It all seemed so normal yet there was a feeling of malignance in the air.

'Do you have anything you want to tell me?', the doctor asked, pulling his chair up directly in front of me so that he could stare into my eyes.

'What sort of something?' I replied, puzzled.

'Could you be pregnant?' His voice dropped as though we were sharing a secret.

'No.' I was suddenly angry at him for asking me such a question, and for all the implications it carried. 'No. No. No.'

He stood up. 'Well, I want you to think about that, and I'll come back and talk to you again in a few minutes.' The door closed gently. I peeped over at the papers on his desk, read my name upside down, some other writing which was indecipherable, and in block letters in red ink, the word, POSITIVE. A red cloud rose up before my eyes and blocked out the room.

Suddenly, the door burst open again and I heard a gasp. I looked about me and was shocked. Papers from the desk were screwed up, torn and thrown around the room. The posters were torn from the walls. I was sitting on the floor and had no idea how I'd got there. In my hands were pieces of something hard and black— fragments of the broken telephone which had been torn from the wall. I kept hearing someone simultaneously wailing and laughing, an awful demented sound, and realised then that it was coming from me.

The doctor smacked my face sharply. A white-uniformed nurse hovered in the background behind him.

He hauled me to my feet and flung me back into the chair.

'She's right, Nurse. I can handle things here.' The door closed. He leaned into my face and asked, his teeth gritted together, 'What do you think you're doing?'

'I . . . I was attacked,' I managed to whisper through parched lips.

'No. You did this,' he said, his arm indicating the room.

'No. I was attacked another day. At night. By dozens of people.'

'Listen, there's something seriously wrong with you. I'll fix up about this, this mess that you've made of my office, but I want you to go and see the social worker.' He looked at his watch. 'She's probably gone for the day, but I want you to see her tomorrow. You're pregnant and you're going to need care. I can't give you a certificate for your work at this stage. Just tell them you need some days off.'

He rifled on the floor, located a file, then scratched some writing on a page.

'Here.' He folded the sheet and handed it to me. 'This is the name of the social worker and where to find her. See her tomorrow, you understand? I don't have time for you. You're her problem.'

It was almost dusk when I came out onto the street. I walked through the crowds waiting to catch their buses and trams back to their suburban houses and families. I walked past the turnoff to my own house, right to the end of the long street then turned and walked all the way back again. The footpaths were emptier now. I continued to walk, aimlessly, and found myself across the street from the milk bar frequented

by the deaf and dumb people who had helped me cel-
ebrate my birthday just a few weeks earlier. Some of
them were already at the tables, silently joking and
laughing amongst themselves. I watched them through
the window from across the street for a long time, then
turned to go back to the boarding house.

I walked down roads and lanes I hadn't noticed
before, always in the general direction of home. In an
otherwise closed street, one door stood open, cracked
a little, with light spilling out. A wooden sign screwed
to the building told me it was a church, a Catholic
church. I stood outside considering whether I could
find help in there. The wind had blown up and I was
very cold.

I slipped in through the door. A priest was in the
front of the church, gathering up books and stacking
them in a pile on one of the pews. I didn't really notice
his face, only his black cassock.

'Can I help you?' he asked when he noticed me
standing in the back. 'Do you want something?'

'Father,' I answered, but I didn't know how to go further. He walked towards me and I thought he looked
unfriendly, but he was a man of God and I was a
despairing person.

'Father, I was attacked. I was beaten up by men and
raped. I don't know what to do.'

His eyes narrowed. 'What do you want? Money?'

'No, Father.' I was shocked by his response.

'Well, get out of here and come back when you're
ready to tell the truth! Come back when you're ready to
confess.' He put his hands in the slits of his cassock
and shook the long black garment at me, shooing me
away as one might shoo a dog. I turned on my heels
and left.

When I got home I lay down on my bed in the dark, fully dressed and still wearing my jacket, and stared up at the ceiling. When my room-mate came in, she turned on the light and was startled to see me there.

I changed and put on my pyjamas, to make her feel more comfortable, and when we'd turned out the lights I lay there again staring up into the darkness. When she woke next morning I was still staring, and she asked me if I had been asleep. I said yes, but that I wasn't feeling well and was taking the day off work. She dressed and left.

Apart from the few new scratches I'd received from falling on the stairs at work, all the swelling, abrasions and bruising had slowly disappeared from my body, leaving just a few scars. When I touched the bridge of my nose with my finger and thumb, I could hear a crunching sound, but I preferred to ignore it and pretend it wasn't there. I had also experienced an increasing burning sensation around my private area, which I'd also decided to ignore.

Overnight, a plan had somehow hatched in my mind. The world and the problems I now faced seemed so huge and without any possibility of resolution, and my life so worthless, that any person, any lout on the street, any priest in his church, any doctor in his office, could see and judge my worthlessness and treat me accordingly. If this was my reality, I didn't want to deal with it. I wanted to go to sleep and never have to wake up. That became my plan.

With everyone at work, the boarding house was quiet and peaceful. I took out my pen and writing pad and wrote a letter to Mum which ran to several pages. In it I sketched what had happened to me, implied rather than stated what I intended to do, and told her not to blame herself for anything that had or was about to happen. Writing the letter took a long time because I kept being overwhelmed with tears of grief, but I remained resolute.

Then, for the first time since I'd been in that house, I took a bath instead of a shower. Sitting in the warm water was an irritation to me, causing my private region to burn very fiercely, and for the first time also I decided to inspect myself there to discover the cause of this pain. I was appalled, disgusted and horrified to find small, almost clear, lice burrowing into my skin to get away from the soap and water. Crabs! I had heard of them in some revolting joke which Leila had told me years ago, but I'd never seen them, never heard anyone else mention them, and probably hadn't really believed something so disgusting could exist. I crawled out of the bath and over to the toilet to dry retch.

I returned to my room to get the razor I used to shave my legs, then completely shaved off all my pubic hair. It wasn't enough, the creatures clung to my bare skin, burrowing away into my pores. I found a bottle of kerosene under the sink in the kitchen and poured a little on myself to see if that killed them. It didn't. I put two more pennies into the gas meter which supplied hot water in the bathroom, and turned the water to a dribble so that it would be boiling when it came out of the tap. I seared my pubic area with the steaming water, letting it run on me until I passed out.

I dressed loosely and walked painfully to the nearest stores, looking for a chemist shop. On the way, I posted the letter to Mum. The assistant in the chemist shop became suspicious of me, she seemed to think I was shop-lifting, as I picked up various bottles to read their poison content. When I'd selected something, she took the money from me sourly. From the little knowledge I had gained about pharmaceuticals while working in the hospital, I knew I was unlikely to be able to purchase any over-the-counter medication that would do the job. Instead, I'd have to ingest a large quantity of a range of products, and it wouldn't be wise to try to buy them all at the one time or at the one shop.

I decided to take home the bottle I'd bought before going to another chemist, in case I was suspected of shop-lifting there too, and searched. The walk home was again painful. I looked at myself when I arrived and saw that large blisters had formed over the scalded area.

'Well,' I thought, 'Mum will be terribly embarrassed if they find me like this and have it in the report when she has to bury me.' At least the crabs had gone. I put Vaseline on myself to hasten the healing, and decided there was no rush to complete the task as my problems would still be there the next day, and the next, and even the day after that. Nothing was going to change for the better, things could only get worse.

Once I'd come up with the solution and my resolve was firmly fixed in my mind, I felt better. I was able to go out into the kitchen in my dressing gown when the other girls came home from work, heat myself some baked beans and put them on toast, and even eat them as if nothing was wrong apart from a mild passing flu.

The next day I called at two other chemist shops, and added my pill purchases to my store. I also returned a book I'd promised to bring back to the book exchange, and washed out my clothes so that nothing would be left for anyone to have to clean once I'd gone.

That evening, my room-mate was excited, she had a date for the following night, and would be late home or, if things worked out, she might not be home at all. Perfect, I thought, as I had been worried about the timing. I had only one more day, Friday, during which I'd collect more pills, and sit around until she'd left. I was pleased at how smoothly the plan had come together, how easily it had been to assemble and prepare everything, and now an opportunity had been tossed right into my lap.

I was also pleased that by the next morning the most severe signs of the scalding had subsided. The day was pleasant and I even sat in the sun in the park for a while. It was to be my last day, and in a perverse way, I wanted to enjoy it. Things, I thought, can only get worse from now on, so for me, this is as good as it's going to ever be.

That night I had a light supper, sitting in the kitchen with a few of the other girls while my room-mate bathed, dressed and perfumed herself for her date. Then she came into the kitchen to be admired and to sit with us until a knock came at the front door. I took a jug of water and a glass and, saying I was going to read, retired to our room.

I could only take a little sip with each round of pills. I didn't want to make myself sick by overloading my stomach with water. I mixed the pills up so I was taking one of each with every drink. When I'd got through what I thought was enough, I dressed and lay down on my bed and closed my eyes to wait.

Through a fog I thought I heard someone tapping on the door. Then strange people were standing around me. Later, a strong hand kept my head turned sideways and for a moment I thought I was in a car.

I woke up in a hospital bed but refused to open my eyes. I knew I was awake because I could hear voices, and I knew I was in a hospital because of the feel of the bed and the antiseptic smell. I'd spent so much time in hospitals already during my life that I could identify them even with my eyes closed.

I felt myself beginning to weep. I was crying because I'd been unsuccessful, and the sorry tale of Leila's many suicide attempts flooded into my mind. I hadn't wanted to be like her, and now I was. A nurse held my hand. I slept.

When I woke up again I was alone in the room, which was some sort of surgery. My clothes were over the back of a chair beside the bunk and I jumped up, took off the white hospital gown and put them on. I walked out and saw no one in the corridor, no one in the foyer, and so I just kept walking until I was out in the street. I walked back to the boarding house.

There was an immediate hush when I came in. The other girls stared at me, but were afraid to ask me anything. I walked around and put the kettle on to make myself a cup of tea as if nothing had happened. The more normal I acted, the more normal they became. One of them told me the manager had gone away for the weekend and wouldn't be back before Monday. I took my tea back into the room.

My room-mate came in and began to cry. She had come back to borrow a coat I had which she thought looked good and which I'd said she could wear whenever she wanted. When she saw me on my bed, she'd roused the other girls, and one of them had called an ambulance. I didn't tell her what had transpired at the hospital, she just thought I'd been discharged. It pleased me to have her and the other girls believe that. I said I wouldn't do it again, that I'd accidentally taken a few too many pills for my flu. She knew better from the wide assortment of bottles she'd found in my bag, but she wasn't game to challenge me. I could see the edge of her fear in her eyes.

Well, what to do next? My problems haven't been solved by that episode, I thought when she had gone, but I'll have to proceed slowly now in order not to draw any more attention to myself, or people will start watching me too closely.

My lack of success and the awesome weight of my problems plunged me into depression, and I spent the next day focussed completely on not crying, not allowing a single thing I was feeling to break through on my surface. This enabled me to answer when I was spoken to, and to sit with my nose in a book even though no one, I hoped, realised I rarely turned the pages.

I spent Monday dodging the manager of the boarding house. It was the day she changed the sheets and generally inspected the rooms. I told her I was in the process of finding a new job, was going to the employment agency, and, instead, I went and sat in the park. I was waiting for another wave of inspiration to hit me. When I lay in bed at night it was as if someone had switched off a light in my head; I fell into a long and dreamless sleep. The knowledge of the peace I'd experienced while sleeping lured me again towards making it permanent.

On Tuesday I was laying down again in my room when the manager knocked on the door. She said there were police outside and they wanted to see me. I thought it might have had something to do with my ambulance ride and the visit to the hospital on Friday night. Perhaps there was some law against walking out of the hospital before you were discharged.

Instead, they said they wanted to speak to me in

their office. I was reluctant to get into the car with them because I didn't know where I'd end up. They said I could help them with their inquiries. The manager looked distressed and urged me to go.

At the station, we went up to a room on the second floor. I sat in a chair, one of them stood and the other perched on the edge of a table. The room was empty, but for the table and a couple of plain wooden chairs. I noticed that the policemen were both fairly young. One carried a folder, and after he'd told me their names again, he pulled out—Oh, dear heavens—the letter I had written to my mother. I'd completely forgotten either writing or posting it, such was the state of my distress.

I was deeply unhappy about having to tell them the details of that terrible night. I had pushed it away, pressed it down until it had disappeared altogether, but it seemed that, first the doctor and now the police were trying to force the whole incident back into my mind.

They looked at me politely and attentively, and took notes while I spoke. They asked me to describe this and that, elaborate on one point or another, and after perhaps an hour they said they would take me home. When they left they said I would hear from them again. The manager came out to meet me, and from the look on her face I could tell that they had spoken to her earlier and that somehow she had picked up the gist of what was going down.

Over the next two days she kept assuring me that it wouldn't matter if I fell behind in my rent. I received a letter from Mum, too, in which she said she had sent my letter, marked urgent, to the Chief of Police in the state. She enclosed a few pounds with which I was able to pay my rent, but the manager only took it under protest.

Three days later, two more detectives came to the house, and they also took me away to talk. We went to a different room this time. I told them the same things as I'd told the others. They had different questions, went over different points.

The next day, another detective came, alone. He was older than the previous four, middle aged, and instead of going to the police station, we drove around for a bit. Then he parked and we talked in his car. He had either read the reports of my earlier discussions or perhaps he had listened in somehow, because although I hadn't spoken to him before, he was able to tell me a great deal of what had been said.

His questions were very precise, he knew exactly what he wanted to learn and this was no fishing expedition for him. At the end of the questions he said, 'I want you to know I believe you. The other chaps you spoke to, they didn't. But there's something about what you're saying that keeps ringing up 'true' on my buttons. I've been a detective longer than they've been in the force. To me, you ring true. I'd like you to trust me. I want to get some justice for you here.'

He also said that he'd be in touch with my mother, and asked me how I was faring for money. I told him that I'd been working at Firth's, but that I hadn't been back. He said he'd speak to them during the following week, and then take me around there to pick up my wages. It felt good to have someone else doing the thinking for me, because I was so exhausted from carrying everything all on my own.

The relief I felt at being believed at last was enormous. At the same time, I couldn't summon up any trust to give him, because emotionally I had nothing left to give anyone. I resented anything and anyone with any part at all to play in this reality. I badly wanted him and everything else connected to this time just to disappear so that I could wake up and find my earlier life restored.

10

My relief at being believed was short lived. Instead of this feeling being positive, it gave the awful events which preceded it a reality in my mind that they did not have before. I'd been able to block everything out, find a new place to live, new job, and even sit in the sunshine with nothing to think about but luxuriating in the warmth of the winter days.

Now even the sun became my enemy. I hated to go out in daylight and I feared to go out at night. Mum wrote to me constantly, but she used her letters as a means to sermonise. I began just taking out the pound notes she included and stacking the letters, unread, in my suitcase. My own emotional load was too heavy, I couldn't carry her grief and frustration as well, nor her attempts to direct the police inquiry from Townsville.

She wrote to the police asking them to send me home. The detective came around and discussed this with me. By now I was sleeping both day and night. Occasionally, when roused by sounds from the other lodgers, I would wake up and go out to get a hamburger or tins of baked beans and spaghetti. Whenever there was mail or anyone called, I had to be woken.

As he'd promised, the detective escorted me to Firth's factory. He'd already spoken to the manager, and when we arrived the manager and many of the staff gave me looks of great pity. They'd drawn up my pay, with holidays and anything else they could think of to give me, and the manager said that if I felt I could handle the work, I'd be welcome to stay on for a while. I was already having trouble distinguishing night from day, so the very idea that I'd be able to arrive anywhere at a set time was a responsibility I couldn't possibly have shouldered. I thanked him for his kindness and he asked the detective if he could be kept informed about my welfare. I didn't hear the reply but suspected that it was 'Sorry but no'. I was glad. Even the thought of people's pity being spent on me was repulsive.

The peaceful blackout sleep I'd been enjoying changed. Although I spent long periods asleep without any thoughts in my mind, I began to have flashbacks and to be overcome by fits of fear and terror from which I'd wake suddenly, shaking and sweating. Then I'd sit for hours watching the shadows in the room, in case anything emerged from them.

The detective seemed to make it his business to visit regularly, and he often brought me food. Sometimes he had another policeman with him, but generally he came alone. He advised me that I should stay in Brisbane as they would need my identification of the suspects when they were caught. I didn't believe they'd be caught, so it was no effort for me to agree. Besides, the energy required to contemplate the simple acts of packing or riding in the train was beyond me. I felt I was melting away, becoming smaller and smaller, draining into the earth. The few chores which I was still capable of, such as showering and changing my clothes, were all that were required of me until I, along with my insignificance, somehow disappeared completely.

The detective became my only lifeline to the outside world, as the girls in the boarding house increasingly withdrew from me. My room-mate disappeared without fanfare, shifted to another room no doubt. She and her things just weren't there one day when I woke up. I'd stopped taking notice of who was or wasn't in the kitchen or bathroom when I got up to use them, and the names of all the girls and even the manager deserted me.

But the detective came by and was always kindly and courteous. I even stopped getting up when the manager told me he was at the door. He would come into my room and, if it was daytime, pull back the curtains letting in the light and fresh air. He'd talk to me, tell me details of the inquiry, even when I didn't respond, even when tears streamed from my eyes, soaking the pillow. Everything seemed such a blur.

One evening, he came in and was a little more animated than usual. I became panicky even before he spoke. He was now hot on the trail of the culprits, he said. He had identified them from sources he had on the street, and within the next few days I'd be called in to make the formal identifications.

My stomach turned over and I was swept by fear. For the first time, he patted my shoulder and tried to comfort me. I had agreed to stay in Brisbane because I'd thought they wouldn't be found. Now, the notion that something, anything, was required of me, over and above living with the pain, was itself distressing. Even more profound and terrifying was the thought that I'd have to look at the faces of the animals who had attacked me, who had reduced my life to nothing. Those who had shaken the foundations of my belief in the intrinsic good nature of the world so that it had crumbled forever. Now I believed that only pure evil existed and I wanted no part of it.

The detective and his partner came for me. The manager had helped me to recognise the day and be prepared to go with them. I was dressed, but in my mind, I wasn't ready. We went in an unmarked police car, the detective in the passenger seat in the front, the other driving, and me in the back. We drove for a while, then parked in an ordinary street. The detective told me that inside the tall fence near where we were waiting was a factory, and that when a siren sounded the workers would come out through a nearby gate. I was to indicate if I saw anyone I recognised. I'd suppressed so much about that night that I was worried whether my mind still held any images of any of the men involved in it. I shouldn't have worried. Eventually, a small flood of workers surged through the gateway. I saw none of them but for the tall fair-haired man who had told me to hold out my hands.

'That's him,' I whispered. My voice had become dry and scratchy. I watched him walking away and thought the detectives hadn't heard me. 'That's the one, the one who's wearing—'

'Yes. We know. A one hundred percent identification. Good. Very good.'

I began to really panic now as he was disappearing along the street while we still sat comfortably in the car. I feared that we would lose him.

The detective turned to me. 'Don't worry. We know

where he lives. In fact we know everything about him now. We'll pick him up when we're ready. He's not about to get away.'

Over the next few days I was taken to various locations and line-ups. I surprised myself by being unable to describe people in any detail but then being able to identify them immediately when I saw them. The tally of identified suspects reached four.

Then the detective came for me again, this time, he said, with good news and bad news. The bad news was that, apart from the four who had been in the car with me, the police were having trouble making cases against the men who'd been in the other cars, one of whom was the last man I'd identified. He said that while I could place him at the crime scene as a face in the crowd, and he admitted to having been there, he denied taking any part in the assault or attack on me. And, he said, at least one carload of the men involved were from New South Wales and were not known personally by anyone police had questioned. He was sorry that their inquiries couldn't extend beyond the border. He didn't have enough information about these men to pass on to the Sydney police to follow up and make arrests. Through their inquiries the police had determined that eighteen, possibly even twenty, men had been present in some capacity at the shed that night, but the likelihood of them all, even the guilty ones, being brought to justice was remote.

My heart plummeted. But the good news, he continued, was that their main quarry, who had beaten and kicked me in the face hoping to kill me, had been found. I was to accompany them to the city lock-up for an identification line-up. This man was already in police custody on another matter.

We travelled in silence, with a policeman I hadn't seen before at the wheel. The detective, unaware of how much it would upset me, said he wished that the crimes had occurred two weeks earlier as, by law, I'd have been still under-age and the crime would have attracted a longer penalty. I was devastated. How, I thought, could anyone wish that I'd had two weeks less of peace and innocence? And particularly, how could he, this policeman whom I regarded as my saviour, have thought such an awful thing?

By the time we reached the lock-up I was over-wrought with anxiety about what lay ahead. What if I couldn't identify the culprit? Could I have forgotten those evil eyes, that sneering face? Would he look different, perhaps have grown a beard or cut his hair differently, and I'd be unable to recognise him. I had to be helped from the car and given a steady arm to hang onto in order to make it inside the door. I recall only a courtyard where the police car was parked and the vague impression of some sort of huge solid brick or cement building. Immediately inside the door was a counter, with no furniture on the side we stood on. I was left leaning against the counter while the detectives went away to ensure the line-up was ready.

When the detective returned, he drew me aside to inform me of the process. 'When you walk in,' he said, 'there will be a line of men. You are to walk along the line and look at each man. On your way back along the line, you're to place your hand on the shoulder of any man you recognise and say, "this is the man".'

From somewhere, probably films, I'd had the idea that I was going to be able to make the identification from behind a screen, or that, having walked along the line-up, we'd all go back outside and I'd say, 'He was the fourth person from the end'. Never in my wildest dreams had I imagined that I'd have to touch the person. I began to weep.

The detective waited for me to get over it, to summon up some inner strength and begin the sickening task. He said we had all the time in the world, but that the sooner I did it, the sooner it would be behind me. In a few minutes I nodded. 'Okay, I'm ready.'

When I stepped through the door, I saw him and only him. My legs were shaking and I was anxious to get it over. I began to walk directly to him, and was stopped by a word from the detective as he repeated his earlier advice that I was to start at the beginning of the line. Looking at these men was a waste of time, and they got a scant glance from me. When I was nearing 'him' I was aware of him staring at me, his eyes again slitted and evil, his malevolence filling the room. I again forgot the instructions to pass by him and go to the end of the line, and instead I turned quickly towards the detectives and said, 'This is the man.' A quick head shake reminded me that this wasn't sufficient. I had to place my hand on the man's shoulder. I looked around to ensure that the police and warders were nearby to save me, as I had to go close enough to touch him and therefore close enough for him to grab me by the throat.

My heart stopped beating when I stood in front of him and put my right hand out towards his shoulder. His stare unnerved me. Then I turned quickly. Behind me, I heard a fumbled rush as the warders closed in on him. I kept walking, not looking back. I was out the door of that room, through the office and into the carpark before the detective caught up with me, grabbed my arm and gently drew me back. I had to sign something before I could leave.

Although I knew that the man was behind bars, I seemed to become worse. This had nothing to do with him, I felt, as he didn't enter my consciousness again once I'd walked away from the police station. I lapsed back into the grey world in which day and night were indistinguishable, and I rarely woke, even to eat.

A few days later, the detective visited in the evening and he was, to say the least, distressed. He made me get up and change out of my pyjamas because he wanted to talk to me outside. We went to sit in his car. He produced a hamburger he'd brought for me, perhaps to soften the blow or to have me engaged in doing something while he talked.

The man I'd just identified was out on bail. I choked. It was an administrative mistake, he said, and there were now fears for my safety. The man had been in the lock-up on other charges, including one of shooting at a policeman, and police had thought those charges were serious enough to keep him confined. The additional charges that had been laid against him had passed through the system too slowly, and he'd appeared before a magistrate only on the other charge—and had been given bail.

There was more. He was a known offender, a criminal with no respect for life, who'd already spent time in prison. The detective patiently explained that the man would know I was to be the main witness against him on a charge that would probably put him back inside for life. The chances of him coming after me were great. The detective asked me if this man could know where I lived through any of his acquaintances?

I didn't know who he knew, but the answer as far as

I was concerned was no. I hadn't stayed in touch with anyone from the Chermside house, even if he knew the people who lived there, which I doubted. I didn't have any friends. It was highly unlikely he'd know any of the women who lived in the boarding house. Nevertheless, the detective said, we had to start taking precautions. He got out and scouted around the front of the boarding house while I sat in the car and watched him. He disappeared up the side path, examining the windows and testing the strength of all the external doors.

He spoke to the manager, and when he returned he had a key to the front door. He was going to personally come by at odd times during the night to check on me, and he wanted to be able to silently move in and out of the house. I was not to go out onto the street. The manager or other girls would bring in anything I wanted in the way of food.

I returned to my room. My inability to take on everything that was happening exhausted me, and I lay down to go to sleep. Tension, however, prevented me from drifting back into unconsciousness. Feelings of worthlessness overwhelmed me again and I thought I'd be better off dead. I got up and opened the curtains wide so that if the madman came he could find me. I thought I'd sleep with the light on so that he could see me through the window.

I woke up later with a start when my bedroom door swung open and the detective was standing there with a torch in his hand, a torch which he didn't need because the overhead light was still blazing. He looked at the curtains and rushed over to close them. He stared at my face, tear-stained from crying in my sleep, and saw through me. He sat on the edge of the bed and patted my hand. 'You don't want to die,' he said, and I knew he'd been reading my mind. 'We've come too far for that, and we're too close to the end. When these men go to jail, you'll feel better, I promise. You can't die now, you'd be letting me down. We're in this together now.'

He gave me a peptalk, reminding me how he'd been the only one to believe in me, and calling on me to believe in him now. He would see me through this, he said, we were a team.

I didn't feel like a team, and he could see his talk wasn't getting the response from me which he'd hoped for. He told me to get up, have a shower and get dressed, he was taking me out to ride around with him. He'd wait outside in the car.

Obedience was about the only thing I had left, and I felt relieved of having to make any decisions as I show-ered and dressed. I sat in the back seat as the detective and his driver made their calls, drove through city streets and watched who was leaving which nightclubs and with whom, and listened to the scratchy voice which squawked intermittently from the police radio. When I became tired of peering through the window, I lay across the seat and slept.

Riding with them at night, and sometimes even during the day, became a regular pattern. I began to regard the back seat of their car as my own space. There was tremendous security in knowing that two men were just a few feet from me, alert and ready to protect me from any danger, should it arise. They knew the crimi-nal by sight, and I was sure they would see him before he had a chance to see me, so I slept easy.

One evening at the boarding house, I woke up with a start and realised I hadn't heard from the detective and I panicked. I decided I had to go outside and look for him myself, perhaps he had forgotten me. I took the camping knife and sheath which I'd had ever since my days at the YWCA group in Townsville, just in case I needed to protect myself.

The detective had never taken me to the station from which he worked. So, when I walked down to the only police station that I knew the location of, I suddenly realised that it may not have been where he operated from at all. The streets were full of people, and it occurred to me that it was Friday night. Suddenly I had a deep longing to see Josie, to share what had been happening to me with someone with whom I'd already shared a great deal. I imagined that if she was in Brisbane she'd be dancing at the Railway Institute, and, though it was a fair way, if I walked quickly I could be there in no time at all. I set off.

Having a purpose gave me a determination, but my paranoia was raging. I shifted my knife to where I could pull it out quickly, and practised pulling it out each time I found myself walking in a dark street or along a deserted block. By the time I arrived at the small city park which many people walked through on their way to the Institute, I was tired and seeing movement in shadows even when there was none.

I stood at the entrance to the park and gazed up the dark pathway, staring into the trees and bushes which grew along its border. I waited until several little groups and couples had walked in and out of it, then when the path was completely empty I made my move.

I was about a third of the way along the path when I saw him. He was walking alone, carrying something clutched to his chest, and coming towards me. Even though he was still quite a distance from me, I recognised him. Panic rose up in my throat. I had brazened it out with him once before, when I'd identified him at the line-up, and I could do it again now, I knew I could. This time the odds were more in my favour. He couldn't know where I was headed and therefore he didn't know it was me. More than that, I had my knife.

He must be wearing rubber soled shoes, I thought, because I don't hear his footsteps. He is almost upon me, get ready, ease the knife out from the sheath. There he is now! I raised the knife and plunged it into his side. The knife moved in smoothly, and I drew it out again. See, it was easy. Keep walking, don't look around to see his startled face, his grin and sneer floating off in the air.

When I reached the end of the path, I paused and looked back. A group of people were walking towards the body on the path, chattering and laughing. One of the men in the group broke away and ran towards the lump he saw ahead. I wanted to scream out that perhaps he wasn't dead, to be careful. Suddenly the air was filled with a scream from one of the women in the group. My feet were rooted to the path. Another man yelled out, 'Hey, you! Come back here.' At last, an order for me to obey. I moved towards them, hastily pushing the knife back into its sheath because it was obvious I didn't need it anymore. I was safe.

They told me to sit on the grass while we waited for the ambulance and police to arrive. When they saw me up close, they seemed to have decided I was a witness. It didn't occur to them that it was I who had stabbed this evil man.

Some police officers must have been nearby, because in no time at all uniformed officers were everywhere. I continued to sit on the grass, my knees drawn up beneath me, staring up at the wonderfully clear stars shining in the sky. Hubbub went on around me, I could hear people from the group giving their versions of how they had stumbled across the man lying on the path. More people had flocked into the park from the Institute and the streets, and I could feel them surveying the scene, trying to guess what had transpired.

At last an officer squatted down on his haunches beside me and asked, 'What did you see?' I looked at him and saw his expression turn from one of inquiry to surprise, and I realised then that tears were streaming down my face. When I didn't answer his question but just kept gazing at him, wondering how he didn't know it was me—me who was guilty now, me who had done it, he asked me, 'What's your name?'

'Roberta Patterson.' He stood up, took a notebook out of his top pocket, scribbled something in the dark and walked away. The police began to form little groups and look towards me. Between their legs I saw that the man on the path had been pulled into a sitting position. They must be getting him up to dump him on the trolley and trundle him off to the morgue, I thought, and I looked up again at the beckoning stars.

I was shaken to hear a familiar voice beside me. It was the detective, who had abandoned me by not coming to get me tonight to let me ride around in his car and be safe. He put his hand under my arm and helped me up. I was surprised when he put his arm protectively around my shoulders. Somehow I'd thought he'd be angry with me.

I whispered to him, 'I got him. I got him before he got me.'

He said, 'I know. Come, let's go and look at him.' He moved police and ambulance officers out of our way, and drew me into the middle of the circle. As we got near I was shocked to hear the 'dead' man talking, to see him moving his shoulders and turning his head. We approached him from the back, and already a wave of apprehension was sweeping over me. In the lights from the torches held by the officers I could see that there was something different, different hair, different hair colour maybe, there was something wrong here. The back of his head was the wrong shape. My feet stopped moving but the detective still held on, pushing and guiding me around to show me the man's face. When he looked up at the sudden hush and our approach, I already knew the face I was going to see was not the one I expected to see. I had stabbed the wrong man.

I turned my face into the detective's coat and uncontrollable sobs shook my body. He steered me away and out to the street where his partner, someone I'd seen once before, was waiting behind the wheel. I crawled into my safe space in the back and we left.

I would have liked to have curled up and gone to sleep in the security of the police car, but the detective had other ideas. We pulled up instead at a restaurant which had a separate room at the back, and after passing a few words with the man behind the counter, he ushered me there. His partner remained at the counter, chatting, and eventually he came in carrying cups of tea.

I was grilled, though not harshly, about my activities that night and the reasons for my being where they'd found me. Towards the end of my story, the detective put his face down in his hands, his elbows on the table, and slowly shook his head from side to side. When I finished, he looked up.

'You didn't do much damage to the fellow. Superficial wound. You're lucky.'

I didn't feel lucky, I felt robbed. I had put in so much effort, and thought I'd been able to rid myself of the central cause of my pain and stress—only to find out that I hadn't been successful. The man was still alive, and still free to hunt me. I felt tired, too, as the long walk to the Institute had exhausted me because I hadn't been having much exercise recently. I could feel my eyes starting to close, but they opened again quickly when the detective snapped at me.

'They're going to say you're crazy, you know. We might have trouble keeping you here. I'll have to speak to the lad's parents, he's only young, and see if they want to press charges.'

Charges? I was surprised. It hadn't occurred to me that I'd done something wrong. I'd got the wrong person, and I was really sorry about that, but I was even sorrier that he hadn't been the right man. Then I wouldn't have been sorry, I would have been glad, and I said so.

They took me back to the boarding house, the detective going into the building first to make sure the right man wasn't laying in wait for me. He left me with a stern warning that I wasn't to move beyond the front door. It was now early in the morning, close to dawn, and it didn't take me long to drift back to sleep.

I don't know when that detective ever slept, because when I next opened my eyes it was because he was tapping on my door. It was afternoon, he said, and we were to talk. He was alone and we sat in the car.

'I hear rumours that "somebody up there" wants you examined. That little caper of yours last night got the wind up some people. Someone's already spoken to the chap's parents, and I don't think we're going to have any trouble there. We had to tell them a bit about your case and all this other stress you're under, with this crim out and about looking for you and so forth. I understand they were very upset to hear it. And their lad's okay, with just a few stitches and a pain in his side.

'But tongues are wagging upstairs. There's a very real possibility that someone thinks you should be committed. There's talk, too, that a hospital, right now, would be a safer place for you than this boarding house, you know what I mean? Someone's loading the dice.'

I didn't know what he meant actually. But I knew what 'committed' and 'hospital' meant. It meant being in a place like Broughton Hall in Charters Towers, which I'd visited as part of my training, and to where patients with very strange behaviour had been taken.

I let him finish talking.

'Now, my advice to you, and you can do with it as you like, but my advice to you is not to let them get to you. It'll do your case against these animals no good at all for these chaps' lawyers to be able to point their fingers and say to the jury that you can't tell what's real from what isn't. Everything you've told us up to this point has been solid. You've walked through the identifications, which are often the hardest part, the part where cases start coming apart at the seams. We've got one more thing we want you to do, and when you've done that, you can go home to your mother in Townsville. I think it's going to turn into a choice— either you go there, or you'll probably end up being put into a hospital here. We've already had dozens of letters from your mother, saying she wants you and will look after you. You were here to help us with the cases, and you've done that, or you've almost finished doing it. Just one more thing to do. Can you hang on?'

I wished he would give me an order, not ask me to make a decision. So, I just nodded. He took that to be the answer he wanted, and he went on to make arrangements based on what he thought I'd wanted. It was all the same to me.

Later that afternoon, another policeman came by and took me to a maze of a building where we seemed to walk for miles, ending up at a little desk with another man sitting behind it. It seemed as if that man was guarding a door. The officer with me signed some papers, got me to sign my name on a form, then we were let in. After the narrow corridors, the room we entered felt vast. A bench at about hip height ran across one wall. The officer now explained that he'd been told to show me some basic things about guns. From the briefcase he'd taken from the boot of the police car when we'd arrived, he pulled out a gun and began to explain something about it. I was startled as I'd not been told what to expect from this outing, and much of the first part of his talk was lost on me as I stared at the weapon. I don't recall what sort of weapon he said it was, and he went into a lot of technical details such as calibre bullets and so on. I then watched him load the gun with bullets. I already knew something about rifles from my holiday at Torrens Creek years before, when Reg and I had gone out after sheep, but my concentration on everything the officer was telling me was a bit scant. It kept running through my mind that this must be connected to the crim making threats against me, and I was confused, because I thought it couldn't be that they were going to give me a gun to replace the knife, which had been taken off me the previous night.

Eventually, I began to suspect that this was something which had been set up for me some time before, and that orders to cancel it hadn't made their way through the system.

The report from the shot was deafening, even through the earmuffs I'd been given to wear. The policeman fired all the bullets but one, then handed the gun to me. I shot the last one at the target in the distance, which he'd indicated to me. Then we left. The strong smell of burnt gunpowder lingered in my nostrils as we made our way back out to the car. The officer had been uncommunicative the whole time he was with me. He was either unfriendly towards me, or he didn't approve of the task he'd been given. The gun, which he'd returned to the briefcase and put into the boot, remained there when he dropped me home.

On my return, the boarding house manager gave me a message that I was to be ready to go out early next morning, and to bring a swimsuit if I had one. I slept soundly that night, wakened only slightly by a now-familiar torchlight being flashed around my room and the quiet click of the door closing. Generally, the detective made these checks on me himself, but occasionally someone else, perhaps his partner, was behind the beam.

In the morning, two young officers whom I hadn't seen before came to the front door. I was mystified, especially as we didn't speak until we had driven a good distance up the road.

The officers were pleased with the job they'd been given, they told me. They were taking me to the beach. I found it hard to believe, but couldn't think of any other reason why I'd been asked to bring my swimmers. Then they talked and laughed between themselves and gossiped about people they referred to by their initials.

It must have been more than an hour later—I nodded off now and again in the security of the car and the warmth of the sun streaming in through the windows—that we pulled up at an almost deserted beach. There were few houses about, and no other cars where we parked. They left me alone to change into my swimmers in the car, while they walked a little way along the sand. When I opened the door and climbed out, my shirt over my togs, they returned and took off their shoes and socks and put them in the boot. Then it was my turn to walk along the sand while they changed into shorts. I was glad. I'd thought how strange we'd look with them sitting beside me, guarding me, fully dressed on the beach.

The three of us went for a long walk along the water's edge, seeing only occasional figures in the distance, and they talked a bit about the sort of music they liked, films they'd seen, scenes from films which had stayed in their minds, funny lines from cartoons, everything except anything serious, and they kept trying to draw me into their conversation. But mainly we just walked along in silence. Then they took out sandwiches and soft drinks from the boot for our lunch.

Afterwards, I lay down on my towel, and they promised to wake me if I started to get sunburnt. I was already brown as a dark berry from having grown up in the sun in North Queensland, so we had a bit of a laugh about the differences in our tans.

The whole day stood out as separate from the rest of my life. It was the detective's day off and he'd organised it. I don't know if the two officers were supposed to be assessing whether I was crazy or not, it didn't feel like it to me. After my nap, we walked along the beach a little way in the opposite direction to the path we'd taken that morning. The tide had changed and they picked up little shells and other flotsam and jetsam from the shore. I was sorry when they said it was time for us to get going. On the way back, they laughed and joked that this was the hardest day's work they'd been given since joining the force, and how they hoped they'd be given such a hard job again.

When they dropped me at the boarding house, I felt like we were good mates, but I never saw them again. On their departure they told me I had to be ready to go out again the next morning, but that they wouldn't be the ones coming for me.

The sun and fresh sea air had stimulated my appetite, and that evening I had the first halfway hearty meal I'd had in months. I opened several of my cans, instead of just one, and made myself a concoction.

But instead of sleeping soundly, I was plagued again with bad dreams. It seemed that the day had served to heighten the difference between how I thought life should be—safe, out in the open and carefree—and how it really was for me. By morning, I had sunk back into my depression.

The detective and one of his partners came to fetch me, and we drove to an outer suburb. He kept asking me to say if I saw anything familiar. We pulled off the main road and travelled on tarred side roads, where a farm house could be glimpsed through the trees occasionally. Then we turned off onto a dirt road. I looked around but nothing appeared familiar.

Eventually, the car drove onto a rough path, travelled a few hundred yards and stopped. When we got out, I thought we were stretching our legs. I looked around and could see an old dilapidated building in the distance. Suddenly, I felt hot and cold, and leaned over because I thought I was going to be sick. I knew why they'd brought me here.

They were watching me, and when they saw that I'd made the connection, we walked single file through the bush to the shed. It seemed to be in worse shape than I'd remembered. In my nightmares it had also grown much bigger, and, even though it made me sick, I felt a sense of reassurance when I saw it in broad daylight, as it seemed to bring it, and the people, back to a size I could cope with in my mind.

The detectives had me go over whatever I could remember: where the cars had been parked, where I'd stood, where I'd woken up. We retraced my steps as far as the gate, with them making notes as we went along, then we got in the car and drove out. We had arrived from a different direction, and I showed them first where I'd walked to the road, then the direction of the milk truck and the route I thought the market gardener had taken.

The detective asked me why I hadn't gone straight to the farm house we passed on the way to the tarred road. I told him about the dogs barking, and even as we paused at the driveway, we heard them again. They sounded further away than they had on that night, but he still seemed satisfied with the answer.

The property on which the shed stood, he said, belonged to an uncle of one of the men they had arrested. When the police questioned the man in custody he told them about the shed and had taken them to it.

On the way home, I looked out the window and blanked my mind as I felt very close to the edge. I was relieved when the detective said he would make arrangements for me to travel back to Townsville. Mum had even offered to come down on the train and get me. But he thought I'd probably be able, and happier, to make the journey alone.

I didn't ask whether or not they had re-captured the offender out on bail, and since the random night visits continued, I assumed that he was free. This meant, of course, that I was still the prisoner, unable to walk out on the streets alone, day or night.

I didn't tell the detective that I would like to see Aunty Glad before I left, although I knew Mum would ask me if I had, because I felt that I'd already been a lot of trouble to everyone. The whole process had taken months, and it wouldn't end until I got on that train. Even then I wouldn't know if it was really over. Would it ever be really over?

A few more nights of cruising around in the back of the police car, sitting alone in the dark while the detective and his partner responded to calls, went into houses and questioned people, and even picked up cartons of beer and parcels of big fish, which they stowed away in the boot. I'd wake up at times and sit up to find that we were driving slowly and quietly, the lights out, and I'd whisper, 'Who are we looking for?'

'Two youths, milk money thieves, stealing from their neighbours,' was the reply once. Another time it was, 'Anybody we find, we've got no description on this one. Break and enter. Keep your eyes peeled. Speak up if you see anything move.'

The detective took me to the train himself. He had come by the day before to tell me that Mum had made an inquiry about abortion some time ago, and that a magistrate was considering the request. I hated being reminded that I was pregnant. When I wasn't forced to talk about it, I was able to ignore it, as I ignored everything else. No one had told me to go to the hospital for more tests or anything, so I was receiving no medical care. Perhaps all official concern had been directed at the pursuit of the criminals, or maybe they thought I knew that I was supposed to be getting medical attention and had decided not to seek it out.

Either way, this conversation about abortion was an alarming reminder that things weren't going to sort themselves out when I got home. For me, at least, it wouldn't be all over.

'From my wife's reckoning,' the detective said, 'you're over four months pregnant. By the time you get home, and they get the paperwork done, you'll be five months. The risk to your own life at that advanced stage would be great, even if you had the abortion the day you received the court order. If I were you, I wouldn't go through with it. That's my advice and my wife's advice, and she knows about these things.'

There were no female officers in the Queensland Police Force at this time, no rape crisis centres. So, as the only contact I'd been allowed was with the police, it had all been with males. I don't know if there'd been some tacit agreement not to discuss pregnancy with me, but I doubted it. Instead I thought that it was just men's way not to bring up anything of a very personal nature.

I didn't respond to the detective's attempt to open this discussion, but he continued regardless.

'It was wise of you not to have sought out an abortion yourself, they're illegal, you know.'

I didn't know. In fact, since I'd been in deep denial about the very nature of the conception and about the pregnancy itself, the notion that I might have even considered a termination was somehow shocking to me. I'd

heard of them, of course, at Charters Towers Hospital—
'dilation and curettage, D & C'—but this was an
abstract concept for me.

'I think your mother might still have some ideas in
that direction herself, and if she suggests it to you,
you'd be wise to tell her it's illegal. You hear?'

Yes, I heard. But every word seemed like a nail being
driven into my coffin. My desire for relief from this
nightmare, this situation not of my own creation, kept
blood hammering through my head. His talk, which he
probably regarded as fatherly advice, served only to
make real my nightmares. When I couldn't stand him
talking any more, I wept. He then put his arm around
my shoulder and pressed me to his side.

'You're a good girl. You're a strong girl. You've
already been stronger than any of us thought you could
be. You're even stronger than you think you are. It's
been a real pleasure working with you.'

His words made little sense to me. I was a snivelling
weak person who couldn't get through an entire day,
barely even an hour, without tears streaming down my
face, no matter how hard I tried. I cried when I was
alone, I cried when people were trying to talk to me. He
was just trying to cheer me up, I concluded.

He continued to be there for me, patting at his pockets and asking me if I had enough money for food on
the train, and carrying my suitcase. He'd keep in touch
through the Townsville Police, he said. They wouldn't
be like him, he added, but they weren't too bad, I ought
to start liking them.

11

Mum met me at the station when the train pulled in at about six in the morning. Although I'd slept almost all the way, for one day and two nights, I still didn't have my wits about me. Mum looked more tired and a bit more haggard than when I last saw her. As I hauled my suitcase through the narrow door of the Sunlander, I realised her eyes were full of tears.

'My,' she said as she approached me with downcast eyes, 'they're real bone buttons!'

I looked at her and saw that her gaze was fastened on the buttons of the blouse I was wearing—one I had bought with one of my early pays from the Golden Circle factory.

'It's second hand, I got it from a used-clothes shop.'

'You didn't need to have second-hand clothes, Roberta. If you'd written and asked me, I would have sent you money for a new one. But they're lovely buttons!'

I knew she was referring to her willingness to have sent me money during the last three months, and I didn't have the heart to say that I'd bought the blouse long before then.

Mum was getting on for sixty years old, but still she tried to drag my suitcase from my hand so she could carry it herself. Arthur was waiting a little further down the platform, and he hurried up and took it from both of us.

When we were in the car Mum said, 'I've got a surprise for you. I bought a new house.'

This 'new' house again wasn't new. We passed through Hermit Park, close by where we used to live, and continued right on out of town. We began to pass fields and long grass bordered parts of the road.

'Where are we going?'

'You'll see,' chirped Mum. 'It's not far now.'

We made a right-hand turn and pulled off onto a side road. The few houses stood on very large blocks of land, and some sites had nothing on them but scraggly grass. A left turn a short way down that street, and we were on an even smaller road.

'Where are we?'

'Aitkenvale.'

The house was smaller than the Norris Street house, but similarly perched on typical North Queensland stilts. It had one main bedroom and two smaller ones, which came off the loungeroom. My piano stood in the corner of the lounge. Mum had Arthur put my suitcase in the main bedroom.

I turned and asked Mum, 'Where do you sleep?'

'I've put you in the big room because I want you to be comfortable,' she rushed towards me, her arms outstretched, 'you poor little thing.'

'Mum, don't do this.' I took a step backwards.

She composed herself and we continued our walk

through the house. Kitchen on the left, directly behind the room she had given me, a large enclosed verandah room in which sat the old dining table and wooden chairs which Mum obviously carried with her from house to house, and the bathroom to the right. As was expected of me, I walked to the bathroom door and peered in. Mum stood behind me, waiting for a comment, an approval of some description.

Close to the bathroom was a toilet, but I could hardly see it for the boxes and cartons which had been stacked all about it.

'Well, the house was somewhere else, closer to town, and then it was moved out here and put up on these poles. This is too far out of town to have sewerage, the pipes don't reach out here. So we use this room for storage.' Mum was smiling, she obviously thought this made our location very quaint.

My eyebrows shot up. 'So where's the toilet?'

'Down in the yard. We have night soil pans and they're collected twice a week.'

She raced off to the kitchen to put the kettle on, and I sat down at the table and rested my head on my arms. Arthur had gone downstairs and was pottering around under the house, staying out of the way, probably giving us time to say whatever needed to be said.

Mum returned with the teapot and cups. She sat down with me at the table while the tea brewed.

'Roberta, I bought this house for you. You're going to want privacy and you don't want to have to have your baby under prying eyes. You can see, there's hardly anyone out here.' She sounded so proud of herself.

Tears flowed again from my eyes at the sound of my future. Mum patted me on the shoulder. 'There, there, dear. You're home now. We're going to make sure you get everything you need.'

Nobody could give me everything I need, I thought. I need to go back to four months ago and say no when Josie asks me for my cash. No, this isn't Josie's fault, this is my fault for being so stupid and ugly. I need to go back and say no when I'm asked if I want a lift. I need the chance to walk all the way to Chermside, or to sit on a tram stop for a few hours, waiting for the early morning trams.

'You're just tired from your long trip, dear. Drink up this nice cup of tea and then go in and have a nice rest. Arthur?' she raised her voice to call, 'Tea's made. Come in and have a cup.'

I couldn't stand to sit around and play happy families, so I said I had to take a shower, I'd not had a shower for two days now, and the train trip had made me feel gritty.

'Well, you go right ahead, dear. When you come out, we'll be gone. We have to go to work now. I arranged to start a bit later this morning, I'm still at the Central Hotel, so you'll know where I am. I'll be back as soon as I get through. Will you be okay?'

I felt that I would never be okay ever again, but I nodded and went in to get pyjamas and toothbrush out of my suitcase.

I woke up hours later, startled to find myself somewhere I didn't recognise, and to the sounds of dishes and plates being moved around in the kitchen. I briefly wondered where my sisters were, since neither of them had been at the house when I'd arrived in the morning.

Mum came to the door, a small tray in her hand.

'I've made you a nice cup of tea, and I noticed you haven't even been in the kitchen so I made you a sandwich too. Vegemite. You need iron. You look so rundown. I'll make you a good solid meal later, when Arthur comes home from work.'

The course of least resistance with Mum was to eat whatever she put in front of you.

'Where're the kids?'

'Oh, Leonie's at school, and Dellie's at work. They both go off early in the morning.'

I ate the sandwich and promptly went back to sleep. Some time later Mum came to the door again.

'Dinner's ready. Everyone's home. Do you want to eat with us or would you rather have a tray brought in?'

I wanted to put off having to talk to anyone, and opted for the tray. Leonie brought it in, staring at me, her eyes huge, as though she didn't quite know who I was or what was the matter with me. I wasn't hungry and merely picked over the food. Mum came back and tried to spoon feed me the vegetables; she said I had to build up my strength.

'Tomorrow,' I said, and waved her away.

'I'll be back in to talk to you as soon as the washing up's done, so don't bother going back to sleep. There's a lot we have to sort out.'

'There's nothing to sort out that won't wait until tomorrow,' and I put my head down and crashed out again.

Mum began to worry after a few days—I slept all the time. Sometimes during the day she'd come tearing in to find me sitting up in bed, sweating and trembling. 'You were screaming,' she'd say, 'are you alright?'

No, I wasn't alright, but I couldn't talk to her about the demons that had started visiting me in my dreams—ugly figures with hard faces and short bodies.

Mum said that she had talked to Dr Ward, our old

family doctor, and that she was taking me to see him on the following Monday.

Dr Ward was a kindly soul, by now grey-haired, but he and Mum talked about me as though I wasn't sitting in the room with them. I didn't want to have to talk with anyone, but I resented them talking and making arrangements about me. Their conversation was in a sort of shorthand, leading me to believe that they had already had several discussions about me.

'An abortion, well, it's possible, even at this late date, but it's dangerous. I don't think that's the way for her to go.'

'Yes, I agree with you, Doctor. But I understand there are papers coming up now, a court-ordered abortion, which she might want to consider.'

'Vitamins. She needs vitamins. I'll give you a list of some things to get for her. She's very underweight, but I'm sure now she's home, you'll be looking after that.' And finally, to me, 'Just hop up on that couch, Roberta, so I can examine you. And you could step outside, if you would, please, Mrs Patterson.'

When Mum returned after the physical examination, they started again.

'The baby could be put out for adoption. But, of course, you know the orphanage is full of coloured children. Nobody wants them, poor little things.'

'Yes,' replied Mum, 'and we'll have to think about that when her time comes.'

It was obvious to me that they were going to make all the decisions for me, a situation I felt I had no control over, even if I wanted to.

'She's asleep all the time, Doctor. That isn't normal, is it?'

'Her situation isn't normal, Mrs Patterson. No doubt

she's having some sort of mental problem, which is not surprising in her situation. But I'm not an expert on that. You're to see that she gets half an hour of exercise every day. Outside. She needs to walk in the fresh air for half an hour each day. I can make an appointment for her to see a psychiatrist if you like.'

'No, I'm sure that won't be necessary, Doctor. She's just sleeping all the time. You're right, she probably just needs the rest.'

As we were leaving, Dr Ward said to Mum, 'Bring her back immediately if she has any problems. Otherwise, I'll see her in four weeks, and after that every two weeks, and in the last month, every week. There'll be no cost. It's the least I can do.'

'No,' said Mum, 'we can pay. I'd rather pay. I appreciate the thought, but have the nurse draw up a schedule of payments.'

Arthur was waiting outside to drive me home. Mum, when she arrived home that afternoon, woke me to show me a few pieces of fabric she had bought.

'I'm going to make you a couple of blouses, big loose tops that gather in just below the hip. Everyone's wearing them now, they're the latest style. And then you'll be able to walk in the street like anybody.'

When I woke up there were two big blouses hanging up on a peg on the wall. I immediately hated them with a vengeance.

Mum also took me to a dentist. 'Babies sap all your calcium. You have to lose a tooth with each pregnancy so the baby can have all the calcium it needs.'

She and the dentist decided which tooth they were going to pull, and Mum waited outside while the dentist yanked it out. The physical pain was somehow a relief to me, as, for a few hours anyway, it gave me something to think about other than the pain which was in my head and in my heart.

For the next three months I slept, fighting demons and nightmares, waking in the night crying, my pillow soaked with tears. Grief kept me choked up much of the time.

Dellie, at fifteen, had a job at Woolworths Supermarket and was the first coloured person to be employed by them in Townsville. She started as a shelf packer, but soon impressed her bosses with her intelligence and charm, and they trained her to work on the checkout, dealing directly with the public. This was a real coup.

She also had a boyfriend, and Mum was delighted. She didn't want all her daughters turning into 'old maids', she said. She was going to let her get engaged when she turned sixteen.

Arthur was still involved with the soccer teams, and players sometimes came and sat around the house waiting for him. Leonie was learning to be a coach, which pleased Mum very much. 'The number of young lads who want to play soccer has more than doubled since Leonie started showing up on the field,' she told me proudly. Leonie was thirteen. She and her friends became used to what Leonie called my 'ghosting', as I quietly appeared and disappeared on my occasional rounds between my bed and the outside toilet.

'One of the players wants to take you to the pictures,' Mum said when she woke me for our afternoon walk around the block. 'Have a rest and then get ready. He'll be here just after six. He'll take you on the six-forty bus into town.'

George Dean, a tall newly arrived Englishman with

short cropped hair, arrived that evening. Mum pushed me out the door with him, whispering to me that I wasn't to be rude. 'Talk to him,' she said, 'and don't go on with any more of your sulkiness.'

George came every week for a few weeks, and when we arrived at the theatre I'd put my head on his shoulder and go to sleep. The bus we caught back to the house was the last run, the 'picture bus'. Mum would give him a cup of tea and then he would trot off into the night, running all the way back to his home in town. 'Good exercise, keeps me fit for soccer,' he told us, as he bolted off.

One day, after my appointment with Dr Ward, Mum said she wanted us to have a cup of tea and a talk before she put me on the bus to go home. She'd bought a cot, she said, and it would be delivered that afternoon. But that wasn't the good news, she added. The good news was that George Dean had asked her if he could marry me!

'And what did you say?' I inquired, shocked that such a puzzling thing could have happened and I knew nothing about it.

'Well,' said Mum, 'I told him you were having a baby. He hadn't noticed, you see. Your little stick legs and arms are so deceptive, and although the doctor says you're going okay, you seem to be carrying the baby so far towards the back that you don't look pregnant at all, especially in the blouses I made for you. Anyway, he said it didn't matter, that he'd look after the child as though it were his own. And he's coming out this afternoon to talk to you about it too.'

I got up and walked out, caught the bus home and climbed back into bed. Some of the nightmares I was having didn't seem half as bad as some of the things that were really happening around me.

The cot arrived soon after I'd gone to bed, and I called out to the man just to leave it on the verandah. A few hours later, George Dean arrived, and when I got up to open the door, I could tell from the shock on his face that, until he saw that cot standing there, he hadn't really believed my mother.

I told him that Mum would be home soon and he could talk to her. Then I left him sitting in the lounge room and went back to bed.

When she came home from work, Mum came in and shook me. 'Get up. Get up this minute. That poor man's sitting out there, breaking his heart to speak to you, and you won't even get out of bed to talk to him.'

I put my walking-around-the-block clothes on, as Mum suggested, and George and I walked around the block. 'No, George, I won't marry you. I'm sorry. I'm grateful, but no, I don't love you, in fact, I don't care about anything or anyone right now.'

'But you'll grow to. I'll look after you. I'll do everything for you. You'll never want for a thing. I'm making good money, and in a short time we could afford a home. I'll buy you a ring. We can get married now, before the baby arrives, and everyone will think it's mine. I don't mind. Actually, it would be great.'

'I'm sorry. I don't think you know how sick I am of everything. Please go away and leave me alone.'

Mum was furious. A perfectly good man, she said, and not only had I let him get away but I'd *sent* him away. Did I have any idea how hard it is to find a good husband? One who wouldn't beat me up? One who would agree to take on a bastard child? Didn't I have any sense?

My afternoon walks became an ordeal, with Mum seizing them as an opportunity to give me 'a good lecture'. 'Somebody has to talk sense to you, Roberta. You seem to have lost all the brains you used to have.'

It was time for me to snap out of it, she said over and over. My gloom was affecting the whole house. I had to stop thinking about myself and think of others. 'Think about your poor sisters, they're hardly game to raise their voices in their own house. They're only young, and they don't know what's going on. Leonie even asked me if you were dying.

'And think of this baby you've got coming. This little mite hasn't done you any harm. You start taking an interest in it, you hear!'

She bought more fabric and began sewing tiny baby's clothes. She bought fancy-work cottons and told me I had to spend half an hour every day embroidering them. She ironed transfers of little flowers on the tops of the dresses and nightgowns and gave them to me to sew. To avoid her wrath I stitched one. When she came home from work and saw that the little flowers were all black and the leaves a dark blue, she scolded me and took all the dark coloured cottons away and hid them in her room.

She bought nappies in packets of a dozen, and layettes, and crotcheted bootees. She laid all these things out in a cupboard in my room. She bought a new mattress for the second-hand cot and sewed small sheets and a mosquito net, and when she thought it looked wonderful, she put it in my room too.

My dreams grew worse, nightmares often linked together, one hot on the heels of another. The same grotesque figures popped up in most of them, and I even began to become familiar with these demons:

I am sitting on the floor of a deep canyon. I know it's deep because I can see a fair way up the walls and there is no light anywhere. The air is full of agony. The agony manifests itself in sounds, awful sounds which go on relentlessly.

Near me, a demon is sitting on a rock. He is wearing nothing but he's very hairy, and the skin on his round face is somehow layered in folds. His teeth are stained. He's talking to me but I have my hands over my ears. I can tell he is getting angry; evil eyes—the eyes I remember so well from my living nightmare—begin to strain out of his head.

I jump up and try to scale the wall in order to escape. Pieces of shale rain down on me as I scramble and claw at the rockface. I reach a very narrow ledge and perch there, crouched and making myself as small as I can so that I can't be seen. From somewhere behind me I hear dogs, big dogs, barking and baying and gnashing their teeth.

A whooshing sound from above captures my attention. A large piece of rock has dislodged from the wall and is plummeting towards me. It is growing larger and larger as it hurtles down, and it feels as if there is nothing I can do to get out of its path.

Sometimes I woke up here, but at other time the dream continues:

As it passes, the rock knocks me from the wall, somehow damaging my left shoulder and heart.

The floor from which I'd scrambled has gone, and I'm falling now, faster and deeper. There is no point in crying out, I somehow know, because nobody's going to help me. I pass other people, who seem also to be squatting on tiny ledges. They watch me fall with their big eyes.

I look down at myself and see that my heart has dislodged from my body. It is falling at the same speed,
still tied to me by thick cords which keep us together. I
grab it and feel it pulsing. It feels awful, sticky yet slip-
pery. I try to push it back into my chest, but it slides
around in my fingers.

I suddenly know I'm a goner, and give myself over to
death. As soon as I have this realisation I feel peaceful,
my arms and legs stop thrashing around trying to stop
my fall, and instead of falling I'm floating.

The demon laughs, a fearful sound, just below me.
He is standing with his arms outstretched, waiting to
catch me. I'm unable to stop myself floating down
directly into his arms and I scream, 'No, no', in an effort
to avoid this contact. Death I don't mind, but him I do.

Mum continued to scold, nag and lecture me during my
every waking moment. I almost didn't mind this, however, because it was a break from the dreams. From
somewhere in her past, Mum recalled that scrubbing
floors on your hands and knees was a good exercise to
strengthen the muscles for childbirth. My afternoon
walks were reduced to twenty minutes, followed by ten
minutes of scrubbing. Mum prepared soapy buckets of
water and told me which patch of the floor to scrub
each day.

Arthur became solicitous, asking me if there was
anything I wanted to eat. He was concerned about how
thin I was, even though Mum continued to force food
on me that she said I had to eat, such as carrots, pumpkin, spinach and liver. She mashed them so as to conceal any flavours I objected to, and made fried patties
out of the ingredients I said I detested. When invited
by Arthur to nominate something I *would* like to eat, I

found I hankered for prawns. Later, when he heard me stir in my room, even at midnight, he'd get up and go out in the car to wake up the fishmonger and bring home a parcel of prawns. The fishmonger, who lived above his shop, didn't mind, Arthur said, because he knew about 'women's cravings'.

Mum's delight at the approaching baby was so thick that people began to say that they thought she was acting as if she was having a baby herself. At the same time, my displeasure at her constant scolding about what pregnant women should and shouldn't do, coupled with my inability to articulate my problems and the horrors going on in my mind, caused me to seek bizarre forms of relief. If I was awake in the afternoon when Mum was due home from work, I would put my hands around my throat and squeeze until I fell into unconsciousness. After one such episode, Mum became furious when she noticed bruises on my neck. So, from then on, I experimented with locating the exact points on which to put pressure to gain the same effect.

The blackouts usually only lasted a few minutes, but they left me dazed, which was sort of euphoric. I welcomed the spinning lights in my head, a vortex into which I could disappear, no dreams, no reality. I kept hoping that I wouldn't recover from them, that by some accident my heart would just stop and all the pain would be over.

Dellie's sixteenth birthday-cum-engagement party was drawing near, and the house became a hive of activity. Food and soft drinks were brought in by the bootload, and it sounded as if the entire soccer team had come to string fairy lights up in the garden. I stayed in bed.

On the Friday before the party, I had to make my now weekly visit to Dr Ward. Mum told him that the court hearings in Brisbane had been put on hold until after I'd given birth, as I was too weak and too close to time to travel. When she shared this information with him, I momentarily wondered how she kept abreast with what was happening in regard to the police proceedings, and why she told the doctor rather than me.

He explained to Mum that this would be my last visit. He would see me at the hospital before the week was out. She left me at the bus stop in the main street to catch a bus back to Aitkenvale, and she said that if I felt anything between then and when she arrived home from work, I was to call out to a neighbour who would ring her at work. Mum, of course, still had no phone.

While I was waiting for the bus, I was delighted to see my dear friend Jeannie from years ago. She was very obviously pregnant, and because I knew her to be non-judgemental, I told her that I was too. I walked with her down the street a little and would have gone further, even to her home, had she indicated I would be welcome to tag along. Instead, she seemed anxious to get rid of me, although she'd been pleased when we'd first spotted each other. I thought she must have been meeting some guy who she didn't want me to see.

When I left her I walked to the next bus stop where I ran into yet another friend from the past—my old dancing partner with whom I'd won jive competitions, Renata.

She was pleased to see me, and said, 'I'd heard you were back in town. There's even been a rumour that you're pregnant. It's because of that blouse you've got on. Come out, come out with me tonight. Let's wear our dancing gear again. God, I've missed you.'

We chatted briefly and when I walked away I realised I was lonely. The isolation Mum had established for me by buying the house at Aitkenvale had served its purpose very well.

When she arrived home, Mum came into my room and said that she was putting Leonie in to sleep with me in the double bed from now on.

To my protests she replied, 'If you think I want to wake up one morning and find you've had the baby in there all by yourself, you're mistaken. I know you, my girl, and I wouldn't put that past you at all!'

I still didn't believe that a real baby was going to be the end product of all this discomfort, and I hadn't made any arrangements. Mum packed a little suitcase from a list Dr Ward's office must have given her, and left it by the door of my room.

The next day was a blur of noise and comings and goings. Mum was screaming out orders, tinting her hair while ensuring that all the plates and cups which she kept packed in the upstairs toilet were washed, dried, and put on tables under the house. She tried to interest me in cutting crepe paper into streamers, but I refused to come out of my room.

There was a lull in the evening as friends who'd been helping around the house all day went home to get dressed for the big occasion. Mum said I was to get out of my pyjamas, put on a smock, and sit in her bedroom where I could watch the festivities from the window. When I baulked, she said the real reason she wanted me to sit there was so that she could keep her eye on me from the garden.

In Mum's bedroom I put my head down on the sill and went to sleep, unfazed by the music that blasted out from the speakers in the yard. I was woken by the presence of a man standing in the doorway. He startled me because I didn't know him. He introduced himself as 'Skip' and asked if I was alright, why didn't I join the party?

Shortly after he left, Mum came upstairs and told me that the oldies were going to Aitkenvale Hotel for a drink, and to let the young people enjoy themselves for a while. They were only going for an hour and I was to come along with her.

Her's and Arthur's cronies were all there, and we sat in a big circle in the beer garden. I was put into a soft lounge chair so that I'd be comfortable. Skip was amongst them, although he didn't look as though he was even legal drinking age yet. He seemed to make it a point to sit near me.

A waiter delivering a full tray of drinks walked past the back of my chair and stumbled, accidently hurtling his load of glasses and beer onto me. Everyone gasped as beer soaked through my hair and clothes instantly. I tried to get up, but was so advanced in my pregnancy that I was clumsy, heavy and awkward, and fell back into the chair. Skip raced away and got towels from the bar, but nothing could remove the sharp stench of beer which filled my nostrils and made me nauseated. The drinking session was cut short as Arthur took me home.

I showered immediately but the smell remained. The odour of beer was one of the strongest associations I had with the night of my nightmare. I screamed out and wept so much all night, as I struggled with the demons and flashbacks evoked by the incident, that Mum had Leonie move back into her own bed and leave me alone.

Everybody spent the following day clearing up. Dellie was proudly showing off her engagement ring and musing over the gifts she'd received, working out whether they were meant as birthday or engagement gifts, or a combination of both. Her fiance, she told me, was entitled to regard half the engagement gifts as his own, so it was important for her to sort this out.

Over the next few days, Mum wouldn't let me be alone for more than a few minutes. If things went on this way, I thought, my sisters would be rostered to accompany me to and from the toilet. In all these months I hadn't shared anything with them, either about what had happened in Brisbane or what I was going through now. When I was around they stared at me warily, until they became involved in a conversation of their own which took their attention from me.

I was sitting on the front verandah with the two girls on the floor playing at some game when Leonie looked up at me, watched for a moment, then yelled, 'Mum, Mum, you'd better come.'

I was surprised by her call because nothing was the matter with me, apart from a twingy backache which I had from sitting upright on the wooden chair. Mum came and stood beside me.

'Got pain?'

'No.'

She remained standing there for a few minutes. I was watching the girls play and thinking that as soon as Mum saw for herself that everything was normal she'd go back inside. Again the discomfort fluttered across my spine.

'That's it, Roberta,' Mum said, as I twisted slightly.

'No, Mum, that's not it. There's nothing happening at all, I'm just uncomfortable on the chair.'

'Well, you're going to have to be uncomfortable on a chair up at the maternity ward.' She raised her voice,

'Arthur, come out and drive this child up to the hospital.'

Dellie and Leonie leapt up and began dancing and chanting. 'We're going to have a baby. Oh, goody, we're going to have a baby.'

I was disgusted, and glad to get away from them. Mum accompanied us in the car, rushing ahead when we arrived to give the nurse my name and details. The nurse called the sister, and they consulted a chart and began nodding their heads and whispering. I heard them say Dr Ward's name.

I was taken into a room and helped to change into a hospital robe, then taken into another room and told to lie down for a while. A clock on the wall said it was twenty minutes to five in the afternoon. A nurse sat beside me with her fob watch on her chain. The sister came, rubbed my arm and said she was going to give me a very small needle. Almost as soon as she had done so, the hands on th clock ceemed to jump to five-thirty, and I could see it only mistily through my tears. I heard their voices as they talked, 'Dr Ward said he's coming immediately. She's to feel nothing. You stay with her, Nurse, that's all you have to do.' I drifted off again and remember very little.

I woke up surrounded by white—white ceiling, white curtains, white sheets. My hands fumbled onto my stomach and encountered a wide elastic binder of some description. My stomach was still raised and I thought, 'Oh, a false alarm. Mum will be mad at me.'

A wardsmaid woke me again when she brought a plate of soup on a tray. I sat up, took two or three sips, which were enough, and slid back down again.

Through a chink left in the curtains by the wardsmaid's entry I could see beds diagonally across from me. Women sat up in them, and nurses hurried back and forth handing babies wrapped in bunny rugs out here and there. I briefly wondered why I'd been put in this ward to wait for my labour to begin when everyone else here had already had their babies. I turned over and went back to sleep.

Voices talking just beyond the curtain in sharp but hushed tones woke me.

'Has she asked to see her baby yet, Nurse?'

'No.'

'Doctor said she's not to be given the baby until she asks.'

Who was this strange woman they were talking about who didn't even want to see her baby after all the trouble she'd gone through in having it, I thought, and drifted comfortably back to sleep.

'Mrs Patterson.' I opened my eyes, someone was calling my mum. A sister stood at the foot of my bed.

'Mum's not here,' I answered groggily because she was looking at me. 'I'm Miss Patterson, her daughter.'

'We call everyone here "Mrs",' she told me archly, her voice loaded with meaning.

'Your doctor gave instructions to bring your child only when you asked for it,' she continued. 'But a whole day's gone by and you haven't asked. Visitors will be here soon, and I thought I'd give you the opportunity. You can say no if you want.'

'Have I had the baby?' I replied.

'Does that mean yes?'

'What was it? What's the baby?'

'A son. You have a fine son.'

'Oh, oh yes. Bring him. I'll see him.'

She walked away briskly and soon returned with a bundle which she placed across my knees. I'd hauled myself into a sitting position, the better to look at what appeared to be a present. A very small sleeping face lay at the top of the bundle, just visible from the folds of the bunny rug.

'Can I open it?' I asked.

'He's yours, Mrs Patterson. You can do as you like with him,' she said, and brushed her way out through the curtains.

Between the wider gap she had left, I could see women peering across at me. They were silent. I suddenly thought that they were worried that I might dash the child to the floor.

I drew the bundle up onto my stomach and began to unwrap it. A small wrinkled arm, and then another, emerged. I counted the fingers on each hand to make sure none were missing. Then opened the rest of the wrapper and counted the toes. I saw a wide strip across the child's stomach and realised this was covering his cord. I was too afraid to pick him up in case I hurt him, so I just unpinned his nappy and peered in to make sure the sister had told me the truth about the child being a boy.

A boy. I wrapped him up again with a feeling of satisfaction. At least here was something I'd done right. The child had all his fingers and toes, and even a great swack of hair on his head. I sat waiting for the nurse to come and take him away again, after I'd assured myself that he had arrived with all his pieces intact.

As the nurse's rubber-soled shoes approached, squeaking towards me on the highly polished floor, I heard a woman's voice say to her in hushed tones, 'Nurse, she didn't even hold her baby.'

Tears sprang into my eyes. If somebody had told me what it was I had to do, I thought as the nurse removed the bundle, I'd have done it. Never mind, I'll do it next time.

Just a few minutes later the curtains were drawn back a little and Mum and Arthur came crowding in. Mum looked anxious.

'You're supposed to be in a private room. I paid for a private room. The sister said all the private rooms were full, and they had to put you here. Are you alright?'

'Yes, Mum.'

Her face brightened. 'Here's some fruit for you, and a milk chocolate bar. You're to eat them all up, you hear! You've had a son, have you seen him? Have you put him to the breast?'

Put him to the breast? What was she talking about? How was I supposed to have 'put him to the breast'?

I looked shocked. Mum patted my hand. 'It doesn't matter,' she said kindly. 'I'm sure they're feeding him alright. I'll just go and look. Come on, Arthur.' She steered him out and as he passed through the gap in the curtains, he looked back at me with a very pleased expression on his face.

This whole event had been a new experience for him, and when they returned from the Baby Viewing window, he was beaming.

Mum pulled a magazine out of her bag and put it on the bed. 'We've got to go. Dellie and Leonie are in the car, children aren't allowed in, you know. As soon as you see Dr Ward, you tell him you want that child circumcised.'

I was still flicking through the magazine when Dr Ward walked in. He pulled the curtains closed and bent over me, speaking softly. 'How are you, Roberta?'

'I'm fine, thank you.'

'Well, you've had a healthy son, and as you know, your mother has decided you're to keep him.' I knew nothing of the sort, but I suppose I should have guessed from all the arrangements she'd been making at home. Still, I was surprised that something like this could have been decided without my ever being a party to the consent.

'Mum said he's to be circumcised,' I said, grasping at something to say to sound knowledgeable.

'He doesn't need it. They're not done automatically anymore, and he doesn't need it. You'll have to start thinking of a name for him soon.'

I couldn't argue about the circumcision because I didn't know what this conversation between the doctor and my mother, via me, was all about.

'Yes,' I said, in answer to whatever it was he was asking me. Whatever he said, I'd agree with. It seemed safer that way.

Next morning a nurse came to my bed and said that Dr Ward had given instructions for the baby to be bottle fed, but I could feed him the bottle if I wanted. They were going to give me some pills to dry up my milk.

'Okay. Yes.' There seemed to be no choice left to me in all the decisions that were being made, and I felt too insignificant in the process, and too ignorant of the details, to be involved anyway. The nurse showed me how to hold the baby and put the bottle in his mouth. It just felt as if I was feeding a baby for someone else. He drank it all, then gnawed on his fingers until the nurse came to take him away.

I was surprised the next day when a visitor arrived during the afternoon. It was Skip, the young man who'd come to see me during the party, and who'd sat beside me when the tray of beer was accidentally dropped on my head. Could it have been only four or five days earlier? It felt like a hundred years.

He was clutching a gift for the baby and wearing an extremely embarrassed look on his face.

'I went out to your house looking for you, and they told me you were here. I couldn't believe it. You didn't look at all like you were having a baby. But when I thought about it on the way in, I remembered you couldn't jump up out of the chair. At the pub, remember?'

Now it was my turn to be embarrassed at being discovered in the maternity hospital.

'What do you want? What are you doing here?'

He looked around, pulled a chair around from the other side of the bed and sat down. He put his hand over mine on the cover.

'You're going to need friends now, and I'd like to be your friend, if you'll let me. That's all.'

I pulled the sheet up over my head, so that he wouldn't see the tears which I felt welling up in my eyes and spilling over. I felt that I didn't deserve a friend, I had somehow attracted evil and therefore had become evil myself.

He sat there in silence for a while, then asked, 'Do you want me to go? I'll go if you want me to.'

'Yes.'

'Well, don't forget about me, because I'll be back.'

When it was time to be discharged, Arthur came to the hospital to fetch me. Mum, he said, had had a bit of an accident, nothing major, but she hadn't been able to come.

I'd been given a list of things I was required to buy

from the chemist. Arthur stopped the car outside the store, and I thrust the baby upon him so that I could walk in quickly. Bottles, teats, lactogen, sugar of milk— it took me a while to locate them because all these things were strange to me. When I carried them back to the car, I found Arthur in a great panic. The baby, he said, was 'snuffling', and he was afraid of the sound; scared the child was choking or something. I was glad then to have held the baby during his feeds in the hospital and to have had the opportunity to get a little used to the noises and gurgles of a newborn infant.

Mum had somehow dropped a boiling hot pot of tea into her lap, and was very badly burnt across her thighs. Despite the pain, she thought it was a bonus because she could stay home from work and help look after the baby.

Help? She completely took over the child, and I was able to climb right back into my bed. She put him in a box on the dinner table near her, so that she could keep a constant eye on him from wherever she was. I resumed sleeping between eighteen and twenty hours a day, but I found that the demons had waited at the house for me to return and plagued my dreams constantly. Mum didn't mind me sleeping all day now because she had something much better to occupy her time. If I was out of the way, so much the better. But a week or so later, her burns healed and she had to return to work.

Mum had been pestering me to name the child. 'I'm getting tired of calling him "Boy". Give him a name or I will. I have to take his birth registration papers into the registry office and they must have something on them.'

I felt this child had been foisted upon me; I'd had no real role in his arrival, and wanted a name that somehow projected that. I also wanted a name which might evoke for him from the spirit world the strength and power he would need to survive in this overwhelmingly white racist society. I thought of the only child I'd heard of whose mother had played no sexual role in his conception, and told Mum, 'I'm going to call him "Jesus".'

'You are not! No, I absolutely will not have it.' Her face puffed up with rage.

'Jesus is a good name, and a fairly common name in South America, too.'

'This child does not live in South America! He must have an Australian name. He'd be taunted unmercifully at school and throughout his life. Those South Americans called Jesus who come to Australia to live change their names to things like Peter or John. Have you ever met anyone who said his name was Jesus?'

She brought home baby name books, and made lists from magazine stories and from novels she'd read at some time. I said she could name him anything she liked, the whole thing was becoming a terrible bother to me. I'd already picked a name and she'd ridiculed it.

She took the papers in and got an extension for lodging the baby's first name. With the heat off now, a name came to me as if in a dream, in the same way my poems came to me, and I got up and wrote it down. Russel. In the morning, when I showed her the name, Mum said, 'That's not how you spell Russell. My maiden name was Russell, and it's spelt with two l's, not one.'

'He's not named after your maiden name, Mum. I didn't even know it was your maiden name. This child is a single "l" Russel. His name will attract the right spirits for him, because the spirits told me what to name him.'

I had few dreams, only nightmares, and they came as often and were even more disturbing than before. Mum frequently came and took Russel out of his cot to sleep in her room. She said I was upsetting him, screaming and yelling out all the time.

One night, the main dream started playing itself out again:

I was sitting on the floor of a deep cavern. The demon was there, trying to talk to me. My hands were over my ears. Instead of scrambling up to scale the wall, I was too tired and I continued to sit. Through my hands, I could hear what the demon was saying. He was trying to get me to agree with something, and to some-how be tied to him. If I didn't, there was going to be worse in store for me.

I was looking at the floor, and the floor was solid. I suddenly knew that I was on the bottom now, the rock-solid bottom; there was nowhere else left to fall. A sense of peace came over me, and when I took my hands from my ears there was silence. I had struck no deals, and yet there was peace. I started to get to my feet and realised I was weightless. I was so light that I began to float upwards of my own accord and without any effort from me. I floated past the shelf from which I was always knocked by a falling rock, and when I floated even higher, I saw the big brown and black mas-tiffs. They were in a cave, baying from behind a solid glass window that was stretched across the entrance. I could see their teeth in their snarls as they heavily hurled themselves, over and over, at the glass wall between us, but not a sound from them reached my ears.

As I floated, my body started turning around, slowly at first, much like a corkscrew being twisted out of a cork. At the same time, I began to see daylight filtering down from the top of the long tunnel I was in. The spinning grew a little faster, then a little more, until I experienced almost the same sense of vertigo and euphoria I'd previously got from choking myself around the neck. As the daylight became stronger I opened my eyes, and was surprised to find myself awake.

After I had this dream, the nightmares stopped, as suddenly and inexplicably as they'd begun. I remained suspicious that they'd return as soon as I let my guard down.

During my waking hours, I still felt bad and worthless. I wasn't eating much; I felt I didn't deserve food, so my energy level was often very low.

One morning I woke up and the baby was in his cot. He was lying on his stomach, facing towards me, with his eyes open. Mum had told me that small babies can't really see yet, as the nerves in their eyes have not fully developed.

The baby smiled, arching his back to do so. He couldn't be smiling at me, I thought, because I was across the other side of the room and he couldn't possibly even see me. I sat up in the bed and moved from one side of it to the other. He followed me with his eyes, his head held steady. So I got up and left the room.

The experience embarrassed me because, for the first time, I'd felt there was somebody else in the room with me. Until then, his presence had been about as remarkable as a dent in the paintwork or a picture on the wall. Now I felt a real person was in there and the whole dynamics in the room were changed.

Whether he was asleep or awake, I began to feel his presence all the time. Awake, he watched me constantly, twisting himself about in the cot to enable himself to do so. When I looked over he'd catch my eye, and smile. A gummy but increasingly delighted smile, it was obvious he was pleased to see me.

Eventually, I began to take him out of the cot and bring him onto the bed to look at him. He'd lay there happily, waving small hands and feet in the air, and sometimes even quietly falling asleep. Whenever he could, he'd catch my eye and try to engage me in his gaze. I would often lay on the other side of the bed, staring at the ceiling, preoccupied with the turmoil of the awful things that passed through my head. Yet suddenly, I would find that, almost of its own accord, my hand had reached out to touch him to make sure he was still there, that he hadn't moved towards the edge of the bed. When I turned my head, he'd look at me and beam.

The child had separated himself from the nightmare and become an entity in his own right. I had begun to care about him despite myself.

12

Mum came into my room one afternoon and said the police had been to see her at work. The police in Brisbane had begun to schedule the court cases.

My first thought was that I couldn't afford to go back to Brisbane because I had very little money. I had not given any consideration to money in all this time. Earlier, Mum had told me that the Department of Social Services gave unmarried women an allowance to cover them for six weeks before and after the birth of their children, and she made an appointment for me to go in to see them. 'Your visit is a formality, I've already told them your circumstances,' she'd said, which turned out not to be the case when I got there. I was grilled at the counter by several clerks, within hearing of the other clients, about who the father of the baby was. This experience upset and embarrassed me.

Mum always got me to sign the Social Services cheques when they arrived, then she would cash them and buy food and whatever else I needed, as well as everything in preparation for the baby. Whenever I thought about the cost to her, I was overwhelmed with guilt because she was still having to rise early and leave the house at daylight to start her job, boiling up dirty laundry in a ramshackle lean-to at the back of a hotel.

'The police will issue you with a travel warrant, and they'll give me one, too, so I can go with you,' Mum told me. 'The court will also pay you a daily allowance to appear, and we'll stay at Aunty Glad's house, so that'll be enough.'

Then I began to worry about going to the court. Would I still remember the faces? What would I be asked? The memories were very strong but they appeared to me only in nightmares and flashbacks; I was able to keep them at bay when I was in control. Now I had to prepare myself to rake them all out in broad daylight, and found I couldn't even bear the thought of doing this.

Mum carefully picked out the few clothes I was to take, and packed for herself, me and the baby. We caught the train for the long journey, and Aunty Glad was at the station to meet us when we arrived.

I was glad to see the familiar detective. However, probably because Mum was with me and he thought I no longer needed him to be so supportive, he was very businesslike. As he'd predicted, it had been impossible to trace any of the others involved. Even one of the five whom I'd identified had had the charges against him dropped through lack of collaborating evidence of his guilt of the more serious offences.

The detective told me that each of the four men charged was to appear first in the Magistrate's Court, and if the magistrate found the men had a case to answer, they would be tried in the Supreme Court. This meant that I would have to make eight court appearances. In between these cases, unless they were scheduled for consecutive days, Mum and I were to be issued with travel warrants to enable us to go to and from Townsville.

The Magistrate's Court was on the second floor of an old wooden building, with peeling paint and a verandah on which I had to wait. Mum and Aunty Glad were allowed into the court, but as I was involved in the case, I wasn't permitted to hear anyone else's evidence.

Mum or Aunty Glad sat with me most of the time, but when the decisions were being made in the court, they both wanted to be present and left me sitting alone, looking after the baby. Russel was also not allowed to be taken into the court, we were told, because the defendants' solicitors would claim that I was trying to manipulate the court into feeling sorry for me instead of concentrating on the justice of the case. The only way I found out what the verdicts were was when Mum, Aunty Glad or one of the detectives came out at the end to tell me.

Three Magistrate's Court appearances went well. I was asked very few questions as, no doubt, the prosecutor had already outlined the case against the defendant and all I had to do was substantiate it. So, apart from having to force myself back into the terror of that fateful night, nothing more occurred to add to my trauma. It was embarrassing to be on the verandah when the defendants were being walked into court by their lawyers, but once I was inside, I had other people, such as the magistrate, solicitors and the court attendants, to look at. This meant that I was able to ignore the man in the dock, while still appearing cooperative, if and when the defendant or his lawyer looked at me.

At the end of each hearing we were taken to an office where I signed a form and received a court appearance fee. Ironically, although not a lot of cash, these payments amounted to more money than I'd received from any of the jobs I'd held. I was pleased to be able to pass most of it over to Mum to help repay her for the wages she was losing by accompanying me, as well as the huge expenditure she'd incurred as a result of having had to look after all my needs during my pregnancy. Even after this, I still had a couple of pounds left to spend on Russel and myself.

A nerve-racking ritual for us all—Mum, Aunty Glad, the police, the defendant, defendant's lawyer, and sometimes members of the defendant's family, as well as, occasionally, the men who were introduced to me as the prosecutors—was having to be together on the verandah at the same time every morning, during the lunch break when suddenly everyone came pouring out of the court, again after lunch, and yet again when court finished in the afternoon. The detective cautioned me against glancing towards anyone from 'the other side' in case anything could be made of my look. He said the defendants' solicitors would tell them the same thing, and that if they were smart, they would do as they were told.

So I, and everyone else, was surprised during the hearing for the tall blond man. When the court recessed for lunch, he stepped away from his solicitor and his group so quickly that no one could stop him, and he came towards me. But Mum was even quicker. She was beside me already when he stopped, leaned over me and said, 'Can I see the baby?' Russel was wrapped in a bunny rug, asleep on my lap, and the man looked only at him, not at me when he spoke. His solicitor was there in a flash, dragging on his arm, pulling him away. We could hear him being heavyied—'What did you think you were doing?' and 'You want to act guilty? Well, that was a fool's way of doing it!'—as his party closed in around him and escorted him down the stairs. A man on a rape charge wanting to see the baby was an unheard of admission of guilt.

Mum, Aunty Glad and the detectives were all scandalised, as no doubt was everyone from the man's own camp. During lunch, Mum and Aunty Glad couldn't stop talking about the implications of his actions. When we got back to Aunty Glad's house later that afternoon, they were still burning with outrage, and shared this titbit with the few people whom they had made privy to what was going on.

Just before the final hearing in the Magistrate's Court, the detective told me to brace myself, because the fourth man had decided to defend himself. Did that mean he could ask me questions himself, not through a lawyer, I asked? Yes, we're sorry, that is the case, I was told. This was, of course, the main assailant, now known to be a violent criminal, who had turned in the front seat of the car to knock me out and, later, stomped on my head with his boots and left me for dead. Then he had been inadvertently released on bail. The thought of having to endure him even speaking to me, as part of the process of justice, terrified and sickened me.

The fourth hearing was a great ordeal, and I felt as if I'd really earned the court appearance fee, not so much for what had been asked of me in court, which had turned out to be little, but because of the anxiety I'd experienced. I was completely unnerved by having to look at my interrogator, a situation which the

magistrate alleviated by telling me I didn't have to look
at him. I could give my answers to the bench instead,
as long as I spoke loudly enough for the defendant to
hear me.

Mum and I spent a lot of time on the train, going
backwards and forwards on the two thousand mile
return journey. Then, while talking to the detective one
day, I learned that we could have flown back and forth,
but Mum had refused air-travel warrants.

So, the next time she was preparing to make the trip,
I asked her why we weren't going by plane. I'd never
been on a plane, but the idea of spending a couple of
hours—as opposed to a couple of days—travelling to
these cases, while attending to the needs of a small
baby, was very appealing to me.

'Go by plane?' Mum roared at me. 'Are you crazy?
When I was a little girl, men were jumping off chicken
coops with bits of wood strapped to their arms, trying
to fly! And now you think I ought to go up there in one
of their contraptions? No fear! We're going by train,
and that's the end of it. I'll hear no more about it.'

At our first appearance at the Supreme Court, we
were met by the detectives, who were waiting for us
outside. They were more neatly and smartly dressed
than they had been before. When they took us into the
vestibule, where I was to spend my time waiting, we
saw a number of other men, none of whom I instantly
recognised, all neatly and soberly attired. The detective
introduced them to Mum and me, and it turned out
that the group included the milkman whom I had
flagged down, the vegetable gardener who'd given me a
lift, doctors, and others connected with the case. Most
were obliged to sit in the vestibule until called to give
evidence. When those who were allowed into the court

had gone inside, both the milkman and the vegetable gardener, at different times, approached me to tell me how much they wished I had spoken out at the time. They would have taken me to a police station, and the milkman especially was deeply regretful that he had left me by the roadside when he'd gone off to deliver his milk round.

I was very pleased when, a little later in the day, another policeman arrived and ushered Josie in. She was happy to see me, but reticent in the court environment and police presence. We exchanged a few words, but because she was called almost immediately, we didn't really have a chance to talk.

Once witnesses were called in to the courtroom, I had no idea what happened to them. I learned that there was another vestibule on the other side in which the defendant's witnesses, family, character references and whoever else gathered, and that as long as I sat in my own vestibule and moved in and out of the court only under police escort, there'd be no chance of running into any of them. The police, I was told, were there to ensure that no interaction between potentially hostile groups occurred.

The examinations in the Supreme Court made those held in the Magistrate's Courts feel like informal chats by comparison. I was nervous and edgy by the time we arrived at the court for the first hearing, and Mum had made me wear one of her only two good dresses, which was probably much too old-fashioned for a girl of my teenage years, so I didn't feel comfortable either. Aunty Glad rented a stroller from somewhere so that I wouldn't have to hold Russel all day, or lay him down on the wooden bench. Either Mum or Aunty Glad was to stay outside with the baby while I was giving my evidence. We were all very tense.

When finally I was called, the prosecutor made me go through my life history—where I'd gone to school, what sort of jobs I'd held—then asked me questions about the night of the assault. His questions were precisely phrased and I was only allowed to answer yes or no. I had thought that, at last, I would have an opportunity to tell my side of the story, so that the judge and jury would get a complete picture, but this wasn't to be. After the prosecutor led me through the evidence which he needed, the defendant's barrister was then allowed to ask me any questions he wanted. However, he, too, only asked me set questions to which my answers were to be yes or no.

'Now, I put it to you that you put your arms around the defendant and kissed him before you even got into the car. Isn't that so?'

'No.'

'And I put it to you that you whispered to him that you wanted to go off somewhere with him. Isn't that right?'

'No.'

I could see what he was trying to imply, and the romance he was inferring didn't make any sense to me, but I was unable to say so in my answers.

I was relieved that, with the guilty verdict which was brought in, the accumulation of the defendant's evidence didn't add up for the jury either, even though I'd not had the chance to tell them so myself. They saw X-rays of the shattered bones in my face, and heard from others their descriptions of how I looked, where they had seen me and what I had said to them. From all these things they'd been able to deduce that this was no lover's tryst which had got out of hand.

Once the first guilty verdict was in, Mum was obviously relieved and felt that her actions in notifying the police had been vindicated. I didn't experience anything like the same relief, as my pressures were coming from different directions from hers. Nothing would be 'normal' for me ever again. Apart from this, I also knew I had three more gruelling interrogations to get through.

By the time the second case came up, Mum and Aunty Glad had already heard the evidence from the witnesses—which remained the same and was formally repeated at each trial—and they became more relaxed. Aunty Glad even left the court to go shopping, and Mum prowled around the place, going out occasionally to stand in the sunshine and fresh air. To my eyes, the building was enormous, with pillars and marble, some sort of slate or ceramic tiles on the floor, and large polished wooden panels, doors and staircases. I remained confined within its grandeur.

There seemed to be so many people involved in the cases that I lost track of their names almost as soon as they were introduced to me. They became just so many grey suits or brown suits or dark blue suits, with little to distinguish them. The second of the 'lesser role' defendants was also found guilty, with his barrister also putting very few real questions directly to me. They spent a lot of time with their suppositions with which they hoped to impress the jury, 'I put it to you that on the night in question you . . .' type of questions, and kept me sitting in the witness box for hours. Apart from the frustration I felt about the process denying me an opportunity to give my version of events, my fears were generally not increased through the activities in the court.

When there were two cases left to go, the detective told me to expect the worst. Both these 'main players' were looking at very long sentences, and their barristers would become low and dirty in their efforts to get their clients off the hook. But he also said that all I had to do was tell the truth, and that the truth hadn't let me, or him, down so far, had it?

These two cases bothered me. The faces of the men bothered me. I hated the fact that the tall blond man had tried to look at my baby, confirming for me that he realised his guilt. Nevertheless, it was all the same to him because he was still happy to plead 'not guilty', and attempt to further destroy my life by having his barrister try to hack away at my respectability and credibility.

On the day the tall blond man's trial began, Mum came into the vestibule from one of her jaunts out into the hallway with her eyes brimming with tears. The detective had given me some background as to what had already transpired in relation to this defendant. His girlfriend, to whom he'd been engaged, had called off the engagement when he'd been charged with rape and completely broken off her relationship with him. Her family had cut him off. He had never been in trouble before and his family were devastated. Then, in a bizarre stroke of fortune, he'd won a lottery, the Golden Casket, and with the money had hired a man reputed to be the best and toughest barrister in the business.

When Mum came in, I thought someone must have said or done something really untoward to upset her. But I was perplexed when she kept looking around and edging me towards the back of the vestibule so that no one would hear her when she spoke to me.

She'd been approached, she said, by the parents of the defendant, who had laid in wait around the hallways after our arrival, to see if either of us re-appeared. She said they had wept, that they were afraid this child of mine could be their grandchild, and that they were distraught that they would never have the opportunity to know him. They had made an offer to Mum to give me money to help bring him up, which she had refused on my behalf, and they were desperate to catch even a glimpse of him.

By the time she had finished telling me this tale, she too was weeping openly and patting her face with her handkerchief to stifle her sobs. Russel was sleeping by my side in the stroller, and Mum reached into it and lifted him out. I knew what she was about to do, and I knew it was wrong, but she seemed so overwrought and distressed that it was beyond me to stop her. She heaved him up onto her shoulder and stood up. Her expression of grief became mixed with pride, and she walked out of the vestibule to show him off and also to ease the grief of the possible other grandparents, who would never have what she had—the baby in her arms.

When she came back with him, she told me, 'I couldn't help it. Those poor, poor people, my heart goes out to them. They're decent people. They did everything they could for their son, gave him a good education so he'd have a good job, and look how he's repaid them!'

'Did you let them touch him? Put their hands on him?' I wanted to know if he'd been somehow sullied, had become contaminated by some source of evil.

'No, they just looked at him and cried,' she replied.

Perhaps she was thinking of her own son, my brother, who had taken off when I was one year old and had refused to contact her for all those years. Who knows?

Their son's barrister, of whom I'd become quite fearful because of the detective's warning, turned out to be only a little different from the others. He, too, implied that I had thrown myself at his client, even asked me if I thought his client was good-looking, and he tried to twist the words I'd answered to the prosecutor's questions to his client's advantage.

'I understand that you said earlier that you asked my client to hold hands with you, isn't that right?'

'No. He said, "Give me your hands."'

'Objection, Your Honour.'

The judge cut in, 'Yes, just answer the question, yes or no. You are not to elaborate on your answers unless directed to do so.'

The detective had previously told me that, with all the lottery money this defendant had to spend, the defence had most likely hired someone in Townsville to poke around and explore my background, find any old boyfriends, and would use anything to try to discredit me. The defence would try to sully my reputation in any way they could. There was pathetically little to find, but they weren't to know that when they set out. I was afraid that, in the absence of real dirt, they might try to invent something, and I didn't know how I could deal with that.

'Tell me something about your previous boyfriends,' the barrister asked me, implying that his client obviously fell into the category of a boyfriend of mine.

'About who?' I replied.

'Oh, there's been so many then? Well, just tell me about any one of them that comes into your mind.'

'I don't have a boyfriend. There is no boyfriend. There's nothing to tell.'

'You were a nurse, and you never had a boyfriend? That's a bit far-fetched for the court to believe.'

'Am I allowed to answer that, Your Honour?'

'Yes, go ahead. There was a question in there.'

'I was a nursing aide, in Charters Towers. There's seven girls to every boy in that town. I didn't stand a chance of having a boyfriend there.'

A twitter of laughter ran through the jury, but I didn't feel they were laughing at me.

There were other questions, more personal in nature, about whether I thought there'd been enough blood around at the scene to verify whether I had been a virgin, and if not, why not? When I said I didn't know, that I'd been unconscious and it had been dark in the shed, he nevertheless persisted with this line of questioning. Surely I would know whether I'd been 'ruptured', he asked me.

'It's not always possible to know about these things,' I replied. It was really embarrassing to have to have this discussion in a courtroom overwhelmingly full of men, policemen, court attendants, the judge, barristers and solicitors, and an almost entirely male jury. The few women I could see in the seats at the back and in the balcony must have been friends or relatives of the defendant, as they weren't known to me. So, I could draw very little comfort from looking at them.

'Why isn't it always possible to know?'

'With people who wear tampons, it's not always possible to know.'

'And you—you wear tampons?' He raised his voice

as though wearing tampons was tantamount to harlotry.

'Yes.'

'And how old were you when you began wearing tampons?'

'About fourteen. I had to wear them. I was a swimmer in Townsville and we had to train every day.'

In the end, his efforts to embarrass me did neither him nor his client's case any good, and actually ended up embarrassing him. He had tried to make me admit that I had witnessed the police making an arrest without giving a caution and that, later, police officers had coached me in my evidence. Unfortunately for him, I was able to recite the police caution word for word.

'You have that down very pat,' he said. 'Did the police tell you to say that?'

'No. I've heard it before.'

'Oh, you've heard it before? How many times have you been arrested, that you've heard it so often?'

I've never been arrested. I heard it on Aunty Glad's television.'

'You did? And just what program did you hear it on?'

'I heard it on "Perry Mason".'

The irony of the situation was not lost on the jury, some of whom burst out laughing. I glanced at the judge and he, too, was having difficulty keeping a smile off his face.

The grilling, though, went on for ages. The clothes I'd been wearing on the night in question were beyond reproach. The barrister, however, posed questions which implied that perhaps these weren't the type of clothes I normally wore; that I must have had some fairly seductive items in my wardrobe. My morals, and whether or not I went to church regularly, whether or not I drank alcohol, even the type of films I went to see, all became the focus of his questioning. The jury sat forward, attentively throughout, although I was afraid to look at them. The detective had told me that I was not to smile back if anyone smiled at me, in case it seemed as if I was frivolous or even over-friendly. So, it was easier for me not to look at them.

When I was at last excused from the witness box, I went back to the vestibule, and told Mum and Aunty Glad that I didn't think the barrister was as great as the police had told me he was, and that I'd be surprised if he managed to win a not-guilty verdict.

Although the jury was out for longer than before, they came in with the same verdict as they had for the previous defendants: Guilty.

Fortunately for me, the man who had defended himself in the Magistrate's Court allowed a public defender to appear for him at his Supreme Court hearing. This meant that I only had to look at him when the court ordered me to point directly at the person I was alleging was my assailant.

His friends in the upstairs gallery hissed and made noises during my evidence, either as a means of threatening me, or to distract the proceedings. The judge cautioned them a few times, but I didn't look up towards them even then.

The line of questioning taken during this hearing didn't include anything about this man's release on remand, as the jury was not allowed to know about his prior record. Nor of how the police had had to guard my life against him during that time.

During each case, when the hearings had been completed and the jury retired to make their deliberations, everyone wandered off in different directions to wait.

We had to tell the police or court officers where we were going if we wanted to be notified when the jury was returning. These were difficult and extremely stressful times, during which I was in a state of limbo, wondering whether I had been believed. It was made even more stressful because I had no idea of what other people may have said in the court. Although the process of excluding the victim from the hearing may be to avoid evidence contamination in case the person is called back, and be part of an effort to enable a fair trial for the defendant, it adds enormously to the pressures experienced by the person who has already been devastated by having been attacked.

I was also not allowed into the court even when juries returned with their verdicts, and news of the outcomes were relayed to me only in the sparsest manner. Neither Mum, Aunty Glad nor any of the police, who were permitted to remain in the court throughout, ever discussed with me what had been said by other witnesses, solicitors or barristers, or even the judge. I felt that I had been almost completely left out of a process which was supposed to be of assistance to me.

However, when the fourth of the hearings was over and the jury returned, I heard an explosion of commotion from inside the court. A woman's voice, which police later said came from the defendant's girlfriend, who was up in the balcony, screamed loud and long, although I couldn't hear her words. Closer to me, I heard the sounds of scuffling and bumping on wood, which police also later told me had been caused by the defendant who tried to fight off his police escort and escape. The defendant called out, 'What the hell! She's an Abo! She's just a fucking boong!' He continued to scream these words over and over, as though to explain

his outrage at the verdict to the judge and jury, while he was being dragged, kicking and struggling, down into the holding cells under the courtroom.

When I'd heard the first muffled sounds of the commotion I'd become afraid and snatched Russel out of the stroller, ready, if necessary, to run. Usually the door to the courtroom was kept firmly closed and no sound escaped into the vestibules or foyer, so the door must have been being held ajar for me to have heard anything.

When Aunty Glad and the police filed back out of court, none of them volunteered any information about what had happened inside, and it wasn't until I asked about the screaming that I was given even a brief explanation. No one wanted to repeat the words they'd heard, but their silence compounded for me the importance of what had been yelled. The words burned into my brain and, in my continuing depression, became a mantra of evil in my head. 'Abo. Abo. Just a fucking boong!'

Epilogue

The court hearings had taken a year. The criminals received sentences of five, seven, ten and fourteen years. I had not a twinge of sympathy about their removal from society for these periods. The main assailant received the longest sentence, half of which was to be served concurrent with his seven-year sentence for shooting at a police officer. The menace which he'd projected at me throughout—not only in person but in my nightmares—was such that I felt he would surely come after me and kill me on his release, and that I had only the fourteen years of his sentence left to live. Fortunately, I'd never heard of remissions for good behaviour or my panic would have increased. If any of these cowards appealed against their sentences I was not informed of it.

During that year I was able to earn very little, was not entitled to government support, and my efforts to apply either for unemployment benefits or jobs were hampered by the fact that I often had to travel to Brisbane to attend the court.

On my eighteenth birthday, Mum had encouraged

me to take stock of my life, and I did. I had no job nor job prospects, a baby three months old, no husband or confidante, nowhere to live except in a remote house with my mother and under her domination, kindly though her intentions obviously were, no close friends, no access to a phone, no vehicle. My stocktake plunged me into a different level of depression. Until then my nightmares had mainly been centred on the past, exacerbated from time to time by things happening around me. None of these things had ever been talked about or resolved. Now I faced a bleak future and saw no break in the horror of it, no relief, and no hope.

On the positive side, the time I had spent reading while recovering from meningitis had left me with a near photographic memory. And, despite my fragile appearance, my view of myself was that I was physically very strong. I'd demonstrated my stamina by surviving all manner of diseases and illnesses, and I knew myself to be a good person, regardless of what anyone else may have thought.

My emotional despair, however, contained only one little beacon of light, the tiny baby boy who was increasingly centering himself and his needs on me.

As he grew, he clung to me like a baby koala, always clutched to my clothing with his small fists. His face, in repose, mirrored my unhappiness and my family began to call him 'Little Sad Sackie'; my mother blaming me for his seriousness.

But he was very bright and determined, hauling himself first into a sitting position and then onto his feet by the time he was ten months old. I went back to Tobruk Pool when Russel was six weeks old, in the hope that enough water washing over me would cleanse me of the dirt which had been put upon me. It didn't, of course, but instead, the child taught himself to swim, and by seven months old could splash his way across the width of the Olympic pool, although he was still too young to walk. His joy at his own accomplishments was infectious, and often served to distract me from my personal gloom.

At the time there were no victim services, no counselling, no victim compensation, and single women with children were regarded as immoral and presumed to have very little intelligence or worth. When the twelve-week maternity allowance payments ceased I went to the government unemployment agency. For the staff there, the fact that I was a black woman looking for work caused consternation, that I had a child, a dependant, caused even more, but that I was unmarried with an infant almost caused apoplexy amongst them. One kind woman told me that I'd have a lot of trouble because male employers would think I was loose, and female employers wouldn't trust me around their husbands or male employees.

I saw no point in telling anyone the truth, because even women who had been overpowered and raped were considered to have contributed, if not wholly caused, their own misfortune by having acted or dressed in a provocative manner. The crime of rape held a tremendous curiosity for the public, and, over time, I saw numerous other women who had been raped suffer as much from ignorant and even hostile public attention as they had from the initial assault. I was determined not to become one of them.

Physically, I remained very slight and thin, and strangers often remarked, 'What a good girl you are, holding this baby for his mother,' or asked, 'You look tired—will his mother be much longer, do you think?'

Their comments drove me to become very possessive about Russel, and his striking good looks and intelligence gave me a great pride in my maternal status.

At the same time, I grew concerned by the thought that people were always staring at me and my child. I felt that perhaps their admiration of Russel's features was a mask for unbridled busybodyness. What were these strangers saying about me behind my back? I'd grown up in a racially hostile environment, where being a 'darkie' was viewed with suspicion and distrust. I became very protective of my privacy, sharing little about myself or Russel beyond what people could see with their own eyes. I tried to adopt a positive facade to shield my deeply embedded sorrow which may have prompted questions, and to keep out the negativity which I often sensed in the air.

As my love for the baby grew, I began to fret about what he would think if he ever found out the circumstances of his conception, and how he would react if he learned of the burden I had first assumed he would be. I became determined to protect him from this knowledge, no matter what indignities I had to suffer to do so. I knew enough to appreciate that a Black boy child was an endangered species, living with so many external threats that he'd find difficult to negotiate without being additionally burdened from within.

The state of constant sleepfulness in which I'd spent my pregnancy had passed, and in its place came my former alertness and concentration. So I turned back to reading. I read everything I could find on child development, aware of the complete absence of literature on Black child development and, as I did so, I became increasingly aware that the truth that at first I had not wanted him, had the potential to damage any baby's mind and perhaps turn him into a similar character as those who had perpetrated the crime upon me.

My silence became an imperative, which created a dilemma for me. My mental rehabilitation might have depended on being able to talk about the emotions which were caused by my trauma, but this might have had a very negative effect on my child.

My search for my own identity, I realised, had to take a back seat to the construction of my child's identity and sense of self-worth. My father's identity remained unknown. Did it matter? Would my son also wonder who his father was? And what would I be able to do about that when the time came?

My mother's valiant desire to be a white woman in a world she recognised as intrinsically racist, had, in the end, been a godsend for me. I learned of no other instance in which the rape of a black woman by white men resulted in prison sentences. Perhaps there had been, but throughout my research I'd never heard of it. I felt sure that, initially, only my mother's 'whiteness' had prompted the police to begin their inquiries.

I tried to repay her by becoming the 'white' daughter she, in her mind, imagined she already had. I bought blond hair dye, succeeding, at first, only in turning my hair a dark reddish colour. The second application turned my hair brassy, and the third, which I left on for an hour, caused all but about six hairs in the front to completely dissolve and fall off my head in the rinse. I also, and equally in vain, searched the magazines to find out where I could send away to buy blue contact lenses. Her reward for helping me, a blond-haired, blue-eyed daughter, never eventuated, and Mum even became cross with me and called me a 'dill' when I had to walk around with a beanie on in the middle of our tropical summer to hide my bald pate.

But the extent of my indebtedness to her, for saving me from being put in a mental hospital, for caring for me physically during this terrible period while I was unable to care for myself, and for remaining beside me during the ordeals of the court hearings, was enormous. What sacrifices she had made previously, bringing us children up by herself, and cycling out to her job in the middle of the night, were made insignificant by her efforts to save me as a young adult. I determined not to harass her further, if I could help it, about the things she wanted to keep secret. I, too, had my 'secret', which I wanted to remain private, and, although we didn't need to discuss our pact of silence, our mutual understanding of it has hung heavily between us all this time.

A few months after the court cases were finished, Dellie, who'd changed her name to Della and broken off her engagement, casually informed me that she had a new friend—a brother of one of the rapists whom I had put in jail. She said I couldn't hold him responsible for the sins of his kin and that he was a nice person. I was shocked. It may have been thoughtlessness on her part, but it seemed to me that with the millions of people in Australia, she could have chosen her friends more selectively and with some concern for me. I felt completely betrayed at the deepest spiritual level, and a pain flared up in my heart which time has not erased. It was not, however, to be the only betrayal I would receive from my close family and friends. My capacity to forgive was to be sorely tested throughout my life, and Della's actions were only the first lesson.

I returned to my totem, the snake, and learned 'the

silence of the serpent'. Without vocal chords, in pain the snake rears back and opens its mouth to cry in complete silence, and its agony is only apparent to those who know it well. I engrossed myself in everything I could learn about snakes, and formed my own opinions about how they had become maligned, like myself, and been made symbols of sin in European theology. This was also very much like the situation I found myself in, through circumstances and actions not of my own making. Their innocence in the face of the way society thought about them and struck out against them mirrored my own, and my identification with their situation was both profound and emotionally rewarding.

If I followed the path I was paving, I realised I would have to live on the edge, between truth and light, because the truth would almost certainly have negative consequences for the one small person I cared most about. I was in a perverse situation where the truth represented darkness and only my silence in the face of the pain society would inevitably inflict on me could represent light.

Could I do it? Would I be able to carry the additional burden of silence—without losing my mind completely? Could society change enough in my lifetime to be able to help me recover from my ordeal and assist me with this trial?

Although these were tall orders for an eighteen year old to consider and struggle to meet, I saw no other option but to try, not merely to resurrect myself, but to give Russel a healthy start in his own life. I was to assume the silence of the serpent as a cover for myself and my child, an umbrella to hold over both our heads for the next thirty years.

Apart from these deep feelings of love and duty surrounding my son, I had no idea what the future would
hold for me. North Queensland remained as racist as
ever, but my love for this area, my birthplace, my
cradle, was still strong and abiding. Nevertheless, I felt
the need to run out into the world to discover what else
was out there, and, hopefully, to restore my sanity and
faith in humanity in the process. Yet I knew that the
string with which my heart and soul were tied to the
cradle would tug at me on all levels regardless of where
I moved.

From my foundations it perhaps does not stretch my
readers' minds too much to realise that the racism I
encountered, which all Black Australians encounter in
their childhoods, is the breeding ground of militancy.
We all want to be treated with respect and dignity, and
when we are treated like scum and deprived of opportunities in life, we strain towards those things through
whatever avenues seem open to us. At this terribly
unhappy stage in my life, however, it never once
occurred to me that I would become a prominent
activist in the Black movement, a writer, poet and edu-
cator with publications in foreign languages, a global
traveller visiting and speaking in all continents, and a
Harvard graduate. These triumphs of the human spirit
over adversity lay dormant for many years.